Workplace Culture Matters

Written in a novel format, this book addresses the challenge of changing a "sick" culture.

Some organizations wake up one day and realize they have become something they never intended. Their employees run scared. There is no innovation, only blind obedience. There are warlords within the ranks of management, and they fight over turf without considering the best interests of customers, their employees, or their organization as a whole.

At the Charleston, South Carolina, branch of Copper-Bottom Insurance, the wake-up call comes when an employee files a lawsuit against the company and its leaders. The Charleston division Vice President, Jack Simmons, is put on probation and given an ultimatum: "Change the culture!" Jack understands the "or be fired" implication all too well. He scrambles to find help and runs into an old friend, Don Spears, from Friedman Electronics. With Don's help, Jack begins the journey that will heal his organization.

In the course of their first visit, Don and his Director of Continuous Improvement, Tim Stark, help Jack to make an important discovery: Copper-Bottom's executives are not showing their people respect. Don and Tim point to the following observations as proof. Copper-Bottom leaders are

- Using top-down, "command-and-control" leadership behaviors rather than recognizing their people as Subject Matter Experts and listening to them
- Issuing instructions to their people rather than observing then improving performance through coaching
- Keeping employees in the dark as to the impact their work has on the organization's mission
- Unaware of the obstacles in their people's paths; hence, never use the authority of their positions to remove those obstacles
- Staying in their offices, aloof to the difficulties their subordinates face

As Don and Tim see it, Copper-Bottom's problems stem from the way its leaders lead. After the executive who precipitated the lawsuit is let go, the Friedman team begins the process of teaching Copper-Bottom's executives that a healthy culture begins at the leadership level. Don, Friedman's General Manager, states that cultures change when their leaders change. In short, leaders need to initiate the changes in the culture by first demonstrating the desired behavior. So begins the process of reeducating Copper-Bottom's leaders in the difference between managing and leading.

In short order, Tim begins to work with Jack's leadership team, while Don takes Jack to Friedman's Oakland facility. There Jack learns

- To first concentrate on surrounding himself with the right people
- The importance of top-down metrics to which leaders first hold themselves accountable
- how to cascade their metrics (KPIs) down through their organization and use a dialog about them as a way of developing relationships of respect

Although a long way from complete, by the end of Jack's six-month probation, Copper-Bottom has made significant strides and is well on its way to changing its culture. Jack will learn that he is not the only one to appreciate the new developments.

Workplace Culture Matters

Developing Leaders
Who Respect People and
Deliver Robust Results

Robert B. Camp

Routledge
Taylor & Francis Group

A PRODUCTIVITY PRESS BOOK

First published 2023
by Routledge
605 Third Avenue, New York, NY 10158

and by Routledge
4 Park Square, Milton Park, Abingdon, Oxon, OX14 4RN

Routledge is an imprint of the Taylor & Francis Group, an informa business

ISBN: 978-1-032-37255-6 (hbk)
ISBN: 978-1-032-37254-9 (pbk)
ISBN: 978-1-003-33605-1 (ebk)

DOI: 10.4324/9781003336051

Typeset in Minion
by Apex CoVantage, LLC

The book of Proverbs says, "As Iron sharpens iron, so man sharpens his fellow man." Proverbs 27:17

Keep in mind that, at the time those words were written, the term "man" was gender-inclusive, more properly understood as "human or humankind." In that spirit, I would hope each of you have people in your lives who sharpen you. This book is dedicated to two remarkable humans who sharpen me.

The first is Abisogun Kokumo. Abisogun is the head of the Education Bureau for the Arizona Department of Corrections. Although born into the privilege of the United States, he took the name of a slave after graduating from college. He is unassuming and hardworking. He takes his role extremely seriously, knowing that the 200+ educators who work for him are literally changing the futures of men and women who have hit bottom and are trying to rebound. There are two behaviors that make Abisogun worthy of this dedication. The first is his humility and his willingness to seek and listen to the counsel of others while making up his own mind. His title is not the result of militancy or a reflection of the affirmative action laws of the United States but of his own hard work. The second thing that distinguishes Abisogun is his commitment to changing himself and his organization for the better (Kaizen). In the years I've known him, Abisogun has moved boldly to employ Lean disciplines that have advanced his bureau and his people beyond almost any other. He performs due diligence before adopting new disciplines, but once he is satisfied, he executes swiftly.

The second person to whom this book is dedicated is Tomas Ayala. Until his passing in 2021, Tomas was a Deputy Warden in an Arizona prison complex. He was responsible for the careers of some 200 staff members and the lives of over 1,200 inmates. A servant leader, Tomas took care of his people, both staff and inmates. He fully understood the rules within which he had to work but still found ways to promote those in his care. He employed Lean heavily and, at the time of his passing, was writing his doctoral dissertation on his use of Lean within the corrections industry. Tomas was an inspiration to me, and although he sought me out to mentor him, I found as much knowledge passing in my direction as his. He had an unquenchable desire to be the best personally and raised up others who developed similar expectations for themselves. In short, Tomas was a marvel and is deeply missed.

Contents

About the Author

A graduate of the US Military Academy at West Point, Robert began his career in one of this country's foremost schools of leadership. However, like most, he gained his real impression of skills by watching leaders. He came to realize that leadership is a precious gift that far too many fail to recognize. In the mid-1980s, as Americans began to watch markets they had created be penetrated and then dominated by Japan, Robert started reading the literature trickling out of that country. Each new book pointed to a new technique. "Statistical process control (SPC) is how they're doing it!" proclaimed some. "It's quality circles," countered others. Still others claimed it was just-in-time manufacturing. As it turned out, none was right; all were right.

Over time, as a more complete picture formed, Robert learned that it was the combination of those tools that gave the Japanese their considerable edge. Still, the picture was not quite complete, and it wasn't until the late 1990s that the world came to realize that the tools alone would never make an organization Lean, because their results couldn't be sustained.

By then, Robert had made Lean a full-time profession. Over and over, he transformed organizations. Some succeeded, but most failed. He tried to make heads or tails of the circumstances that made the difference. The answer, he discovered, was right under his nose all the time. The difference was leadership.

He learned that many have been content to manage and call it leadership. Management, however, isn't leadership. In fact, it's a far cry from that. Management faces backward, analyzing yesterday's data and perfecting it today. It's an extremely valuable skill and much needed, but it's not leadership. Leadership, as Robert sees it, is the ability to look forward, over the horizon and through the haze of battle, to define and communicate a new course of action and compel others to follow.

Robert has had the good fortune to work for some of this country's biggest and most successful organizations. Throughout his career, he's been afforded the privilege of working under great men and women who have taught him in both word and deed.

Introduction

Workplace Culture Matters is a novel in the same series as *Sustainable Lean* and *The Lean Leader*. In fact, some of the same characters carry over throughout the series. Unlike its predecessors that focused largely on the mechanics of Lean, *Workplace Culture Matters* focuses on the people aspects of the discipline.

The book opens with the senior executive of a Charleston, South Carolina, insurance branch being hit by a hostile workplace lawsuit. The suit also lists corporate officers, and soon the branch manager is sitting in the corporate boardroom. There he is given 90 days to "change the culture" of his branch. Although it's not spoken, the implication is that if he fails in the pursuit, he will lose his job.

Not having a clue where to start, the branch manager stumbles onto Don Spears of Friedman Electronics. Don, having been through similar circumstances a few years earlier, agrees to help, and so begins a journey to change a culture. Early in the effort, Don's CI Director, Tim Stark, points out to the executives of the insurance company that "Changing your culture is really about changing how you lead." Step by step, Tim and Don take the leaders of the insurance branch through a tectonic shift in the way they lead, and with that shift, in the way they relate to their people.

In the 1920s, Western Electric learned in its Hawthorne, Illinois,[1] plant that, when you pay attention to your people, their performance usually improves. Can the same happen in this instance?

NOTE

1 Often referred to as the "Hawthorne Effect," Western Electric hired a consulting team to adjust lighting in their Hawthorne, Illinois, plant. As they raised the lighting level in this assembly plant, productivity went up. Later, when they dropped it, production went up again. The Hawthorne Effect, as it came to be known, determined that productivity went up not because of the level of lighting but because researchers and supervisors had paid attention to the hourly workers.

DOI: 10.4324/9781003336051-1

1

The Last Straw

"That's the last time I intend to tell you!" shouted Henry. "I'm sick and tired of you always screwing this up. Either get it right, or find yourself a new job!"

Henry Corn stalked off from the Accounting cube farm almost proud of the chaos he'd just created. If he cared, he'd have said, "Just as well. They all need to get the message. I won't tolerate incompetence!"

As soon as Henry and his ill temper left, fellow accountants congregated at Patty's cubical. "What was that about?" asked one of her colleagues. Patty, who had been quietly crying, self-consciously wiped the tears from her cheeks and, in a hoarse whisper, replied, "Darned if I know."

"Really?"

"Really," replied Patty, gradually regaining composure. Speaking quietly, she said, "He stormed in here flashing the latest cost projections and started ranting."

"But ranting about what?" asked Samantha.

"He didn't like the way I'd calculated Operation's projection, I guess," said Patty, still deeply hurt by his callous attack.

Patty's hurt wasn't just because she viewed herself as a professional and didn't feel Mr. Corn's behavior was at all courteous. More than anything, it was based on the fact that she was the sole provider for her household and needed this job. She didn't feel she could fight back and believed Mr. Corn used that fact to single her out for this style of abuse.

"What was wrong with it?" asked Paul.

"Take your pick. Last time he didn't like that I'd included temp labor in the projection. The time before that, it was because I'd overstated inventory ... in his opinion. Anyway, it's anyone's guess what I did this time. He never said. It's just his rant du jour."

DOI: 10.4324/9781003336051-2

While she was still talking, Jerry, the Controller, arrived. Everyone but Patty scurried back to their cubes.

"What was that about?" Jerry asked. By now Patty was rehearsed in the answer. She simply stated, "Honestly, Jerry, I can't tell you what it was this time. It was more like he just needed a dog to kick. It's not like he told me what he was angry about."

"Well," assured Jerry, "We'll find out soon enough. Just don't antagonize him. He's the head of Operations and that makes him our customer, right?" Jerry no longer needed to repeat the slogan that hung outside his office: *The Customer Is Always Right*. With that, he turned and headed back to his office.

"Why does he never support us?" Patty asked under her breath. She was referring to Jerry. He was spineless, and his people all knew they could never expect him to come to their defense. Whenever it came to trouble, they were on their own. That had been what had gained Jerry the nickname of "The Jellyfish." The man had no backbone.

Having been humiliated in front of her peers yet again, Patty went through the motions for the remaining hour of her workday. She felt despondent, hurt, and wished she could go home and just crawl into bed.

Sometime during her sleepless night, the question came to her: "If this were happening to your son, if he were being bullied, would you stand by and silently let it continue?" In that second, she knew she had to *do* something this time, or she'd be showing her son that allowing oneself to be bullied was acceptable.

Even though she had a near-flawless attendance record, no one thought anything was amiss when Patty failed to show up to work the next day.

2

Legal Hot Water

It was a full week before Jack Simmons, the Vice President and head of the Charleston branch, got served with the lawsuit. The suit alleged *Hostile Workplace*, and named Jack, Jerry Falstaff, and Henry Corn (the original perpetrator), as co-litigants. The list of litigants didn't end there, though. It also named their employer, Copper-Bottom Health Solutions, and its officers.

Jack had been served in the parking lot as he'd come in to work. The server quickly departed, leaving Jack to scan the document.

"Son of a … !" he muttered under his breath.

The suit gave dates, times, and places when Henry had embarrassed and harassed Patty Purcell. The suit also named the dates, times, and places when she'd brought her concerns to her supervisor's attention and went on to allege that no action had ever been taken.

Jack had never been served before. This was virgin territory for him, so the moment that Nadine Sommers, his HR Manager, showed up to work, he was in her office.

Nadine read the suit twice then looked up. "Jack," she said, "this is serious. I'm sure the corporate officers will be served as well, but I'm going to have to report this to corporate immediately. They'll get our lawyers involved, but I can tell you that this isn't going to bode well for you, Henry, and Jerry. The only advice I can give you is to get ahead of this as best you can.

"I'll interview Patty," she continued, "but she's probably been instructed not to say anything out of court. I'd recommend you talk to Henry and Jerry."

DOI: 10.4324/9781003336051-3

3

Unraveling the Ball of Twine

As a single mother, Patty couldn't afford to quit without another job to go to. In this economy, there were no jobs to be had in Charleston, especially for an accountant with only a bachelor's degree.

Feeling backed into a corner, she'd opted for *fight* over *flight*. "If the company is going to allow the Henry Corns of this world to treat their employees this way," she'd reasoned, "they are as guilty as he is."

She'd called a labor lawyer whose billboard she'd seen dozens of times. His paralegal had assured her over the phone that the first meeting was free, but would give her peace of mind. At least she'd know the direction she wanted to go.

At the actual meeting, she'd been encouraged to file suit and she had. The lawyer had agreed to take her suit on contingency.

In the beginning, she'd felt self-righteous and indignant, but when the impact of her actions hit home, her feelings turned to fear.

Shortly after receiving the suit, the company lawyers had tried to settle. They offered a small settlement, but Patty's lawyer advised against accepting it.

"I mean," her lawyer had begun, "if all you want is money, then take it. Remember, I'll get 30% of it; however, you told me that it was the principle of it all; that you wanted the company to know how humiliating it had been for you each time you'd had to endure Mr. Corn's verbal assaults and Mr. Falstaff's handwringing."

Reminded of her own words, Patty agreed to continue forward to the hearing. That's not to say that she wasn't scared of retribution … or worse. She lived in constant fear of being called into someone's office at work.

In fact, the longer it took for the hearing, the more her fear got the better of her. She became paranoid: constantly frightened that someone

DOI: 10.4324/9781003336051-4

would kill or maim her (or her son) before the trial. She'd read newspaper accounts of such things. Next, she worried that the company would hire someone to abduct or injure her little boy.

She went to work every day, but the rumor mill had quickly spread the word that she'd sued the company. Now her colleagues shunned her out of fear of becoming collateral damage in whatever fate awaited Patty. Jerry had others deliver her work or dropped it off personally before she arrived.

Her lawyer tried to reassure her, but this was so far out of Patty's comfort zone that she lived in a constant state of anxiety.

By the third week after filing suit, she was a basket case. After she'd gone three nights without sleep, she finally sought a physician's assistance. He'd prescribed an antianxiety medication and sleeping pills. Even then, she developed a skin irritation and constantly felt like bugs were crawling under her skin.

By the time the actual hearing rolled around, she was a mess.

Having watched TV, Patty had been prepared for a courtroom, a jury, days (if not weeks) of testimony and counter testimony. There was none of that.

The hearing was presided over by a Magistrate. They were seated in a conference room, and she could practically reach out and touch the people she was suing.

The company's lawyer argued that Jerry had an open-door policy and suggested that this tragic misunderstanding had been Patty's fabrication.

Patty's lawyer had gotten testimony from Patty's fellow employees, who acknowledged Jerry's policy but went on to testify that everyone knew that nothing shared with Jerry ever led to resolution, nor, for that matter, was it kept confidential.

If anything, they'd said that using Jerry's *open door* identified the employee as a potential troublemaker. After that, the employee was *marked*.

Frequently, this added scrutiny led to mistakes or other problems and more than once had resulted in the employee's termination for reasons other than the original complaint. That was because Jerry didn't want anything that could be tied back to the fact that the person had gone to him seeking support. If anything, his employees learned that you *didn't* go to Jerry if you had a problem.

The hearing also brought out the fact that Henry bullied everyone. "It doesn't mean anything," he'd explained. It was "just his *style*," he'd told the Magistrate.

Others testified that it wasn't just that he was tough—which he was. It was that Henry seemed to take satisfaction in verbally bludgeoning people. Rarely did he give an explanation about what had been wrong. Sometimes, when the facts were tracked back, it hadn't even been the employee who'd been bludgeoned who had touched off Henry's ire. He was roundly feared and universally hated.

The presiding had lasted less than a day. To no one's surprise, the court ruled in Patty's favor, awarding her $15,000 for lost time, ongoing medical bills, and day care. They awarded her another $95,000 for mental anguish.

The company had been further admonished not to take retaliatory action against Ms. Purcell, as it would undoubtedly lead the parties back into court, "and," the Magistrate reminded them, "more money." With that, the Magistrate's gavel had come down.

BAM!

4

What Goes Around ...

The week following the suit, Jack found himself sitting in front of the CEO and his staff. The session had been grueling. They'd wanted to know how this could have happened right under Jack's nose. No explanation was acceptable. No matter what he said, somehow, he was wrong.

Frankly, Jack had never felt as if it was his job to babysit his subordinate manager's etiquette. As he saw it, he paid them for results. They were supposed to be professionals. They should *know* how to behave. Besides, he'd inherited all of them from his predecessor. He'd neither hired nor promoted any of them. He didn't see how this was *his* problem.

After almost two hours, the meeting had ended with Jack being informed that

- A letter of reprimand was being placed in his personnel file,
- He was on a 90-day probation,
- Any further incidents would lead to his immediate dismissal, and
- He had 90 days to change the *culture* in the Charleston plant or there could be serious consequences on his own career

By the time he got to his rental car and headed to the airport, Jack realized that he'd sweated through the armpits of his suit coat.

Jack was in a black mood. The whole episode had been a miserable experience. His mood turning darker and darker, Jack held Jerry Falstaff and the whiner, Patty Purcell, accountable. Jerry was a waste of skin as a manager, a bean counter, plain and simple, but at least he didn't incite problems the way Henry did.

If Jack had his way, he'd have fired Henry the minute he got back, but while in the meeting, the corporate VP of HR had admonished him not to

DOI: 10.4324/9781003336051-5

take adverse action on any employees without first reviewing it with him personally.

Jack felt beaten down, totally defeated. He wanted to get home and crawl into bed.

Little did he think that two years later, and with the clarity of hindsight, he'd be grateful that things had turned out the way they had. Ironically, Patty's suit had saved him and Copper-Bottom's Charleston facility from a much worse fate.

5

Any Port in a Storm

Jack was keenly aware that the clock was ticking on his 90 days, and he wanted to move as swiftly as possible.

In the week following the meeting at corporate, he tried to discover how to change his culture. He'd spoken to a lot of consultants. All had offered to assist, but their programs were expensive and seemed somehow lacking in detail. He finally decided to approach the other executives and CEOs he knew, to see if any of them had worthwhile suggestions.

That weekend, while playing a round of golf at the country club, someone had suggested that Don Spears had turned his plant around within the previous three years. "It's a different place," Jack had been told. "The employees love working there, and better than that, Don's numbers are among the best in his corporation. Let me tell you," the speaker had gone on, "Don himself is a changed man."

Sure that he'd gotten the *hyped* version of the story, Jack nonetheless sought out Don, who, he'd been told, just happened to be in the clubhouse restaurant.

Finding Don with his wife mid-lunch, Jack was reluctant to approach. *Well*, he reasoned, *all I want to do is get on his calendar.* Jack cleared his throat, gaining the couple's attention.

"Mr. Spears," he began, "I'm Jack Simmons. I'm a Vice President for Copper-Bottom Health Solutions. I run their office here in Charleston. I was recently talking with a colleague about changing the culture of my organization, and they said you'd been through something that changed yours. I wonder if I could make an appointment to talk with you this coming week?"

Don broke off the conversation with Honey, his wife, and invited Jack to sit down.

DOI: 10.4324/9781003336051-6

"I don't want to interrupt your meal any more than I already have"—nodded to Honey—"but if I could make an appointment to speak with you, I'd sure be grateful." Jack pulled a business card from his shirt pocket and handed it to Don. Don reciprocated.

"May I call you on Monday?" Jack asked.

"By all means," Don responded. "I'll look forward to it."

Monday's call was brief. Don said he and Honey had been thinking about what he'd tell Jack and decided it would be better to have Jack visit his plant. "Can you make it this afternoon?" Don had asked.

Changing the culture in the Charleston branch was Jack's number-one priority, so he agreed immediately. At 1:15, he was waiting in the lobby of Friedman Electronics.

The old Don would have had his secretary fetch Jack from the lobby, but the new Don arrived in person. He extended his hand and gave Jack a warm welcome.

"Jack," he began, "so glad you could make it. Before we talk, would you let me show off our plant and people?"

Although his mind was consumed with questions about culture change, Jack readily agreed. Besides, no one he knew ever turned down an opportunity to tour someone else's operation.

6

Monday: Starting from the Ground Up

Over the weekend, Jack had read up on Friedman Electronics. Ten years ago, it had been a stodgy organization, well known for its mainstream products but not very highly regarded for its customer service or ingenuity. At the time, Friedman was in the top three manufacturers of electronic cabinets in North America, but its very size militated against its market nimbleness.

Then a little-known Plant Manager became their VP of Operations. He soon turned the corporation on its ear, radically eliminating poorly-performing Plant Managers and hiring young-minded men and women of all ages. This VP of Ops also implemented a new discipline called Lean. He required each plant to employ the technique, and the results had been amazing.

Within a year, the bottom line of the corporation began a significant rise, and the new VP was considered a wunderkind. Not only was Friedman making its old products safer, of higher quality and less expensively, but its customer service ratings had soared.

Friedman became known as an innovator, creating an industry-leading plastic cabinet that offered the insulating properties of plastic, but the strength and rigidity of steel. They had also developed an online application that allowed customers to design their own cabinets with standard components and have them delivered anywhere in North America in two weeks or less. That alone set a new industry benchmark, but the changes didn't stop there.

Based on industry surveys, Friedman ranked as one of the top midsized employers in the country for the last three years running. One statistic that Jack found odd to see advertised was that Friedman employees had an average of 2.6 implemented suggestions per employee per year. Apparently, they thought that was a big deal. All in all, Friedman sounded like a pretty incredible organization.

Now, as he toured Don's plant, he was really impressed. It was extremely clean and well organized, nothing like the image of dark and dingy manufacturing sites he'd heard about.

Friedman's plant, as Don had encouraged Jack to call it, was well-lit and surprisingly quiet. Jack's reading had informed him that Friedman's Charleston, South Carolina, plant was one of their top revenue generators with a higher $/employee contribution than any other, yet, as Jack looked around, he noted that employees were relaxed and working at a comfortable pace. He asked Don about the seeming inconsistency between those two facts.

"Good observation," acknowledged Don. "We use something here called Standard Work. It involves finding the safest, fastest, and most defect-free way to perform a process. We rely heavily on our operators to help us to find that method. Once found, it is then written down, and every employee in that process is trained to perform their job exactly according to the written standard. In time, every employee in the line is trained to perform every job, and they rotate positions regularly, not only to relieve boredom but to give everyone on the line the opportunity to perform every operation.

"The recorded version is called *Standard Work*, as it has become the new standard. Once everyone has demonstrated the ability to perform the new standard routinely, the supervisor still monitors at least once a week to ensure that workers are holding fast to the standard. If they're not, they're retrained and reevaluated.

"Time standards are part of Standard Work. They are set by the employees and based on the most sustainable rate of production. We expect employees to be time-conscious, but not to rush, and never to put schedule ahead of quality."

Don wound the trip up in his office. As they entered, Jack noted that there were three people already seated at the table there. Two of the three looked to be hourly workers, while the third looked like a low-level salaried employee. The trio stood on their entrance.

Don introduced the three to Jack. "Jack, I'd like you to meet Hector, Ginny, and Denise." Turning to the three, Don said, "Perhaps the three of you will tell Jack what you do."

Hector began. "Jack, I'm Hector Santos. I am an assembler in the mechanical assembly line." He turned to Ginny.

"Hi, Jack, I'm Ginny Pierce. I'm an accounts payable clerk." Ginny looked at Denise.

By now, Jack was seated, and Denise extended her hand across the table. "Jack, I'm Denise Cho. I work in shipping and receiving."

Denise turned to Don, who was still standing. He indicated the three should be seated.

"Jack, you wanted to know about our culture," Don stated. "I want you to speak to our employees and to form your own conclusions about whether you want to follow our lead." He turned to the trio. "Will half an hour be enough?" he asked.

"Better make it 45 minutes," said Ginny with an affable grin. "You know us girls when we get to gabbin'."

Jack was dumbfounded on a whole bunch of levels.

- Don let employees sit in his office while he was away? Wasn't he worried about them going through his papers?
- Don allowed these employees to meet with a guest without a "chaperone" present: someone who would make sure they stayed within the boundaries established for them?
- Don was letting three low-level employees talk to an outsider, and an executive at that? He'd have expected to speak with fellow executives; then again, he was here to talk about the culture at Friedman Electronics. Had Don left him to talk to executives, would he have believed them?

Maybe Don was even shrewder than Jack realized.

"We understand you want to learn about our culture here at Friedman," Denise began with a genial smile. "I'm not sure what you're used to, but for those of us who came from other companies, working here was quite a shock, in a very positive way."

Ginny was next. "I've worked here since I graduated from high school. I got my associates degree while working here and the company paid to send me on to get my BA. They're now paying for me to get my CPA.

"I'll be honest, though," she continued, "this plant is *very* different than it was four years ago. It was pretty much common knowledge then that Don was on the chopping block. His boss, Jim, fired Don's entire staff and replaced every one of them. The replacements were all hired from outside, at least from outside this facility. Most were from other Friedman plants.

"Don later told us that one of the reasons he was in trouble was that he'd failed to hire minorities, failed to hire women, and failed to grow leaders below him. That all changed after Jim's visit."

Hector added, "It was really hard for those of us who worked here before those changes. It was common knowledge that it didn't matter what your boss said. The only one who could make anything stick was Don. We learned to go around everybody else and go directly to Don. You could tell he didn't like the hassle, but he never sent anyone away, either. We always got our answer."

The group fell quiet.

"So what's different?" asked Jack.

"Don!" was Ginny's immediate response. "Don's what's different. Night and day!"

"Can you give me an example?" Jack asked.

Ginny swept her hand across the table. "This used to be a leather sofa and matching lounge chairs." Now, gesturing around the room, she said, "Don's desk was a 200-year-old mahogany monstrosity that came from his family's plantation. This place was his inner sanctum. No one got in here unless they were in serious trouble, or here to sign a contract, or something really important." She giggled.

Hector chimed in. "After he went through his transformation, Don replaced it all with this stuff," he pointed to the furniture, "and it's no longer *off-limits*. If we have a concern or a question, we're free to come to him, but we usually don't have to. Our concerns usually get resolved by our immediate bosses. The crazy thing is that, now that Don listens to his subordinates and his subordinates have actual power to make decisions, their decisions are usually the same as we'd have gotten from Don."

"I disagree a little with Ginny," he continued. "It wasn't just Don's transformation. Jim brought in top-notch directors and began changing the way the company was led. Like I said, the new directors really listen to us. They ask us what we think, and there's not a lot of *telling* anymore. They're asking, and they take what we say about our jobs into account as they make decisions."

Denise was next. "We are coached, and our skills are continually assessed. Friedman uses a tool called *the Skills Matrix*. Every job has an established list of skills required for that position. Our bosses rate us at least quarterly and document our performance of those skills. That rating forms the basis of a quarterly face-to-face discussion. If we have weaknesses, we're told what they are. We're offered additional training and an opportunity to retest.

"After we demonstrate our ability to perform all the required skills, we have a dialog with our supervisor where we talk about our desired career path. If we aren't ready to choose one yet, we're given opportunities to shadow employees in careers that interest us.

"Once we choose a career path, the skills needed for the next job in that path are added to our skills matrix, and we get opportunities to understudy someone performing that job. In time, we're given a chance to demonstrate those skills, too. As our performance improves, we are added to a Succession Plan for that position.

"Of course, there is a downside, or maybe it's a second upside, to the skills matrix. If we can't perform the skills required of our job, we're given multiple chances to train and retest. If those don't work, our next one-on-one is to suggest a different career path. Sometimes, however, the only path leads to termination.

"Don's boss has told us on multiple occasions that failing at one thing only narrows down the list of other things we might be really good at. He tells us not to look at termination as failure but as life pushing us toward what we'll be really good at.

"Besides," she continued breathlessly, "we have some great career counselors who can look at our demonstrated skills and suggest different career paths."

"There are other rules around the Skills Matrix," Denise concluded, "but the thing is, it's fair and impartial. Everyone in that skill group is held to the same expectations."

"I agree," Ginny volunteered. "I can honestly say I feel we're playing on a level field here and that we're respected.

"It used to be that we were hired for our hands, and expected to hang our brains next to the time clock. No one cared what we thought, or even *that* we thought. Just put in your eight hours, do what you're told, and go home.

"Jack," she said, drawing his full attention, "I've got a house and car. I've got kids. I've got a checking and savings account. I live within a budget and make big-girl decisions the other 16 hours of the day, so why was I not trusted to do so here?"

Indeed, Jack thought, *so why not here?*

That sent him into a reverie. He wondered what his own employees would say about the way he and his staff managed. He knew he'd never be crazy enough to ask. As one of his bosses used to say, "If you can't handle the answer, don't ask the question."

The remaining time before Don returned was spent having more of the same type of discussion, but Jack had already made his decision. This was what Copper-Bottom needed. He was sold.

When Don returned, everyone stood up, and the three Friedman employees marched out after shaking Jack's hand and wishing him luck. Now, with only Don in the room, Jack said, "I'm onboard. What's next?"

Don served Jack a cup of coffee and they sat back down at the table.

"Tell me why you're interested in changing your culture," inquired Don.

Jack gave a long sigh and explained the events of the last month. When he finished, Don let out a low whistle.

"Now I understand your urgency. Give me a second while I think out loud." There were several seconds of silence before he began again.

"What I'm about to describe is the way I'd go about it. Doesn't make it right. Just means we've seen it work here. At the end of the day, this decision's yours.

"The first thing I'd need to do would be to get my boss's permission to assist you, but I think he'll be quick to join the cause.

"Next, I'd loan you my Director of Continuous Improvement, Tim Stark.

"For sure we'd want to establish a baseline: find out what people think of your culture today. We have a questionnaire we use twice a year. It asks what our employees think of me, the organization, and my staff. It also asks what they think about the way we're managing our business and what we could do better.

"If we use the same questionnaire at your firm, based on our own history, we can expect their impressions to be poor, but that's okay. Our goal is only to establish the baseline, the point from which you'll start to improve.

"What do you think so far?" Don asked.

Jack gave an uncommitted nod, simply acknowledging what Don was saying.

"Next," Don continued, "We'll want to talk to all your managers about *how* they manage. In our experience, middle management is usually the level where employees become disenfranchised, and cultures turn sour."

Don stopped. "You've only got 90 days?" he asked.

"More like 80 now," Jack replied.

"All right, then. Last two things for now:

1. We'll work with you and your staff to create a system of cascading metrics, and
2. we'll begin using those metrics to initiate dialog between leaders and led. While providing you with a daily barometer of performance, the metrics also become a vehicle to coach and grow subordinates.

That last point is going to be crucial," Don explained. "*The way your leaders lead determines your culture.* We'll help you move from a domineering relationship with your people to a collaborative one. We'll teach you how to do that."

"Sound like a plan?" Don asked.

Jack sat silently. Finally, he said, "It sounds good, but I'm not sure how that is going to change our culture. Can you explain the cultural role of metrics?"

"Good point" was Don's response. "It all makes sense to me because we've already been through it, but let me see if I can explain it to you. Can you afford to take a few more minutes?" Don asked.

Jack nodded, and Don launched into a description of how the system worked.

"From what you've conveyed," Don began, "your immediate staff, and presumably those below them, have a directorial relationship with your employees. By that I mean they give your employees direction without making communication two-way. Is that correct?"

Jack thought for a second. "Yeah, I suppose that's true. I mean, it's just been the way we've managed. No one ever expressed a problem with it before," he said, more in defense than as explanation.

"You know, Jack, sometimes marriages grow in wrong directions. Husbands take their wives for granted. Wives see their husbands as walking paychecks. Neither shows the love and respect they once felt.

"If they're smart, they go to a marriage counselor and the counselor holds a mirror up to their relationship. The mirror shows them who they really are, versus who they want to be. Once they have an appreciation for what they've become, the counselor can help them past their *stuck spots* and get them back on track.

"In this example, metrics become the mirror. They show the parties where they are and allow them to monitor progress as they alter course back to where they want to be.

"Does that analogy make sense?" Don asked.

"It does," agreed Jack, still a little dubious about where this was going.

"I can tell you aren't convinced, but there comes a point at which you'll need to trust us. If we start and you don't like the direction we're taking, you can always stop us. Agreed?"

"I just hate wasting the time," Jack said.

"Jack," Don said in as conciliatory a voice as he could. "Take a step back and look at what is happening here. The problem you're presenting us with isn't Friedman's problem, but we're agreeing to help you.

"You've been in our plant and talked with our employees. You can see the relationship we have. You've been on our floor and read what's on our website. You know what we've attained. You need to ask yourself if you want our help, or if there's something better.

"This isn't about my ego," Don continued. "If you've got a better alternative I'd encourage you to embrace it, but I need to know."

Jack was quiet for long seconds. Don knew the next words had to be Jack's and waited patiently until the man was ready to speak.

"The truth?" Jack asked at last.

Don nodded.

"I'm scared and I'm not sure what to do. I'm worried about my job and about the jobs of my staff. I'm defensive and reactive, and I'm afraid I'm not making the best of decisions right now. I also don't have anywhere else to turn. Can you deal with me there?" he asked Don.

"To be honest, Jack, I can't. I can't make you want this. I can't make you get behind what we're offering, but if you don't, we're wasting each other's time. If *you* don't believe in our approach, then I can guarantee failure.

"You're the leader," Don continued. "You can't be half, or even 90%, committed. You've got to be *all in*, or all out."

Jack nodded and was silent. Finally, he said, "Give me overnight to think about it?".

"I'll expect your call tomorrow." Don replied. "I won't do anything until I hear from you, but remember, before I can commit to anything, I need to inform my boss and gain his approval. I'll wait to hear back."

In point of fact, Don had already given his boss a heads up, but he had only informed him about what was happening. He had not asked for permission to help.

The men shook hands and Don led Jack back to the lobby.

"No matter what," Don said as he reached again for Jack's hand, "best of luck."

Principle #1: Leaders need to be fully committed. Only *full* commitment will lead to success.

Corollary #1–1: No one will commit more than the leader. If the leader's commitment is tepid, the battle is already lost.

7

Tuesday: The Work Begins

Jack called Don early the next morning. "I'm onboard," Jack stated. "When do we start?"

"No time like the present," Don responded. "How about you giving Tim and me a tour today? I'll inform my boss and, with his approval, we'll start first thing tomorrow."

Jack looked at his watch. "How does 9 AM work for the tour time?" he asked.

"Done!" came Don's response. He consulted his own watch. "I'll scramble Tim and we'll see you in an hour."

The tour had revealed no surprises. Copper-Bottom Health Solutions was basically a cube farm. It had nice conference rooms and executive offices, the things customers see, but once inside the part of the building where actual work took place, the glamour gave way to grimy carpets, mismatched furniture, and paper chaos.

When people saw Jack coming, they scurried back to the security of their cubes and kept track of him out of the sides of their eyes.

Copiers, printers, bookshelves, open binders, and stationary cabinets (with doors flung open) were all overflowing with loose paper. There were disheveled stacks of documents piled on a small table next to the printer and picked-over piles still in the printer/copier. In what appeared to be an "Every Man for Himself" environment, employees were picking through documents to find what they had printed and leaving the rest.

Nothing was labeled or organized. While the tour watched, employees stood in line to sift through the stacks for what they'd printed. The scene was unadulterated mayhem.

What went on in the cubicles was little better. Filing drawers were open to display folders with handwritten names on them. Papers littered desks

DOI: 10.4324/9781003336051-8

and floors, and workers spoke on the phone as they pawed through files on their desks, in their drawers, and even on the floor. Even with all the clutter, trash and recycle bins overflowed with paper.

"Why," asked Tim, "is there so much paper? Aren't your files available on your people's computers?"

Jack blushed. "We appear to have some kind of a problem," he acknowledged.

When it became apparent that he hadn't answered the question, he continued. "I seem to recall something about files not backing up or something," he offered.

Neither Don nor Tim responded.

Jack switched the subject and began explaining the process they were seeing. "Few calls are outgoing, and incoming calls are assigned randomly based on who is not already on their phone. Customer Service Reps print their notes of the call. I'm told that, if the Customer Service Rep gets another call before they can get to the printer, what they printed sits until they can get to it. As you might imagine, that's a common occurrence during peak volume times of the day.

"Apparently," he continued, "if more than an hour goes by since they printed, it's just faster to print again. It would appear that the old document just sits there until someone throws it away. I believe the janitors do that Friday night."

Tim and Don nodded. It was evident that Jack didn't need to be told how wasteful that practice was, not to mention how hard it was on the employees. As Jack started to move forward, Tim looked at Don and gave an almost imperceptible shake of his head in disbelief.

The rest of the tour was more of the same. On the car ride back to their plant, they rode in silence until Tim finally said what both men were thinking. "No wonder morale is so low. Management has just abandoned their workers. Honestly, Don, do you think we can help them?"

Don thought for a long second. "It's possible," he said at last, "but only if their executives are willing to confront the real problems. The fact that executives can live with things the way they are doesn't give me high hopes. We're going to need to get their commitment before we agree to help them," he stated.

Don continued. "Yesterday, Jack shared with me the incident that set this all off. One of his executives yelled at an accountant and humiliated her in front of her peers. Worse, it wasn't the first time, nor does it appear to have been well founded. This particular senior staff member has a reputation for being a bully. The fact that this guy has been allowed to get away with it before makes their current climate understandable."

"Did you see how employees steered clear of us as we walked around?" Tim asked.

"I did," Don admitted absentmindedly. Shifting gears, he informed Tim, "I've already spoken with Jim but I need to get his approval for this project. Be prepared to start there tomorrow morning."

Jim was Don's boss, COO and VP of Operations for Friedman Electronics.

Later that afternoon, Don called Jack. After exchanging pleasantries, Don began. "Jack, you understand the effort you're being asked to undertake is a *Hail Mary*, right? Cultures are built over years, and you're being asked to change yours almost overnight.

"Here's what Tim and I have been approved to do: We will help you begin your transformation. We will help you improve your organization's morale, and if your leadership team will accept that as a good faith effort, we'll continue for up to six months.

"Is that acceptable?" Don asked.

"Geez," Jack responded, "that doesn't sound as if you're very confident in the probability of our success."

"Time to put the cards on the table," said Don. "I'd be amazed if your jobs aren't already being shopped. A 90-day transformation of a culture is an unrealistic expectation. If I were a betting man, I'd bet the 90-day performance period was more to give your corporate HR folks time to find a replacement for you.

"If you succeed, which your CEO appears to see as a long shot, he can save face by telling candidates that he's filled the job internally."

Don stopped and waited for his words to sink in.

"Holy smokes," Jack said after a pause. "This has all happened so fast, it never occurred to me that there might be something else going on." He paused again before saying, "What you said makes sense, though."

"I'll tell you the truth," Don said, "my boss took a gamble on me, or I wouldn't be here today. I'm sure he'd be willing to do the same for you, but only with your permission.

"Here's the deal," Don continued. "He's willing to contact your CEO and pledge our support if your CEO will extend your performance period to 180 days. May I give my boss the go-ahead?"

Jack was still shaken by the news that his job could already be on shaky ground. "Give me 30 minutes, will you, Don? I'll call you right back."

Don knew this was a big step and that Jack must be thinking through the consequences of Jim calling his boss. Don didn't think Jack had a lot to lose, but Jack might not see it that way. He prepared to have Jack bail on the offer in the next call.

When the call came, it was clear that Jack had decided to stay and fight. "You have my permission," he told Don.

"Okay," replied Don, "I need your CEO's name and cell or home number. Jim, my boss, will call him this evening. If we get a green light, Tim and I will be there tomorrow at 9 AM. Agreed?"

"Agreed," said Jack.

"I'll text you with my boss's response," Don concluded.

8

Wednesday: The Tide Shifts

Jim's call had been unexpected. As a result, Jack's CEO, George Franklin, was a bit on the defensive. Jim introduced himself. "George, I'm the VP of Operations for Friedman Electronics. We have a manufacturing plant in Charleston, South Carolina, and my plant manager there knows your Vice President.

"That's a long way of explaining my connection to you. I'm calling because my plant manager has asked for permission to assist your VP in the transformation of his culture. Before I continue," Jim said, "are you willing to hear me out?"

"Go," said the other man with a note of empiricism.

"I've agreed to allow my plant manager and one of his employees to work with your firm for up to 180 days free of charge. Just to give you a sense of what I'm offering, my firm paid more than two grand a day for the same service, and we've done it in all our plants all over the world."

There was silence at the other end of the phone.

"I do have two concerns," Jim confided. "May I continue?"

"Sure," George replied without betraying any commitment.

"George, as you must know, this is a big deal. Changing a culture takes a long time, because what you're really doing is changing the people in that culture.

"We've learned the hard way that, for the changes to stick, the leaders in that culture need to change: that means Jack and his staff, and that's where my concerns come in."

Testing the waters again, Jim asked, "Okay to go on?"

"I'm listening."

"My first concern is that 90 days isn't enough time to change a culture. Our experience is that it takes closer to three years, but as you know, it's an

DOI: 10.4324/9781003336051-9

endless job. You're never *there*, if you get my drift. Still, you'd need at least 180 days to even begin to see meaningful changes.

"I don't want to get into your business, but if you're serious about changing the culture in Charleston, you're going to need to give your VP more time. I'm asking if you'll extend his deadline to 180 days, if we pledge to assist him?"

The line was quiet.

"Jim, I don't mean to sound like a jackass, but I don't even know who the hell you are. Why would I commit anything to you?"

"Fair point, George. I'll tell you what. Let me tell you my other concern, then give you time to look at our website and speak to your VP. After you've done that, you can call me back with your decision. Sound fair?"

"Better," was all George would concede.

"Okay," Jim plowed ahead, "our other concern revolves around Jack's staff.

"Cultures are built around the personalities of their leaders. In order for a culture to change, the leaders all need to be willing to change. Sometimes, managers aren't prepared to make the *personal* changes needed to make the *organizational* changes successful, and that becomes a major impediment to the transformation.

"I'd like to ask you to grant Jack permission to discipline anyone who refuses to embrace the changes, including terminating them if necessary."

"Wow," George responded, "you don't mess around."

Jim wasn't sure whether George meant that as a compliment but decided to take it as one.

"You can't afford to mess around, George. As my people have learned, this is the single most significant thing that this organization will do since starting the branch."

There was no response, so Jim concluded. "Okay, I've given you a lot to think about. Why don't you and Jack talk? Make sure this is something he wants and that you're comfortable with, and then get back to me."

Jim also gave George the URL to the Friedman website. "Take a look," Jim suggested. "See who we are and who I am. I pledge my utmost support to your Charleston branch, if you want it, but the deal's only good for 24 hours.

"Either way, I'll look forward to your call," Jim stated. "Rather than have my assistant track me down when you call, here's my cell phone number." After giving George his number, Jim said goodbye and ended the call.

It was almost 10 PM in the Midwest when George called back.

"I had no idea who you were when you last called," George began. "I've read your website and about you personally. Clearly you know what the hell you're talking about. I'm onboard."

George continued. "I've extended Jack's timeline to 180 days starting tomorrow, and I've given him the authority to discipline his staff up to and including termination, although I hope it won't come to that.

"Let me ask you," George continued, "how will I know that he's made any progress?"

"Excellent question," Jim stated. "The first thing we're going to do is to baseline the current conditions of the organization. We're going to assess Jack and his team the same way we do our own. That includes an analysis of morale and trust in the leadership team. We'll continue monthly until the 180th day. I'd recommend you make it a precondition of your ongoing support that Jack share those metrics with you every 30 days. Sound fair?"

George agreed that it made a lot of sense.

"One other thing you might personally want to consider," Jim said. "We practice something called *Genchi Genbutsu*. That's Japanese and simply means *Go and see*. The implication is that leaders shouldn't take the word of others—including looking at computer screens—for what's going on. We tell our leaders to *go and see for themselves*.

"Genchi Genbutsu is going to be one of the practices we're going to have Jack implement early on. It will become the agent for much of the change that will take place with his managers. It's going to force them into frequent dialog with their employees, and that will start to show your employees a new face to your management team.

"While I'm on the topic of Genchi Genbutsu, I'd like to encourage you to visit your Charleston facility as soon as you can. If you'll let me know when you'll be there, I'll fly out to meet you and maybe we could have lunch or supper. I'd also like to give you a tour of our own facility there."

"I'd like that," George replied.

"Let me conclude, George, by assuring you that we are going to do everything possible to help your Charleston organization succeed in their cultural transformation. There is no advantage for us to invest the kind of effort we're going to if you and your organization don't succeed."

"I'm not sure why you'd take this project on," George admitted, "but I want you to know we're grateful and will do our utmost to support you and Jack."

"Thanks, George. I hope to see you soon."

Jim checked his watch. It was after midnight on the East Coast. The good news could wait. The following morning, Jim called Don. Don then called Jack.

"Jack, this is Don Spears. Both of our bosses have approved for my organization to help yours. As I promised, Tim and I will be there a little later this morning. I just wanted to review a couple of preconditions to our work. My boss has agreed to allow Tim to work with you full-time and me part-time, *if* you agree to follow our approach. If you stop, we leave.

"Agreed?" Don asked.

"Agreed," replied Jack in solidarity.

"Jim wanted you to know that Friedman paid two grand a day for the same service we're going to give you for free. We're prepared to donate our service, but it's imperative that you and your employees execute the actions we agree to in a timely fashion. Do you agree?"

There was a second of silence before Jack said, "I agree, but why is your approach so militant?"

"Fair question," Don responded. "The answer is twofold. First, it's our nature to get the rules clear before we start. We don't want you to later think we pulled any fast ones on you. Second, your condensed performance period forces us to move swiftly. That means that we can't afford to waste time. We'll answer questions, but we won't debate.

"We know the system we're going to implement works, so we're not going to be experimenting on you.

"That reminds me," Don interjected, "Jim was able to get your CEO to extend your performance period to 180 days, starting today. That means we have twice as long to affect the change your boss wants, but you're going to see that success is still going to take a lot of hard work."

"I'm starting to recognize that," said Jack. In that moment, Jack had realized that his CEO had been betting he'd fail. All of the sudden he felt exhausted, defeated. He questioned whether any of this was worth the effort. Was his dismissal already a foregone conclusion?

Don sensed what was going on and reassured Jack, "If we apply ourselves, success is absolutely possible. I won't deny that hard work will be involved, but this is absolutely within your ability. Look at it this way: if you try and fail, you'll have learned valuable skills that will help you the rest of your career."

Jack was silent.

"We good?" Don asked.

There was a pause before Jack acknowledged in a low voice, "We're good."

Don could tell there was reservation on Jack's part. He paused before continuing in a concerned voice. "Jack, this will only work if your heart is completely in it. You need to be *All In*. You know what I mean, right?"

"I do," admitted Jack, still feeling overwhelmed.

"Your people are going to be watching you. If you believe this is achievable, they will believe it, too, but you can't have a divided mind. You're either *All In*, or we're all wasting our time."

Don paused before asking, "Can you be *All In*?"

When Jack didn't respond right away, Don said, "Jack, it's okay if you can't be, but this won't work unless you are. So, why don't you take half an hour to think about it and call me back with your answer? Just remember this: If you can't be all in, you've already lost. You don't strike me as a loser."

Jack said nothing.

"I'll look forward to your call," Don concluded and hung up.

Jack no sooner hung up than he had three people in his office, all for different problems. He dealt with them, looked at his watch, and realized he still had 10 minutes before he had to get back to Don. He grabbed his jacket and headed out for a walk.

Clearing his head helped. During his walk, he'd realized that this was *do or die* time. Everything he'd worked for—15 years of his career—would end if he just gave up now.

"I'm going to fight!" he told himself. "You're damned right I'm all in."

Still outside, he called Don from his cell phone. "I'm all in," he stated emphatically, "and daylight's a-burnin'. See you at 9:00."

"Great!" Don enthused. "One last thing," he cautioned, returning to his earlier monolog. "With so little time, you're going to need the full support of everyone in the organization, especially your direct reports.

"I'll be honest," Don continued, "of everyone in your organization, the folks who report directly to you are the ones who are going to need to change first, and probably the most. We'll make that fact clear when we speak to them, but be prepared for some to resist.

"Unfortunately, you're not going to be able to tolerate that. If it comes to it, you may need to discipline or even terminate some of them." He paused a few seconds and said, "I won't say this again, but this is literally your neck on the line. You can't afford to equivocate. This is going to be your way, and if they don't want to follow you, then *they're* saying goodbye.

"Clearly you don't want to lead with that." He chuckled. "We'd like to believe that everyone will see the logic of what we're proposing and accept the changes it brings, but experience has taught us otherwise.

"Not everyone may want to accompany you on this journey. You will need to make it clear to your managers that this is the direction the organization needs to travel. If it does, you can assure its success. Otherwise, the only guarantee you can make is that they'll need to go. And, while my boss was speaking with yours, he got your boss to give you full authority to discipline your staff, up to and including termination. That's a really good sign, by the way."

There was no response. "We good?" Don asked in conclusion.

"We're good," Jack responded. Then, as if an afterthought, he stated resolutely, *"All In!"*

The last statement wasn't made with cheerleader exuberance but with quiet resolve.

Principle #2: Change has to be led from the top and continued with enthusiasm throughout the organization.

Corollary #2–1: Lackluster support by leaders is worse than no support. You're either "all in," or you are as good as "out."

9

Thursday: "All In!"

As previously arranged, Tim and Don showed up at 9 AM. They were shown into the conference room where Jack had assembled everyone who held a managerial position.

Without preamble, Jack led with the edict he'd been given: *Change the culture in 90 days!*

He'd thought about withholding the very real probability that the jobs of most in the room depended on their success. In the end, he'd decided they needed to know.

"Let's be honest, folks. If we fail, it's highly likely that none of us will be here in a year. Clear enough?"

There was a low murmuring within the assembly. Jack let it continue for almost 10 seconds before interrupting.

"I won't deny my personal responsibility for the problems that led to this challenge, but I can't change the culture on my own. It will take everyone in this room.

"We are really fortunate that there's a business here in Charleston that's already been through this. They've offered to help us for free. In a second, I'm going to turn this meeting over to them and let them explain what's ahead, then I'm going to need a decision from each of you."

With that, Jack introduced Don and Tim by name and title.

Don addressed the crowd. "Hello, everyone. I'm sure we'll get to know each other in the next few weeks, but I want you to know this: Friedman Electronics is 100% committed to your success. It's important that you know that for two reasons.

"First, you need to know that we're going to measure our success based on your success."

DOI: 10.4324/9781003336051-10

"Second, you should know that Friedman is already doing the things we're going to ask you to do, and we've been doing it successfully for over three years. So, if there's any doubt that we know what we're talking about, banish it now.

"Unfortunately, we've been given a tight time schedule, and that's going to make the urgency of what we do together all the more critical.

"Tim is going to teach you some new things. We guarantee that, if you use them, your success is all but assured. If you don't, your failure is almost a foregone conclusion.

"How can I say that? Because three years ago, we were where you are. We were in big trouble, and the person leading the parade of trouble was me. My boss put me on a 90-day probation. Sound familiar?" he asked, turning to Jack.

There were a few chuckles in the audience before Don continued.

"We made it, and if you'll work with us, you will, too."

Don stopped and surveyed the crowd for several seconds, making eye contact with each of the people in the room.

"Tim and I are *All In*. For the next six months, my boss and I have made helping you Tim's full-time assignment, and I'll be here a lot to help your senior managers.

"I want you to know that we intend to give you every advantage, but in the end, you'll be the ones who will make Copper-Bottom Health Solutions succeed or fail."

Don turned to Jack to let him know he was finished. Jack entered the center of the room as Don retreated to the wall where Tim was standing.

"This, I'm afraid, is crunch time. Like Don and Tim, I want you to know that I'm *All In*, too. I'm going to distribute a card to each of you and ask you to indicate whether you intend to join us. The formality of a card is for your benefit. You can answer the question on it whatever way you want, but in short order, your actions will tell us where your heart is.

"Fill out the card and give it to me on your way out." As an aside he stated, "Some people charge admission to get in. I'm charging it to get out." There was a light ripple of laughter, but he'd made his point.

Date: _____

Name: _____

I'm All In:

    ( ) Yes

    ( ) No

Signature: _____

10

Friday: A Long, Long Day

On Friday morning, Don and Tim were in Jack's office. Tim had a document in front of him and he was going down the plan of attack for the upcoming month.

"First thing we're going to do," Tim announced, "is to meet with all your direct reports." He stopped. "I'm curious," he asked Jack, "did everyone commit to being *All In*?"

Jack fidgeted for a second. "No," he admitted with a combination of frustration and disgust.

"Really?" Tim asked in astonishment. "What do you intend to do about that?"

"I was going to ask you," Jack responded.

Don, who was sitting next to Tim, laid a hand on Tim's forearm, then queried Jack, "Let me ask you, are you going to have two ways of changing your culture going forward: yours and this other person's?"

"No. Of course not," Jack replied.

"Then don't you have your answer?" Don asked.

"You're saying I should let them go?" Jack asked.

"Jack, you know I can't answer that for you. You're the only one who can make that decision. I *am* saying that you gave them the chance to join you and they chose not to. Can you trust them to be part of your team moving forward?"

Jack shook his head in a sad but determined manner.

"Then don't you have your answer?" Don asked again.

Jack looked at the table and said in a low but resolute voice, "I do."

"Then, if you have someone qualified to replace them immediately, don't equivocate. Show them the door. You'll be sending a clear message to the rest of the organization.

"If you don't have a replacement ready, keep the person in place until you can hire someone to replace them. Understand this, though: If you let them stay until replaced, they can't be on your team any longer.

"They'll know something's up," he continued. "I'd suggest that you tell them your plan. Make it clear that, if they attempt to derail your transformation or fail to perform their job, even once, they'll be fired on the spot.

"Now," asked Don, "is what I said clear enough?"

"Yes," said Jack.

"Can you execute that plan?" Don asked. "Before you answer," he cautioned, "remember that whoever didn't sign that card said they are unwilling to follow your leadership moving forward."

"When you put it that way," began Jack, "it really makes it clear: me or them."

"Honestly," Don agreed, "it is that simple."

"Okay." Jack let out a deep, anguished-sounding sigh.

"May I ask who it was?" Don queried.

"Henry, my Director of Operations," Jack replied.

"Isn't he the one who started this whole brouhaha?" Tim asked.

"He is," Jack responded.

Don put his hand on Jack's shoulder again. "I'll be honest, Jack. I'm pretty confident he wouldn't have lasted past the next phase. He's impressed me from the start as someone who doesn't take direction well. Someone like that will be a constant source of irritation in your organization.

"Okay," Don continued, "I'm guessing you'll want some time with your HR person. Want us to come back later?"

Jack thought for a second. He wanted to get started on changing the culture but knew he wasn't going to be in the mood until this was behind him. "Yeah, if you don't mind," he said. "How about after lunch?" he asked. "I'll give you a call."

"Sounds good," said Don. "Let's have the rest of your staff here when we meet, including Henry's replacement, if you have one."

When Jack's call came later that afternoon, it was clear he and Tim weren't going back to Copper-Bottom today. "How are you doing, buddy?" Don asked.

"Had better days," Jack admitted.

"Care to share?" Don asked.

"When I confronted Henry about his vote, he got defensive. I tried to explain to him that we were trying to take our team in a new direction and that he had just voted himself off that team. At that point, he flew into a rage.

"I won't give you the blow-by-blow, but he left me no choice but to terminate him on the spot.

"Fortunately, I'd gone over everything in advance with Nadine Sommers, my Director of HR. We'd mapped out Henry's possible courses of action and how we'd respond in the event of each. Nadine had prepared a termination notice just in case. Nadine and I both tried to get him to sign the termination notice, but he refused.

"We walked him to the front door. He carried on in a loud voice the whole way. Needless to say, that got everyone stirred up and provided plenty of grist for the rumor mill.

"Nadine tried to inform him that she'd mail his final check to his home and arrange a time to clean out his office. I'm not sure he heard any of that. He just stormed off and burned rubber getting out of the parking lot."

Jack took a long pause. "Glad that's behind me, but now I need to focus on what's ahead."

Don had listened attentively as Jack had recounted the story. Now he assured Jack that the worst was behind him.

"Monday you'll start a new chapter. You'd be amazed if you knew all the good that lies ahead. Great stuff, I assure you. In a couple of months, you'll realize what a gift Henry gave you today.

"One recommendation," Don continued, "don't let the rumor mill have another minute to work. Sit down with Nadine and craft a statement *immediately*. Tell your people words to the effect that you and Henry reached an impasse; that, much to your sorrow, you can no longer work together, and that, with great disappointment, you let Henry go.

"Nadine will put words in about thanking Henry for his years of service and wishing him the best in his future pursuits, but the purpose of this statement is threefold:

- First, you need to make it clear that there is only one leader at Copper-Bottom and that's you.
- Second, you want to make it clear that *you* let Henry go and that he didn't fire you.

- Third, and perhaps most important, you need to *own the message*. Don't let other people put words in your mouth. I can assure you that, as unflattering as this message may seem toward you, what the grapevine would say would be far worse.

"Like I said," Don concluded, "*own your message.*"

As it turned out, Jack did publish the memo, but he did more than that. He called in his direct reports and their direct reports.

"I'm sorry to announce that I had to let Henry go today." No one spoke, but Jack could tell he had their undivided attention.

He continued. "Henry returned his *All In* card indicating that he would not join me. I asked him about it today, giving him a chance to change his mind, and he again refused. Since we have neither the time nor money to pursue two courses of action—his *and* mine—I terminated him.

"You're the leaders of this organization. I want you to know what I did and why. I'm going to ask that, if you hear scuttlebutt about Henry's departure, you explain what I've just told you."

Prior to the meeting, Jack had met with Sharon Ferrari, Henry's number two and go-to person. He asked her if she'd be willing to act as Henry's interim replacement until a new one could be found. He assured Sharon that, if she wanted to be considered for the permanent position, she would be. She told him that she'd be honored to act as the interim Director of Operations and that she was definitely interested in the position long-term.

"In the interim," Jack informed the room full of managers, "Sharon Ferrari has agreed to be my *Acting Director of Operations.*" There was heartfelt applause, more than Jack had expected, but Nadine had assured him that Sharon was highly respected.

Earlier, Nadine informed Jack, "Sharon has managed to keep Ops running *despite* Henry. She's toned down Henry's rhetoric and helped to build back people's sense of self-worth after he'd just beaten them down. I'm confident you're really going to enjoy working with her.

"One other thing," Nadine continued. "People are going to see your replacement of Henry with Sharon as a very positive thing. That alone will signal a change for the better around here."

Back at the meeting, Jack said, "That's it. I'm sorry it came to this, but we are on a new and exciting journey. Hopefully, that will be our last departure, but expect a lot of change for the better in the weeks and months ahead. You're good people and Copper-Bottom is lucky to have you."

As Jack finished recounting the story to Don, the latter let out a low whistle. "Jack," he began, "I'm really impressed. You've taken a bucket of lemons and turned them into a pitcher of lemonade. Great job!

"In the weeks ahead, we're going to teach you to take that same bucket of lemons and turn them into lemon meringue." The grin on his face was audible in his voice.

"Okay," Don said, shifting gears, "Tim and I will be there again Monday morning and start what we had planned for today … and for yesterday," he said with a grin that Jack could again hear through the phone. "We're going to need your full staff, including Sharon, present at 8 AM.

"Now, the bad news: we're going to keep them tied up all day for the full week.

"Believe me," he said, cutting off Jack's objections, "this is critical. If it weren't, I wouldn't ask you to do it. Next week, you'll start to understand why.

"Meanwhile, tell your folks to plan accordingly. They're going to need to plan to be out of their offices the whole week.

"Anything else I need to know?" Don asked.

"Like that's not enough," Jack retorted, but there was humor in his voice. "See you Monday. Great stuff ahead," he said, as a reassuring afterthought.

Principle #3: Leaders need to start with the right people around them. Failure to do so always results in slowed (if not failed) execution.

Principle #4: Own your message. Don't let others or the grapevine control the news.

Corollary #4–1: No matter how bad the message, the grapevine can probably make it worse.

11

The Plan

Earlier Friday morning, Don had walked into Tim's office. "Got a sec?" Don asked.

"Sure," Tim responded. "What's up?"

"I've been thinking about Copper-Bottom and what our approach needs to be. I wanted to share my ideas with you and see if we can develop a six-month plan of action. You game?"

"Absolutely," Tim said.

"May I use your whiteboard?"

Tim knew the question was a courtesy and graciously extended his hand, indicating that Don should feel free.

"I've been asking myself where they need to be in six months," Don began. "You and I understand that six months will only get them to the starting line of a lifelong race, but it's a long way from where they are today. Agreed?"

Tim understood the question was rhetorical and nodded his head.

"In my mind, they need to be using KPIs as a way of understanding how they're doing and for creating dialog top to bottom. Do you agree?"

"Without question," Tim said, adding, "They also need to switch from a command-and-control style of leadership to a coaching model. Part of the reason they are where they are is that they let at least one leader run roughshod over their people."

"Agreed," Don responded.

Don wrote "Create KPIs" on the whiteboard, followed by "Command & Control to Coaching."

"If their first KPI is safety, they need to start practicing 5S," Tim offered, "or at least do some major housekeeping. Add to that, they need to up their safety game. I'm not sure there are any data to support it, but with all the

DOI: 10.4324/9781003336051-12

paper on their floors and all the file drawers open, they have got to be having slip, trip, and fall injuries all the time."

"Good point," agreed Don. Distractedly, he moved to his next thought. "Would you agree that they need to invert their method of leadership, become more servant leaders rather than dictators?"

"You said a mouthful," Tim said. "If we could only change one thing, it would be that. Employees need to feel their leaders are doing everything possible to help them succeed and not finding reasons to discipline them, or throwing obstacles in their path. Honestly, Don, everyone in that building seemed scared."

"You're right," Don agreed. "I had forgotten it until you just reminded me. You're absolutely right. It was as if they were more concerned about not getting in trouble than they were about doing their jobs to the best of their ability. That's a horrible way to live."

Don wrote notes on the board, lost in silence.

When he finished, Tim said, "Leaders need to get out of their offices. They've got to *go and see* what is actually going on and observe firsthand the problems their people have."

Don recorded Tim's statement, then said, "We're going to need to conduct a monthly morale audit. Jim promised that to George, Jack's boss. And," he continued, "Jack's got to send those results to George each month."

Don had been writing that down but stopped. "Do you think we can do much more in six months?"

"I think what you already have up there is going to be a tall order," responded Tim, "but if they don't fight us, I think it's doable." He had his own ideas, but asked Don, "Where do we start?"

- KPIs
- Coaching
- Servant Leadership
- 5S
- Genchi Genbutsu
- Morale Audits

Don tapped the whiteboard next to his last entry. "Morale: let's take the pulse and see where we are. I'd suggest we use our own evaluation and have a group of our employees sit down to interview their people. Agreed?"

Tim nodded his assent. "Good news is their staff is relatively small, but it will still take a couple of days to get all their feedback. I can get our HR folks on it, and I'm sure they will do a super job, but can you afford to dedicate that many hours to this project each month?"

"I think we have to do it this month. We don't have time to train their people to do it the first month, but you're right, we'll need to find another way to do it by next month. Meanwhile, can you undertake getting our own HR to send us five employees trained to conduct the survey? Let's plan on doing it next Monday.

"Afterwards, we'll need at least one person from our HR team to train Copper-Bottom's people to conduct subsequent surveys. Can you arrange that, too?"

Tim made notes in his Day-Planner.

Setting his pencil down, he said, "Okay, while that's going on, where do we start with the leaders?"

Oh boy, Don thought, recalling his own journey. Silently he began a new list on the board. When he'd entered several items, he began talking to the list as he wrote.

Leader Behavior

- *Lead by Example:* Leaders need to lead by example; not only *walk the talk*, but set the pace. That means they can't leave this transformation to us or even to Jack. The only way to lead is to be out front yourself. We can teach them, but THEY are going to have to lead their people.
- *Leaders First:* Leaders need to apply any new behaviors, any new programs, any new knowledge to themselves first, and only apply them to subordinates after the leaders have maintained them for no less than a month (six would be better, but we're on a short timeline here).

Knowledge Transfer

- *Leaders Teach:* You're right, we cannot be the teachers of anyone besides the executives. If we are teaching the lower tiers of Copper-Bottom, that would make it seem like this is a Friedman initiative. Their legitimate leaders need to own this transformation; hence, they need to teach.
- *Cascade Knowledge:* Leaders need to learn, then teach their subordinates. That begins a cascading of knowledge and ensures that

everyone speaks the same language; further, when leaders teach, the leaders learn doubly well. When their leaders teach, their people understand that what they're being taught is important. After all, their leaders are teaching them.

Inspiring Performance

- *Key Performance Indicators (KPIs):* Leaders need to establish the key measures of good performance: KPIs. Almost without exception, they apply all KPIs to themselves first, posting their performance publicly on KPI boards in chart form.
- *Leaders Own Performance:* Leaders need to hold themselves accountable. They hold briefings at their own KPI boards at least monthly, and when they don't reach their objectives, they initiate root cause analysis until the reason for failure is understood. Then they develop and execute a recovery plan. That plan identifies: what will be done, by whom, and when it's scheduled to be complete. In short, leaders establish a discipline of not only *reporting* performance but of *controlling* it.
- *Recovery Plan:* Anytime a deadline is missed, the person responsible must respond immediately with a recovery plan that lays out the step-by-step process of getting back on track.
- *Cascading KPIs:* Once they have the hang of holding themselves accountable, leaders cascade their KPIs down through the organization—one management layer at a time. So that everyone knows what's expected of them, every KPI will have a goal that establishes what good performance looks like.
- *Goals, Arrows, and Catchball:* And every measure will have an arrow pointing in the direction of "good." Leaders need to determine how to tailor their own KPIs to their subordinates. Then the leader and subordinate need to jointly establish what the goal for each subordinate KPI will be. They'll do that using a process called *catchball*.
- *Post and Review:* Leaders need to ensure their subordinates are also posting their performance metrics publicly and reviewing their performance at least weekly. The closer to the customer a subordinate's job gets, the more frequently their performance reviews need to take place. Frontline leaders should be meeting daily to discuss the previous day's performance and discuss what countermeasures they'll put in place to reverse poor performance.

Go and See (for yourself)

- Leaders need to make time to visit their subordinates' KPI boards and listen to their subordinates briefing their organization's performance. Leaders use these opportunities to coach their subordinates: asking, not telling.

Tim took a photo of the whiteboard Don had been working on so Don could erase it and start over.

Standard Work

- This will be a lifelong process, but leaders need to make their employees' jobs clear and standardize the way the job should *always* be performed. The standard should be in writing and hopefully in photos. Everyone who performs that job needs to be trained in the new standard.
- Leaders need to monitor their employees' performance against the standard and make sure that employees are adhering to it. Leaders need to continue to monitor and retrain until the standard becomes muscle memory.

Optimize Employee Performance

Leaders need to:

- Remove administrative obstacles from their employee's paths.
- Use the full authority of their titles to help their employees.
- Develop a protocol to transition decision-making authority to their subordinates within clearly established boundaries.
- Catch employees *succeeding* and reward them, if only with praise.
- Create a list of skills that every member of a skill group should be able to perform (skills matrix), and assess all incumbent workers against those expectations.
- Review every subordinate's performance at least quarterly (preferably monthly).
- Identify "Hi Pots" (upward-promotable employees) who have met all the requirements of their current jobs and who are working to be able to perform the job of the next higher level.
- Provide feedback to employees in areas requiring further development while also acknowledging the growth each employee exhibits.

- Begin/continue a succession plan (list of employees eligible for promotion to the next level). Alternately, a list of positions with qualified candidate(s) for each.
- Develop a rapport with every direct report so that subordinates know how their current performance is being assessed and what is needed to advance the next skill level.
- Create clear standards for advancement and make those standards known to all subordinates in that skill group.
- Know each subordinate's growth desires and counsel them on how to achieve those desires.

Before leaving Tim's office, Don took additional cell phone pictures of the whiteboard. He'd later transcribe the lists to a document so he and Tim could follow it.

Principle #5: Establish measures that will tell everyone how they are performing and provide leaders with a tool to coach.

Principle #6: Develop a pattern, from the top down, of coaching subordinates into the right behaviors, rather than "telling" them.

Principle #7: Leaders lead from the front.

Corollary #7–1: Establish a vision for where we're going.

Corollary #7–2: Apply changes and new things to themselves first.

Corollary #7–3: Learn first; then teach their subordinates.

Corollary #7–4: Measure themselves first; then cascade measures downward.

Corollary #7–5: Missed deadlines result in immediate recovery plans.

Corollary #7–6: "Go and See" KPI boards. Use the opportunity to coach.

Corollary #7–7: Lock in optimal performance with Standard Work.

12

Monday: A New Leaf

On Monday morning, everyone was seated in Jack's conference room by 8 AM.

Jack again introduced Tim and Don, then Don gave a quick orientation. "For the next several days, you're going to be creating a top-down system of performance metrics.

"You're going to start out using those metrics to measure your own performance as a management team. Then you're going to cascade the applicable portions of those metrics to your subordinates, and their subordinates, and their subordinates, all the way to the lowest level of leaders. In the future, you'll use these metrics to hold yourselves accountable.

"How's that going to change our culture, you ask? This group is going to post its performance against those measures in a public area. Then you're going to ask all your other subordinate managers to do the same. You're going to use these performance measures as a vehicle to begin *conversations*—not lectures—with your subordinates, and *that's* one of the tools you're going to use to change your culture: honest dialog.

"But let's not get ahead of ourselves. I'm going to let Tim begin taking you through the process and soon enough, you'll see for yourselves. Tim?"

"Good morning, everyone," Tim began. "I'd like you to take everything off the table. Let's start with a clean slate."

As Jack's staff started to put their notebooks and laptops on the floor behind them, Jack handed out the company's mission statement. When everyone had a copy, Tim began.

"What I'm going to start off with is a little philosophy. It may seem inconsequential, but let me assure you, it's not.

"Philosophies guide the way we do what we do. They're at play all the time, even if we don't recognize them or state them formally. We're going

DOI: 10.4324/9781003336051-13

to examine the philosophies of your company and make sure they are compatible with the way you actually work; we'll also want to ensure that your philosophies (your values) represent the way you want to continue to work.

"All right, the first of the philosophies we're going to examine is your mission statement. Who wants to read it?"

When no one volunteered, Tim called on Sharon. "Sharon, you're the newbie on the staff. Lead us off."

Sharon cleared her throat and began: "*The mission of Copper-Bottom Health Solutions is to provide economical healthcare solutions to our clients and their employees.*"

"Short and sweet," Tim said. "Thank you, Sharon."

"Okay, what have we just heard? Somebody, tell me what that all means."

When no one stepped forward, Tim looked at Nadine and said, "Nadine, I'd have called on you, but I don't want the men here to think they're off the hook." He pointed to the man to Nadine's left. "Your name, sir?" he asked.

"Skip Fuller," came the other man's response.

"I'm sorry," Tim apologized, "but the only ones here whose titles I know are Don, Nadine, and Sharon. Can you tell me what you do for Copper-Bottom, Skip?"

"I'm the Director of IT," Skip responded, blushing.

"Great. Skip, tell us what we just heard."

Skip looked down at his paper for a couple of seconds. When he didn't appear ready to respond, Tim said, "Skip, the goal of the next exercise is to develop ways to measure your company's commitments as made in your mission statement. There are a few things we always want to use in our performance metrics. They are Safety, Quality, Schedule, and Cost. How does your mission statement address these?"

Skip hesitated a second longer before stating, "It doesn't. Well," he corrected himself, "at least not directly."

"Good answer," Tim praised Skip. "So, how does it address them indirectly?"

"Well," Skip began, "it says we will provide *economical* healthcare solutions. You could read into that that we are *cost*-conscious."

"How so?" Tim pursued.

Skip had hoped that Tim would call on someone else. He looked at Jack, who nodded his head encouragingly. "Well, one could assume that *economical service* implies low-cost service."

"Very good," Tim nodded approvingly. "What about safety, quality, and schedule?"

"It doesn't address them at all," Skip stated.

"Great job, Skip. That was tough, wasn't it?"

Skip nodded, blushing again.

"Let me drive home a point," Tim said. "Safety, Quality, Schedule and Cost are the bare minimum performance metrics of a company. If you aren't measuring them, how can you tell if you're reaching mission success?"

No one responded. "Which of you is Jerry?" Tim asked the room. Another man awkwardly raised his hand.

"Jerry, you're the Controller. How do you know if you're achieving mission success?"

"When we post a healthy return on shareholder equity," Jerry responded.

"That's it?" Tim asked incredulously. "If your shareholders make money you declare mission success?"

"Yeah," Jerry affirmed his earlier answer. "That's the measure. At least, that's the one I use."

"Good point," acknowledged Tim. "That's the measure *you* use. Sharon, how do you measure success?"

Sharon thought for a second before responding. "We use several: calls per hour per employee, letters answered per day per employee, responses to Internet queries per day per employee, length of calls, number of repeat calls for the same problem." She stopped. "Should I go on?"

"That will do for now," responded Tim. "I didn't hear you mention anything about return on shareholder equity. Don't you measure that?"

"No," Sharon admitted. "Why would I?"

Tim didn't respond to her question. "So, Sharon, what you're telling me is that you and Jerry measure the performance of your groups independent of all the other groups or the company as a whole. Is that right?"

Sharon felt a trap, but there seemed to be only one answer. "Yes, I guess you're right."

Tim addressed the larger group. "I'm sure the same can be said for the rest of you, right?"

There were nods around the table.

"You're not alone," Tim continued. "Ever since the days of Frederick Winslow Taylor and the Industrial Revolution, jobs have been broken down by skill. Like-skilled people were grouped together and given a similarly skilled supervisor to oversee them. That began the *isolation* of groups with different skills from one another.

"Then came Peter Drucker and his *Management by Objectives*. Drucker had intended that managers would ensure that the objectives of their subordinates would be linked, through their own to the organization's objectives. How did that work in practice? In most organizations, only the senior leaders' objectives were tied to the organization's objectives. As long as those goals were met, senior leaders had the flexibility to measure their subordinates based on what they felt important. With each successive layer, the tie back to the top-level objectives became weaker and weaker.

"As we've already discussed, that led to a widening of the gap between what the organization thought was important and what each successive layer of the organization measured."

As he was still explaining, Tim began a quick sketch of what looked like three tin cans. He labeled each: *Accounting Silo, Operations Silo, & Information Technology Silo.*

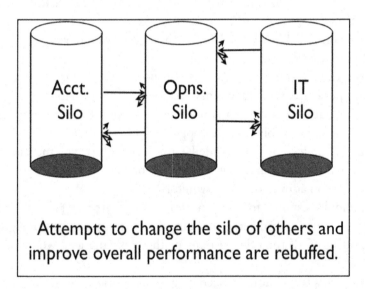

Attempts to change the silo of others and improve overall performance are rebuffed.

"Somewhere in all this, we have the development of *silos*. These occur when organizations isolate themselves and their activities from all the other organizations and become accountable only to themselves and their immediate manager.

"Within their silo, managers measure performance against *their* objectives—what *they* think is important. In doing so, they believe they are serving the needs of the greater organization. Their attitude could be summarized as 'What's good for us *is* good for the organization.'"

Tim pointed to the graphic.

"The owner of each silo becomes lord of their own manor, so to speak. They set their own rules for how other organizations will have to deal with theirs. Those rules are almost always internally focused; improving their own organization's performance at the cost of making it harder for other organizations to work with them. We call this *sub-optimizing* or optimizing the lesser at the expense of the greater.

"Little of this *silo behavior* serves the needs of the external customer, or, for that matter, the greater organization. Sound familiar?

"An example might help," he offered. "Picture Geraldine. She runs the procurement department for a large organization. They have an antiquated computer ordering system that requires her people to perform lots of intricate steps to enter a single order. However, this system also produces excellent reports, including order updates. Those allow others to quickly check the status of their orders.

"Geraldine instructs her people to develop a new online process that will streamline order entry. When complete, the new system requires the organization requesting the product or service to input all the order information. That removes the burden from Geraldine's organization and shifts it to other organizations. However, the new system has no outward-facing reporting. Now to get an update on their orders, other organizations need to call Geraldine's buyers. To get the information, the buyer has to go through a series of machinations that can take up to 10 minutes for each request. They can avoid that by not answering their phones. If they get an email, they get back *when they can*.

"So, while the new system makes it easier for Geraldine's people, it creates a problem for the rest of the organization.

"Sound familiar?" Tim asked. There were a few nods and a mumbled "Yes," while a couple of participants just stared back as if they were watching a TV program.

Tim frowned at the responses but kept going.

"At the end of the day, silos rarely measure the right things. Worse, they fragment the overall organization's response to their clients and shareholders because the various internal organizations are not on the same page. It's a rare organization where that doesn't happen, but we're going to stop it here. We're going to *align* all of your actions so that you support each other, and so that your joint efforts support your organization and your customers.

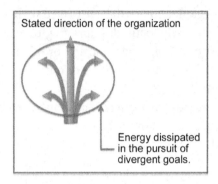

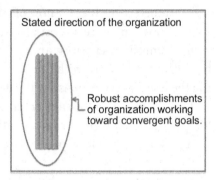

"Does all that make sense?" Tim asked.

Again, there was a lackluster and uncoordinated response.

"Okay," Tim stated. "New rule. From now on, silence isn't allowed to have a voice. When a question is asked, you need to give a verbal response. That's going to be particularly true later as we begin to vote and share ideas."

"So, Sharon, does what I just said make sense?"

"It does," Sharon replied.

"Skip?"

"Yes."

"Jerry?"

"Yup."

"Nadine?"

"Yes, sir."

Tim went around the room asking each person. When he got to Jack, he asked, "So, Jack, does this explanation of selfish silo behavior sound familiar to you?"

"Does it ever," Jack replied. "I've never heard it explained this way, but having heard it, it makes perfect sense."

"Good. We're all on a common page about silo behavior. Let's go back to how we will measure mission success moving forward.

"Although, as Skip has pointed out, the mission statement doesn't address them overtly, we need to develop a way to measure safety, quality, schedule, and cost. After that, we'll create measures to meet the specific needs of Copper-Bottom, like return on shareholder equity. Agreed?" he asked.

There was a chorus of "Yeses."

"All right, let's get started."

"Typically, the first thing we will do is to check your mission statement to see if it really says what you want it to. If not, we'll change it. Then, we'll make sure we are measuring what it commits you to do, as well as safety, quality, schedule, and cost.

"I said that we'd *typically* do that, but in this case, your mission statement is the corporate mission statement, right?"

"Correct," responded Nadine.

"So we can't really change it," said Tim. "In that case, we simply need to ask what does your mission commit you to measure?"

Tim reread the mission statement out loud. "*The mission of Copper-Bottom Health Solutions is to provide economical healthcare solutions to our clients and their employees.*

"Jerry, you're the numbers guy. How do you know when your organization is providing *economical healthcare solutions*?"

"We can't compare ourselves directly to our competitors, but we can look at how we stack up against the industry average," Jerry responded.

"What kind of margin do you want to see?" Tim asked.

Jerry shot Jack a glance. "It's okay," Jack assured him, permitting Jerry to share what was clearly closely held information.

Before continuing, Jerry said, "This stays in this room." Turning back to Tim, he said, "Forty to 45%."

"So, we could say that one of your measures will be to maintain a margin of 40% or greater, correct?" Tim asked.

"Yes," responded Jerry.

Tim erased his earlier sketches and wrote the metric on the whiteboard.

Looking at the greater group, Tim asked, "Is there anything else that your mission commits you to achieve?" When no one answered, Tim asked, "Where does the provision of *economical healthcare solutions to your client's employees* come into play?"

Jerry answered again. "We negotiate the amount of the copay on their behalf," he said.

"And how do you measure whether that's *economical*?" asked Tim.

"We set a target copay of $30 or less," Jerry responded. "Obviously, somebody needs to pay for the whole bill. That comes down to the rates the insurance companies negotiate with hospitals and individual physicians. The more clients an insurance company has, the greater discounts they can negotiate. Copper-Bottom is one of the larger healthcare insurers, so we negotiate some great terms.

"When we get a new client, we shop their coverage around within several of our plans. We then go back to the client with options. Those options look at three basic things: employer contribution, employee contribution, and per-visit copay."

"Thanks for the explanation," Tim stated. "If I understand correctly, you really don't *control* so much as *negotiate* the copay and all the other fees. The employer—your client—then chooses the plan they want. Is that correct?"

Jerry bobbed his head from side to side, as if he were weighing Tim's question and ultimately said, "Yes."

"So," Tim concluded, "what I'm hearing is that the only part of the mission statement against which you measure yourself is your margin. Is that correct?"

"It is," agreed Jerry.

"In that case, let's talk about what else you'd need to measure. How will you measure safety, quality, schedule, and cost?"

Again there was silence. Finally, Sharon raised her hand. When Tim pointed to her, she said, "I'm just spit-balling here, but I'd suggest that we'd have a goal of answering client questions in one phone call."

"Good metric," Tim praised Sharon while writing the metric on the board. "Which of the four measures does that address?"

"Take your pick," Sharon replied. "I could see it addressing either quality or schedule."

Sharon fell silent, then raised her hand again.

"Shoot!" Tim encouraged her.

"I think we'd want to respond to letters within 24 hours and deliver decisions within 48 hours."

The last metric got the rest of the group stirring. Apparently, it was well beyond what was now considered achievable.

"Great. Let's talk about this, but let's do it in orderly fashion. Who wants to go first?"

Nadine was the first to speak. "We don't have enough people to achieve that," she retorted.

Sharon was quiet for long seconds, but it was evident that something was brewing inside her. Finally, she spoke.

"My mom is 73 and a breast cancer survivor. Her health is not good, and I take her to her doctor appointments on my day off. I can't tell you how many times her doctor has ordered a test or a procedure that her insurance company ultimately approved, but it took them weeks and dozens of phone calls before they'd get back to us.

"That's not right. I think we should strive to be better. I'm not saying that we should restructure to give decisions in 24 hours, but I thought the point of this exercise was to set goals for ourselves and then strive to meet them."

Tim responded to that last comment. "It's our objective to determine *what* to measure. You're right though, Sharon, at some point we'll have to establish goals for each of the things we agree to measure. The question is whether this is the appropriate time to set that goal."

Turning to the group, Tim asked, "What do you think? Show of hands, who wants to choose both the metric and the goal right now?" Only Sharon raised her hand.

"Okay," Tim responded, "looks like the first thing the group wants to do is establish the metric. Understand that we'll ultimately need to come back and establish the goal as well, but we can do that at a later time."

Tim turned to the whiteboard and began a table.

Metric	Goal	Origin
Margin	≥ 40%	Mission & Cost
Answer Client questions	1 phone call	Schedule
Respond to Mail		Schedule

Turning back to the team he said, "One thing I would point out, is that we need to make sure that we're covering the metrics of Safety, Quality, Schedule, and Cost, as well as those dictated by the mission statement. It looks like the last two we discussed were both related to Schedule. Can someone think of a measure for Safety, Quality, and Cost?"

Again, no one volunteered, so this time Tim picked on Nadine.

"Nadine, you have to report on Workman's Comp and Lost Time Accidents. What are the company's statistics like?

"Well," she began, "we see mostly paper cuts, scraped ankles, and sore backs."

"Do you measure 'near misses'?" Tim asked.

"I'm not sure I know what you mean," Nadine responded.

"A near miss is a serious accident narrowly averted, for example, someone who *almost* injured themselves when they slipped but caught themselves or a faulty cord that *was sparking but got unplugged before anything* caught fire. Have you had any of those?"

"To be honest, safety is one of those issues that is so minor that, if it's not a problem, we don't waste time on it."

Tim shot Don a glance.

"How about we take a break?" Tim announced. As the staff filed out, Don and Tim approached Jack.

"This can't be good," the other man said with a jovial smile.

Don began. "Jack, you have us here because your organization's culture is having issues. Without something against which to compare it, you have no idea what that means, but both Tim and I come from organizations other than Friedman Electronics. We've seen enough organizations to know that a good number of your problems emanate from the people in this room.

"Let me explain what I mean. First, have you noticed that no one was answering Tim's questions without him having to call on them directly? That's not a good sign. Next, with the possible exception of Sharon, the answers that are given only answer the question asked and don't venture an inch beyond.

"Something in this room is intimidating your staff. Do you know what it is?"

Jack looked quizzically at the other two. "I can't say I do."

"Well, the only one in this room who can begin to change the rest is you. When we reconvene, I'd like Tim to turn the meeting over to you. I'd like you to get to the bottom of the issues I just illustrated. Are you open to doing that?"

"Sure," acknowledged Jack. "Tell me what to do."

"You just need to clear the air," Don replied. "Something's keeping them from commenting freely. They're scared of something. My bet is retribution. They're afraid that someone in the room will later hold things said here against them. If that's true, your culture change dies here. You've got to get them to open up. To do that, you're going to need to figure out what's holding them back.

"I'd recommend you put it to them as straightforwardly as you can. Don't shillyshally. Tell them what we've observed and ask them why they're holding back."

"Okay," Jack said, scratching his head.

"Do you want us in the room or out?" Don asked.

"There's nothing they're going to say that I'm afraid for you to hear," responded Jack. "You might as well stay. If I sense that they won't talk with you in the room, I'll ask you to leave. Will that work?"

Don nodded and Tim gave Jack a thumbs-up sign.

13

Monday Continued: Clearing the Air

When everyone was back in the room, Tim called them to order and then turned the discussion over to Jack.

Standing in the center of the room, Jack opened in a soft voice. "Hey, folks. I came to Copper-Bottom right out of college. I've never worked anywhere else, so I'm accustomed to you being reserved. Tim and Don have worked enough places that they feel you're being restrained, held back by something. They've asked me to get to the bottom of that before we go on."

The room remained silent, and everyone just stared back at him.

Turning to Don, he said, "I see what you mean." There was a nervous titter in the room.

"Okay," he began again. "I've seen all of you in other settings and know you can be a lot more animated and opinionated. What gives? Why is this different?"

Again, silence.

When no one else stepped forward, Sharon cleared her throat.

"I'm not sure this is it, Jack, but I know that there are a lot of us who have felt our opinions have been unwelcome over the years, especially by people in this room."

Jack was unprepared for anyone to be that honest, but Sharon continued.

"Again, speaking only for myself, I have always presumed that you were the one who was behind that. Although it was Henry who was ruthless with his words, the fact he was allowed to continue … well …" She trailed off. "Well, I always assumed you knew and condoned it." She stopped and was quiet for a long time. The room was deathly still.

Finally, she started again.

"I figure my job's toast anyway, so I may as well say it all."

DOI: 10.4324/9781003336051-14

In a strong voice indicative of her resolve to get through her statement, Sharon continued. "I'm surprised that it took so long for someone to stand up to all of you," she said, implying Patty Purcell. She was now flushing brilliantly, but she continued. "And what surprises me the most is that you're surprised." She finished the last statement with hot tears splashing on the table in front of her. She stoically got up and left the room. She didn't rush. She walked with a normal but determined gait. It was obvious that she was exerting a great deal of self-control.

Jack was beet-red and clearly hurt by Sharon's statement. The room remained still. Eyes were downcast. No one dared look at Jack or even in his general direction.

At length, Don stood up and said, "I don't know how all of you feel, but I feel I just witnessed a tremendous act of bravery. Sharon put her career on the line to say what she did, but I hope you all agree she said it for the good of the organization, not out of spite. I can't speak for you, Jack, but those are the kind of people with whom I want to surround myself.

"As for the rest of you," Don continued, "is she right?"

Silence.

"Show of hands." Don was unwilling to let the moment pass. "Who believes that what Sharon said is something they also feel?"

Skip timidly raised his hand. Skip was followed by Jennifer Rosario, Jack's Director of Sales, and then by Nadine and the others. The only one who didn't raise his hand was Jerry Falstaff, the Controller.

Avoiding putting Jack on the spot, Don addressed the rest of the room. "This is a defining moment. You've set out to change your culture. Would you agree that you can't achieve that goal while even one of you is feeling as you now do?

"Doing what led you to this crisis, ignoring the hard truths, can't take you past this juncture. The next question each of you needs to ask yourself is, what do you intend to do about it?"

There was a long silence. Tim was prepared to call a break, but Don began to talk again. In measured words he said, "This is a pivotal moment for this branch of Copper-Bottom. Jack, I see several options.

"ONE: As leader of Copper-Bottom, you can let Sharon go. She already admitted she expects you to do that, so she won't be surprised. Of course," he continued, "if you do that, you'll kill any chance of hearing honest feedback from this point on. Oh," he continued almost as an afterthought, "and you'll scuttle any chance of achieving cultural change. Letting Sharon go will only galvanize everyone's beliefs that the old behaviors were intentional and part of your management style."

He paused a beat, looking at the back of the room and avoiding eyes.

"TWO: You can keep Sharon, get past this awkward moment, and just go back to business as usual. However, if you do that, you really can't expect anyone else to sign up to change anything, since you weren't willing to.

"THREE: You can humbly offer Sharon and everyone else an apology and ask for their forgiveness. You're not apologizing that you behaved like Henry Corn, but that Henry had done so on your watch. You'd also want to assure them that you will do your level best to ensure no one treats them that way in the future."

Jack raised his hands in a defensive gesture, but before he could speak Don said, "I know, Jack, you did that the other day, but one 'I'm sorry' doesn't erase years of perceived disrespect. Remember, we're not dealing with what you intended, but what others perceived. Healing is going to take some time. Besides," Don continued, "you're not the only one at fault."

Now, turning to make eye contact with Jack's subordinates, Don continued. "Henry's behavior and the culture of fear it precipitated could be laid at your feet, too. You could all hide behind the belief that 'It's all Jack's fault,' but that wouldn't be true, would it?

"Don't get me wrong, as senior leaders we should know what's going on in our organizations and take appropriate action when necessary. But this moment isn't about finding blame. It's about finding forgiveness and hope. To get there, each of you needs to look inside him or herself and admit they were silently complicit in Henry's behavior.

"Tim will remind you of this later, but I'm going to steal a little of his thunder to illustrate a point. Your customers perceive you as a company, not as individuals, or even as departments, but as a unified group: *Copper-Bottom*. If one of you acts inappropriately toward your customer, the customer is left believing that's the way Copper-Bottom treats all their customers.

"Likewise, your employees see their leaders as a unified group. They don't think of you as the director of this or the director of that. They see you collectively as *management*. Isn't that what Sharon just told you?

"When one of you messes up and the others don't take them to task for it, then, in your employee's eyes, you all just messed up.

"Nadine," Don asked, "does that ring true?"

"It does," she responded.

"Jennifer?"

"It does."

"Skip?"

"Yes."

"Jerry?"

"I can see your point" was all he'd commit.

"Jerry, this is one of those things you can't sidestep. You either believe it or you don't. Let me ask you again. Do you believe that when any one of you acts inappropriately and no one counters them, then in the eyes of your employees, it's as if you all did it?"

Jerry was silent, choosing to avoid answering. Don was having none of it, so in an even voice he asked again.

"Jerry, this is a yes-or-no question. Do you or don't you believe it?"

"I know you want me to say 'yes,' but I don't believe it. I believe we're each accountable for our own actions and that, if I act badly, no one else is responsible for it."

"That isn't the question, though, is it, Jerry? What we're dealing with here is the *perception* of your people."

Don was getting irritated with Jerry, so he turned to Nadine. "Nadine, do you agree that in the eyes of the perceiver, their perception *is* reality?"

"I do."

Don turned back to Jerry. "Jerry, the woman Henry bullied worked for you, didn't she?"

"Yes," Jerry stated flatly.

"Did she report the incident to you?"

"Yes."

"And how did you deal with it?"

"I reminded her that Henry was our customer."

"Did you say anything to Henry?"

"No."

"Did you report the incident to Jack or Nadine?"

"No."

"You know what I think, Jerry? I think you, not Jack, should be on probation.

"You left your boss swinging in the breeze. But worse than that, you let one of your employees be verbally battered, and then you victimized her again by telling her that it's acceptable behavior for a senior leader to treat her that way because he's your *customer*.

"You might just as well have told her that it was okay for a senior manager to touch her inappropriately. In that moment, you created a hostile work environment and she's got you dead to rights.

"Jack"—Don whirled around to face him—"do you see my point about perceptions?"

"Yes," he replied a bit dispiritedly.

"Do you agree?"

"Yes."

Turning back to Jerry, Don said, "You probably think I'm making a mountain out of a molehill, but this was the crux of the lawsuit against your company. And," he went on, "this is the crux of your culture problems: your people"—he swept an accusatory finger around the room—"don't think you care about them. They believe you only think of them as a necessary evil to get what *you* want."

Don fell silent for two beats to let his words sink in.

"Let's take a break," he said next. And then, as an afterthought, he said, "What just went on in this room needs to stay in this room. By that I mean you can't talk about it with anyone who wasn't in this room. We good?" he asked, pointing to each staff member in succession. Each nodded or said, "Yes."

"Five minutes," he instructed them.

Still in the conference room, Don turned to Jack. "If I overstepped my bounds I apologize, but as I said, this is a defining moment in this organization's history. What you do next will be pivotal in determining whether you succeed in changing your culture, or not.

"I'd recommend that you keep this group together today until you can work through your next steps. You don't need us for that. Tim and I will head back to Friedman. If you want us tomorrow, just give me a call. If not, I'll understand."

Don extended his hand and Jack shook it. "Good luck," Don said.

As he and Tim left the conference room, Don could see the four women in an adjacent office, crying and hugging Sharon. Sharon noticed him, broke away from the group, and ran over to hug him. "Thank you" was all she could sob out before returning to the other women.

Later that afternoon, he got a call from Jack. The other man sounded bone-weary.

"Before I say anything else, I want to ask for you and Tim to return tomorrow. Can you make it?"

Don said he could make it in the morning but had a conference call in the afternoon. "Tim can be there the whole day, though."

"Great," said Jack as if a burden had been lifted. "The other thing I wanted to say is 'Thank you.' You were right. I should have seen what Henry was doing and said something, and I didn't; shame on me.

"After you left, the whole staff came back in, including Sharon. I apologized to them for my complicity in Henry's behavior and asked for their forgiveness. I told them our past wasn't going to define our future and that we were going to become better, stronger, healthier. I asked them for their help.

"I told Sharon that I was grateful for her honesty and that I was unworthy of it but would work to become so. I told her I hoped she'd stay and help define who we were about to become. She was crying again but nodded her agreement.

"As you might guess, Jerry was quiet throughout all that. He looked pained by my admission of culpability in Henry's behavior, as if Henry had done nothing wrong."

Abruptly, Jack asked, "What am I going to do with him?"

"What's your heart tell you?" Don asked.

There was silence, as if that were the first time anyone had ever asked Jack such a question.

"I … I," he stammered. It wasn't that he didn't know what his heart told him. It was that he didn't want to say the words. He started again. "Don, after hearing Jerry's take on things, I'm not sure I can afford to keep him on staff. I mean, aren't I just inviting another incident?"

Don knew that they were talking about a man's career. He also knew that Jerry was the product of years of conditioning in the *old* way of doing things. The question was whether he was willing to unlearn all that behavior and become something new?

"Jack, letting someone go is always my last choice, and in this case you don't have to. I'd give him a letter of reprimand and put him on probation for his part in the Henry incident.

"Talk to Nadine and let her work through the language of the letter with you. That way there's a written record of that incident and his role in it.

"In addition to the letter of reprimand, you'll want to verbally explain to Jerry that, while his behavior may have been acceptable at some point in the past, it isn't any longer. Instruct him on how he should handle a similar situation in the future, and tell him that any additional incidents of that nature will result in further disciplinary action.

"From that point on, it's Jerry's decision what happens to him. If he wants to stay, he'll change his behavior. Remember, though, behavior is learned, and it took him a while to learn it. It may also take a while to unlearn it.

"I'd suggest that, for the next couple of months, you go out of your way to meet with Jerry and just talk about what's going on in his department, how he's doing, what help he needs from you or from corporate. Make him continue to feel like part of your team. By the way, it wouldn't be a bad thing to do that with all your people.

"In the next two weeks, we'll teach all of you new skills that will give you lots of opportunities for positive interaction. Until then, I'd recommend that you take an approach like the one I just suggested. What do you think?" he asked.

When he spoke, there was new hope in Jack's voice. Don realized that he'd been dreading that his only course of action was going to be to let Jerry go. His voice now carried none of the earlier strain and fatigue. He wasn't letting Jerry off the hook, but he was leaving Jerry's future with Copper-Bottom in Jerry's hands.

In a flash, Jack realized that, in his fear, he'd had developed tunnel vision, seeing only one option. Don's input had been invaluable.

"Thank you, Don. That makes so much sense. Jerry's a good man. I think he can work through this. I was afraid that you were going to tell me that I needed to let him go. I'm so glad you've revealed another option that holds him responsible for his past but leaves the burden of his future on his own shoulders.

"Thanks," Jack said again. "I really mean it. If you don't do another thing, you've helped Copper-Bottom move past a terrible moment in our history."

"You realize," Don said with mirth in his voice, "we still haven't drained the swamp, right?"

Both men laughed. It was a moment of bonding.

Principle #8: Outsiders (customers and employees) perceive our organizations as a monolith: a single, cohesive, like-minded body. Under such circumstances, the actions of one member are often perceived as a reflection of the way the entire group acts and thinks.

14

Tuesday: Take Two

The following morning, everyone was already in the room when Don and Tim arrived at 7:45. The two men could both feel a new sense of purpose in the room, almost a static electricity of excitement.

Don asked Jack for permission to address the group. Jack nodded his assent.

"How is everyone doing today?" he asked the group.

There was a chorus of cheerful responses.

"Great," Don said. "I only want to make one point and then I'll sit down.

"Yesterday I did something that I'm not proud of. I spoke harshly to Jerry in a public setting." Turning now to Jerry, he said, "Jerry, I can't take back those words any more than I can un-ring a bell. All I can say is that I'm sorry. I hope you'll forgive me."

Jerry seemed stunned, almost embarrassed that Don would make such a public apology, but nodded in the affirmative. Don knew that this kind of sincerity and forthrightness are often viewed as a weakness by those used to a *command-and-control* leadership style. Still, he also knew that he was setting an example for them, as if to say, "Do as I do; it should match what I say."

After his apology to Jerry, Don sat down and Tim took over.

Tim went to the whiteboard and reviewed what he'd written the day before. Although they'd agreed not to create goals at this point, he'd written the ones that had been volunteered with dry erase pens, knowing that they could be easily erased.

Metric	Goal	Origin
Margin	$\geq 40\%$	Mission & Cost
Answer Client questions	1 phone call	Schedule
Respond to Mail	≥ 48 hours	Schedule

DOI: 10.4324/9781003336051-15

"Okay," he began, "does anyone recall which question we were discussing?"
Skip raised his hand.

"Shoot," Tim instructed him.

"We were discussing a metric for safety," he said, consulting his notes. "You'd asked Nadine about our safety record and then about whether morale was important here."

"Thanks," quipped Nadine with mock derision. "You had to remember that I was the one in the hot seat." There was modest laughter.

Tim realized that this was a completely different group than the one he'd addressed a day earlier. They were already volunteering information, and there was genuine cheer in their banter.

He'd just learned an important lesson from Don. Sometimes it's important to clear the air of anger, mistrust, and misunderstanding, before forward progress can be made. He tucked that away for future use.

"Okay," Tim said, picking up where Skip left off, "let's go back to my last question about *near misses*, but this time, let me give you the answer I'm looking for.

"Morale is going to be critical to your future. Your immediate concern is to improve your culture, and employee morale is central to achieving that goal. However," he continued, "*beyond* improved culture is the real pay dirt: continuous improvement. That's what you ultimately want to achieve.

"You want employees to find better ways of doing their jobs. You want them to discover new products based on customer feedback or their own experiences. You want them to find and resolve problems faster and make their work easier.

"Employees who have low morale or are frightened are uneasy about their own jobs. They focus more on avoiding trouble and not making mistakes than on improving the work they do. Their sole aim is to get home each day without being reprimanded or terminated.

"Think of that!" Tim challenged them. "Think how paralyzing that is. Think of all the opportunities you miss because your employees' whole world is focused on avoiding something negative. What a waste!

"Next point: employees who don't trust you to care for their personal well-being, that is, their safety, won't go out of their way to help you. Let me repeat that. Employees who don't trust you to care for their personal well-being, meaning their safety, won't go out of their way to help you.

"So, if you're wondering about why I'm making a big deal about safety, it's because of its implications on your future. Ensuring employee safety turns out to be really important to continuous improvement.

"How many times do you have employees trip on an extension cord or bang their shin into an open filing cabinet drawer or slip on piles of paper on the floor?" Tim asked the group.

"Not many," responded Nadine.

"You know why reports are so low?" Tim asked. Answering his own question, he said, "Because they look around and realize that you accept things the way they are. You accept conditions that harm them, so why report it?

"Or, how would you feel if the drawer on your desk constantly opened on it's own, so that when you got up, if you weren't careful, you'd run into it or snag your clothing on it? Would you feel like an important part of the team? Would you feel like going the extra mile for *that* team?"

Tim could see he'd made his point.

"Notice that I haven't gotten into time lost from work because of risks that, with a little effort, could have been avoided. I'm asking what's already happening that you aren't even seeing because you filter it out?

"All right, let me tell you what Friedman measures. We have a survey that we conduct twice a month in every department. The survey asks questions like, 'Are guards missing? Are temporary power cords properly covered with tape to prevent trip hazards? Are all maintenance repairs for safety completed within 24 hours?'

"We don't wait to have a recordable incident. We want to catch issues when they are still only a *potential* problem.

"Some terminology I'd like you to understand," Tim offered. "A problem that actually occurs, and that we report after the fact, is called a *lagging indicator*. That means that it's already too late to do anything about it. If we can catch it before the problem occurs, it's called a *leading indicator*. When you choose your metrics, you want to choose leading indicators whenever possible.

"What do you think?" Tim asked the group.

Nadine raised her hand. Tim pointed to her, and she said, "Now I get your point, and it makes perfect sense. I'd be in favor of conducting a survey like the one Friedman uses. Any chance we could get a copy of yours?"

Tim smiled. "As a matter of fact, if you'll give me an email address, I'll send it to you today. Keep in mind: we're a manufacturing plant, so our conditions are different than yours. You'll want to tailor our survey to fit your circumstances. The way we do that is to put a team of interested employees together who will tailor the survey to your conditions and needs."

"That would be great," said Nadine. "Maybe you could help us?" she asked, batting her eyelashes. That drew a laugh from the rest of the leaders.

"Wait!" interrupted Jerry, "Who's going to pay for all this?"

"Good question, Jerry. Here's how we do it. We created a special account within our chart of accounts where we accrued all such costs for the first year. The other account we create is the one in which we accrue all the income (savings) derived from the same activities. Those may be sparse the first year, but it's good to be prepared.

"However, the short answer to your question is that Copper-Bottom Charleston will pay for the improvements and data-gathering. By tracking both the costs and savings, you can get a sense of ROI. You'll also be able to report those costs to your corporate headquarters.

"Now, next year," Tim advised, "you'll want to carve out budget for such activities. You, Jack, and I can discuss that offline," he said.

Jerry seemed mollified by the answer, but Don cleared his throat, indicating he wanted to say something.

"Don?" Tim asked, acknowledging the other man's desire to add to his comment.

"Jerry," Don stated, "to elaborate on what Tim said, next year, a group of you will actually get together to establish a budget for these activities. You'll not only have the advantage of knowing what you paid this year, but you'll be able to identify the activities you'll want to tackle going forward and estimate their cost and projected savings. You'll then compare actual cost and savings to those projected. You'll want to be able to explain any differences and hone your forecasting skills.

"Make sense?" Don concluded. Jerry nodded.

Turning back to Nadine, Tim asked, "So, may I add a biweekly safety survey score to your metrics as your measure of safety?"

"I think so," she responded. "What do you think?" she asked, seeking the input of her colleagues. They all agreed, so Tim filled in the safety portion of the Metrics table.

"We agreed to tackle goals later, so I'm leaving that blank for now. Is that still okay?" Tim asked.

There was a chorus of yeses.

Copper-Bottom Health Solutions		
Metric	Goal	Origin
Margin	≥ 40%	Mission & Cost
Answer Client Questions	1 phone call	~~Schedule~~ Quality
Respond to Mail	≤ 48 hours	Schedule
Bi-weekly Safety Survey		Safety

"Okay," he asked, "how will you measure quality at the senior staff level?"

The room fell quiet.

"How does Friedman measure it?" asked Sharon.

"Well," Tim responded, "we have a physical product, so it's different for us. We measure First Pass Yield, or FPY. That's the number of completed products that pass their initial inspection divided by the total number of products made."

"In that case," Sharon said, "if we change the origin of the second metric from schedule to quality, I think we've got it. That way, if it takes more than one call to answer the question, it failed First Pass Yield. Can that work?" she asked the group.

"I like it," replied Nadine with enthusiasm.

"Me, too," said Skip.

Nadine conducted a quick hand vote and Sharon's recommendation passed.

"Can anyone think of other metrics that are critical to knowing whether you're achieving your mission? Jerry, how about you?"

Jerry shook his head in the negative. Tim went around the room, but no one had any additional metrics.

"One last thing," Tim admonished them, "once you begin publishing your performance, you need to make the decision that this is the information you need and that you'll work to keep it up. You don't want to change from one way of measuring, say, safety, to another way. If you do that, you'll lose all your previous data. For a while, you can add new measures but not change existing ones unless you retire them.

"So, for instance, try to foresee a day when you have a website that is so intuitive that it answers 90% of your customer's concerns. That means there will be fewer calls and whenever it takes more than one call to answer the question, it will have a much larger impact on your Quality metric. Still, you don't change the metric. You simply change the target.

"Last question before break," Tim stated. "How do you feel about having completed the leadership metrics table?"

Sharon was the first to respond. "I like it," she enthused. "We'll have a way of knowing how we're doing at all times, rather than waiting for a financial statement that can be a week or more after the month has closed."

"I like that we'll be addressing employee morale," stated Nadine. "We have good people, and I'd hate to think that they believe we don't care about them."

"Anyone else?" Tim asked.

Jack raised his hand. "I'll be honest, Tim. I want to see how all this works. I'm afraid I'm still a bit skeptical."

"I'm with you," Jerry agreed.

"Thanks for your honesty," Tim encouraged them. "I promise we'll get to that tomorrow. Is that okay?"

Jack nodded. Jerry shrugged. Tim took the shrug as tacit approval.

"Okay," he said, "take 15 minutes. When you get back, we'll start breaking these metrics down to your subordinate departments."

Principle #9: Sometimes it's important to clear the air of anger, mistrust, and misunderstanding, before forward progress can be made.

Principle #10: Employees who have low morale or are frightened, focus more on avoiding trouble (not making mistakes) than on improving the work they do.

Principle #11: Employees who don't trust you to care for their safety won't go out of their way to help you.

15

Leading from the Top

As they left the conference room, Don asked Jack if they could have a private conversation. Jack readily agreed and led the way to his office.

Once in his office, Jack took a seat behind his desk.

Still standing, Don said, "Jack, can I ask you to come around the desk and sit with me?" Don pointed to a set of wing-backed chairs on the other side of Jack's desk.

A little bewildered, Jack complied.

"I know," Don acknowledged with a genial grin, "that seems like a peevish kind of a request, but I assure you it's not.

"My people will tell you that I had a massive mahogany desk in my office. It was a family heirloom that was many generations old and had been a part of my granddad's plantation. I liked the feeling of invulnerability it gave me, but as my boss pointed out, it did not invite dialog or promote a sense of collegiality. He had me visit a peer in our Oakland plant and I found my peer had a nice desk but conducted most of his business at an old Formica kitchen table. It wasn't that he couldn't afford better. He wanted to put visitors and subordinates at ease, the way they'd feel if they visited his parents' kitchen.

"You could ask why you'd want to do that. Sitting behind the desk clearly signifies that you have the power in any conversations held in your office, but the path you're now on is not one of power. It's one of humility." Don waited a beat to let his words sink in. "You're going to need to learn to listen twice as frequently as you speak if you intend to draw out the best from others.

"Don't for a second think that humility is weak. Actually, when you think about it, having to rely on the power of your position discourages both feedback and new insights. In essence, if you are the power in the

DOI: 10.4324/9781003336051-16

room, everyone looks to you for answers. That squelches dialog and, with it, innovation. If you want to grow your organization, you need to encourage dialog.

"That's a long way of suggesting that you'll want to use your office to set people at ease and invite dialog. That is, of course, when you're in your office," Don said with a smile.

When Jack had taken the chair opposite him, Don continued. "Jack, what is coming is all about you. I'm serious. You have the power to change your culture or keep it the same. People will follow you because you have positional power. If you change, they'll see that it's safe, and they'll change as well. If you ask them to change, but remain the same yourself, they'll remain the same, too.

"Oh, they may go through the motions of changing, but that will end as soon as they establish that no one is really monitoring. To change your organization, you need to lead the change, and that entails changing yourself.

"The activities Tim is going to do with your people, you'll need to do as well, but I thought I'd work with you personally, if that's agreeable."

Jack hesitated for a second, then nodded.

"Okay"—Don slapped his thigh to change the mood—"lesson's over. I think we've given you plenty to think about. See you tomorrow?"

Again, Jack nodded. Don extended his hand and Jack shook it.

When Don had gone, Jack suddenly realized that he'd been sweating almost as much as he had the last time he'd been at Corporate.

Principle #12: Don't for a second think that humility is weak.
  Corollary #12–1: If you are the power in the room, everyone looks to you for answers. That squelches dialog, and with it, innovation.
  Corollary #12–2: If you want to grow your organization, you need to encourage dialog.
  Corollary #12–3: If you intend to draw out the best from others, learn to listen twice as frequently as you speak.
Principle #13: To change the organization, you need to change yourself.

16

California or Bust

Shortly after leaving Jack's office, Don called his boss, Jim. "Boss," he said, "as I work with Jack, I'm beginning to see your wisdom in dealing with me. Sending me to Oakland to visit Jorge's shop removed me from all my daily distractions and allowed me to devote my whole attention to observing Jorge and his shop." He paused. Jim said nothing.

"Jim," he began again, "I'd like to take Jack to visit Jorge's shop. Would you have a problem with that?"

"Have you talked to Jorge?" Jim asked.

"I have. He's willing to play host again, but I wanted to get your permission first."

"Thank you," Jim said sincerely. "Have you spoken to Jack? Has he agreed?"

"I have not," Don admitted. "Truth is, I think this is very important and I wanted your advice. Jack can't understand why the things we're asking him to do are important. He's never seen the finished product. I know that's why you sent me to visit Jorge's shop, but you had the authority to do it. How do I get Jack to fly across country to see for himself if he's already skeptical?"

"How about I take care of that," Jim suggested. "I'll recommend it to his boss." There was a pause. "You know …" Jim began and trailed off. "Jack's boss was going to visit your shop and I was going to meet him there. What if we all meet at Jorge's? Kill two birds with one stone. It will be good for all of us."

Don thought for a second and realized Jim's proposal was a stroke of genius, way beyond his own plan. Not only would it show Jack and his boss an extremely healthy culture, but it would also show the tangible results of such a culture. It was a brilliant plan. In an inkling, Don knew that, like it

DOI: 10.4324/9781003336051-17

had him, the visit to Jorge and his plant would spur Jack's behavior for the rest of his career. Truth be told, he also wanted to see Jorge again. He could use an infusion of Jorge's enthusiasm.

Principle #14: People find it hard to imagine what they've never seen. Said differently, "They don't know what they don't know."

17

Oakland

A week later, the four men met for the first time. Jim and Don agreed to meet Jack and his boss, George Franklin, in the lobby of their hotel. They exchanged pleasantries before hailing a cab and driving to a restaurant. There they met Jorge.

Jim and the Copper-Bottom leaders shook hands with Jorge. Don gave him a hug. He and Jorge had conversed regularly since Don's visit almost five years ago.

The meal was good and the company pleasant. At the end of the meal, they said good night to Jorge and agreed to meet at his shop by 7:30 the following morning.

Jim and Don arrived at 7:00 and had a brief meeting with Jorge, more to understand Jorge's plan than to tell him anything. In phone calls before leaving Charleston, Don had already explained what was needed and why.

At 7:30, Jack and George arrived. The five men met in Jorge's lobby and walked to his office. There stood his now-renowned kitchen table.

Jack laughed. "You weren't kidding," he said, looking from the table to Don.

Jorge welcomed them with a carafe of coffee and white ceramic mugs like you'd find in a diner. Sugar and cream were in a matching ceramic bowl and pitcher.

"Let me kick this off," Jorge began. "The goal for today is to expose you to the culture of this plant. Of course, you can't *see* a culture, so you'll be observing our employees and their interactions. In due course, you'll see our products and the processes we use to make them, but let's be clear: products don't make themselves, nor do machines—although," he offered, "we have a lot of automation.

DOI: 10.4324/9781003336051-18

"Our products are all made by people: good, hardworking men and women. Jim and Don wanted to give you a chance to observe them at work. They don't know you're coming, nor do they know who you are. They are used to me escorting folks around, so they won't pay any attention to you."

There was convivial conversation until the last man finished his coffee; then Jorge led them into the plant.

From the moment they walked through the doors separating the plant from the office, the visitors were mesmerized. Instead of seeing piles of material or half-made parts all around, they saw orderly cells of people making things. They observed conversations between operators and assemblers that seemed to end with agreements to do something. Even though this was a manufacturing plant, the concrete floors were epoxy-coated and spotless.

Jorge walked the tour to a wall neatly covered with charts and action logs. "This is my wall," he announced with pride. The men looked at the charts and realized that all were current and showed performance in the high 90th percentile. In fact, many were already at 100% and had been there for months.

"Why do you think I'd start here?" Jorge asked Jack.

It took a second, but Jack finally opined that it was because this wall measured the health of his organization. "Perfect!" Jorge complimented him. "While we're here, let's take a look at our on-time delivery." The chart reflected that they were performing at 99.87% against a goal of 100%. "Let's see if we can figure out why we're underperforming in that measure," Jorge suggested.

Jack and George exchanged glances as if to say, "99.87% is underperforming? Most organizations would consider that performance fabulous."

Jorge led them back to the warehouse, where they read the on-time delivery chart for that operation. It was pegged at 100%. "What do you think?" Jorge asked Jack. "Are we shipping on time?"

"You appear to be," replied Jack, "but how can *your* on-time delivery chart show you're below 100% when this chart shows you are shipping to your customers 100% on-time?

"Ah, right question," Jorge smiled. "I knew I liked you," he added with a heartfelt chuckle.

"Let's go answer your question."

Jorge led the men to another board. This one was outside the procurement area and was labeled accordingly. The on-time delivery chart reflected that they were at 89%.

"The smoking gun," Jorge proclaimed. He grabbed the *Action Item* sheet below the metric. "Says here that our sheet molding compound (SMC) supplier has delivered two batches that failed at incoming inspection. Sure enough," Jorge said, pointing to the Quality chart, "their quality is down as well."

"You mean you measure yourself against your supplier's quality and delivery?" asked George.

"Absolutely," stated Jorge. "Our quality and delivery can never be any better than theirs, so it's important that we stay on top of our supplier's performance as well as our own. If you were to look at my overtime numbers for the month—as Jim does," he said, nudging his boss, "you'd see we're working extended hours to meet our customer's demand and to make up for our supplier's problem. That's all part of the cost of dealing with this supplier.

"Now, it's important for the purposes of this discussion for you to know that this supplier is not yet a *partner*. To become a partner, you have to meet stringent quality and delivery requirements. Partners also receive preferential terms and conditions.

"This supplier is one of three supplying our SMC needs. As Don can attest, Oakland has only recently gotten into the plastic cabinet business. Don, who introduced the product, is now two years into production. He's already identified a partner near him, but because Oakland is just getting started, we have to work with suppliers who are all on the East Coast or in the Midwest.

"SMC is prone to drying out, so the longer it's in transportation or warehousing, the more it degrades. As a matter of fact, I believe Don's supplier ultimately built a production facility near him in Charleston. Transporting SMC from Ohio caused them fits. Is that correct, Don?"

"Yes, it is, Jorge. They recently opened a plant about 10 miles from us outside Charleston. As you already pointed out, we had similar problems when we first started out. The material dried at the edges during the long transit from Ohio to South Carolina. We were having to cut out the dry parts before using it. By agreement, we weighed the scrap and back-charged the supplier for the waste. Based on that, the volume of our business, and the cost of transporting it, the supplier decided to open a small plant near us.

"As Jorge is explaining, it takes a lot of rigor to choose a good partner. Jim has beat it into both of our heads that our product can never be of higher quality than that of our worst supplier, nor our delivery any faster than our slowest supplier."

Don looked at Jim, who nodded with approval.

Picking back up on the conversation, Jorge said, "So, let's go in search of the problem." With that, he led them into the press room, where he issued them safety glasses and hearing protection.

Jorge led them to a press with five people already gathered around it. One of the women in the group was pointing to a spot on a flat part she'd just removed from the press. "See this?" she shouted over the noise of the compression molding presses. "This is non-whetted material. As you already know, it forms an inherent weak spot in our product and makes it scrap." She threw the part into a nearby scrap bin for emphasis.

The supplier's sales engineer took notes. "Did you remove all the edge material?" the latter asked.

"Absolutely," stated the Friedman press operator emphatically. She walked the group to a nearby metal table where the next strip of material had been rolled out.

"And you're keeping the plastic coversheet in place until you use it?" asked the sales engineer.

"Absolutely."

The sales engineer lifted the coversheet to confirm that it was securely attached to the material beneath. It was.

"It's not my job to correct your problem, but based on my experience at another manufacturer, the material seems to be drying out in transit. Any chance you have pinholes in your plastic cover sheets?" the press operator asked.

"It's improbable," the engineer stated, "but I'll check. It is odd that it seems to be drying out in areas of the material other than the edges," she said, pointing to a light gray spot beneath the plastic sheeting. She took photos with her cell phone and scribbled notes for over a minute.

Jorge and his tour hung back, and no one seemed to pay them any attention. Jorge pulled their tour out of earshot and started pointing to the people still at the press. "Jennifer is our press operator," he said, indicating the young woman who had been discussing the problem. "Gavin is our press room supervisor. Erica is the sales engineer, and Justin is the salesman."

"So," George said with a bit of disbelief, "you let your operators talk directly to your suppliers?"

Jorge smiled. "Don't get me wrong," he said, "Gavin is plenty smart and has a lot of experience, but this is the way we develop our people. Jennifer, who deals with this product and process all day long, is the Subject Matter Expert, or SME, at this operation. We push our SMEs out front. If Jennifer had said anything wrong, Gavin would have corrected her, but otherwise, he let her control the dialog.

"This is no small problem," Jorge said, pointing to the bin of scrap. "Once the SMC has been put in the press, it cannot be recycled, nor does it have any salvage value. In addition to paying for it as a raw material, we now have to pay to send it to a landfill. That creates cost without any income, ties up our resources, and causes us to work overtime. We need to get to the bottom of this problem ASAP. While cost aversion is a real concern, our greater concern is our commitment to our customer: on-time delivery and uncompromising quality."

"With all the import of what's going on, doesn't it make sense for more senior people to be conducting the discussion?" George asked.

Jorge smiled as he answered the question. "You make a really great point, George. Be assured that before they leave, the supplier's personnel will meet with our procurement personnel to discuss financial and potential legal consequences of this problem. However, the person who understands the material problem the best is our press operator, Jennifer."

He pointed to a small whiteboard to the right of her press. "That's her production control board," he told them. "It indicates that she needs to press 27 parts per hour to meet customer demand. If you look, she only made 26 in hour one and 25 in hour two. She's already three parts behind for the day, and she just entered her third hour of production. She knows she's got to get this problem resolved quickly. She knows what the problem is and what its impact is on our commitment to our customer. Can you think of anyone better qualified to work with the supplier?"

When no one responded, Jorge continued. "Okay, let's suppose that Jennifer made a mistake. Gavin would correct her immediately, then later speak with her privately to make sure she was clear on what she'd gotten wrong. We refer to such behavior as *coaching*. Gavin isn't there to admonish her but to grow her. Jennifer could be our next Gavin, and we want to make sure she gets every advantage."

Jorge paused for a moment, waiting for what he'd said to sink in. "It's kind of an upside-down way of thinking about leadership, but at Friedman Electronics, we believe that one of the key roles of a leader is to build bench: to grow the people who report to them."

George and Jack exchanged glances, as if this was not at all what Copper-Bottom thought the role of leaders was. Jorge caught the look and said, "I take it you don't agree."

Looking at George again for affirmation, Jack said, "You're right. We don't feel it's our job to grow our people. We hire people for a specific skill and expect them to perform it. If they do exceptionally well, we may promote them, but the burden to advance is on them, not us."

"Interesting," Jorge responded. "Jim, do you want to share your thoughts on the matter?"

Jim laughed. "Was I *that* obvious?" he asked amid good-natured laughter.

Principle #15: One of the key roles of leaders is to build bench: grow their people.

18

First Who

"At Friedman, we believe our future starts with hiring the right people," Jim explained. "While there are exceptions, we tend to hire for attitude and train skills."

"Wait," Jack interrupted, "how do you know you're getting people who can actually do the job you're hiring them for?"

"Good point, Jack," Jim conceded. "First, we try to grow talent within, so most of our openings are entry-level.

"Also, we have created step-by-step instructions—what is called Standard Work—for all our jobs, so even if someone had come in already having done that job somewhere else, we'd have to retrain them to do it our way. We've learned that if we hire self-disciplined people with the right attitude, we can challenge and grow them for the rest of their careers."

Moving to his next point, Jim said, "So, when I talk about hiring people for their attitudes, what am I referring to? First, we're looking for people with positive, can-do attitudes. We're looking for people who habitually see the glass as half-full, and are eager to do their part to raise the level.

"The one thing we can promise candidates is that the world continues to change, and we will have to change, too. We assure them that we don't just want to keep up with the market. We want to lead it. To do that, they need to help us constantly reinvent ourselves.

"Jim Collins, in his book *Good to Great*, says that greatness comes from 'disciplined people, engaged in disciplined thought and taking disciplined action.' Here at Friedman, we look for candidates who are self-disciplined. We then teach them how to engage in disciplined thought and take disciplined action.

"Sorry, Jorge," Jim said sheepishly. "Didn't mean to take over. You know I'm passionate about hiring the right people, though."

DOI: 10.4324/9781003336051-19

"If I could," George interrupted the exchange, "how do you know you're hiring disciplined people?"

"Jim?" Jorge asked.

Jim took his cue. "Good question, George. As you imply, getting the future right is all about getting the right people in the beginning. The answer is really pretty simple. Our HR people observe the candidate for *tells*. Our folks actually use a check sheet that asks questions like:

- Did the candidate arrive on time?
- Are the candidate's shoes clean and, if leather, shined?
- Is the candidate's outfit pressed?
- Would the candidate's outfit be considered at least business casual?
- Did the candidate arrive with something on which to take notes?
- Was the candidate respectful?

"Let me make one more point," Jim stated. "Collins also says that the transition from good to great begins with getting self-disciplined people on your bus, and that self-disciplined people don't need a lot of bureaucracy to keep them in line. That fact has allowed us to focus more effort on the mission.

"Again, sorry, Jorge," Jim said apologetically.

"Let's see," Jorge said, starting over, "Where was I?" Everyone laughed easily, suspecting that Jim had stolen a good part of Jorge's thunder. If it bothered Jorge, he didn't act like it. The truth was, most in Friedman Electronics were a bit in awe of Jim, including Don and Jorge.

"Leaders ..." Jorge paused and started over. "Leaders' top priority is to make sure that safety, quality, schedule, and cost expectations are met. We are very firm in that regard. Our employees' well-being is our highest responsibility. We operate on the belief that if we take care of our employees, they'll take care of our customers. Over and over, we see our belief validated by employees who go above and beyond not only for customers but for each other.

"Of course, another of the roles of leaders is to define the path forward. In Gavin's case, that means his talks tie daily goals back into the mission and make clear how everyone's jobs fits into the overall plan for the department and company. He makes sure everyone understands their daily production requirements. He also ensures that everyone is following Standard Work: the one best way to do their job.

"The next role of the leader is to hold their subordinates accountable. Each employee is given individual or team goals they are expected to meet. I don't need to tell you that things happen sometimes to prevent that, but we try to give our employees enough authority to respond to foreseeable problems. Gavin's job is to provide the next layer of support. He gets his people the resources they need to resolve the immediate problem quickly. If there is an ongoing element to the problem, say a machine that needs corrective maintenance rather than a tweak, Gavin will work with the maintenance organization to schedule it.

"After the dust of an emergency settles, Gavin hosts an after-action meeting and, with members of his team, sets about identifying the root cause of the problem and putting a long-term solution in place to prevent that problem from ever happening again. If there is a problem with an individual's performance, Gavin's first role is to coach: make sure the employee knows what they did wrong, as well as lead them through the process of discovering the correct response to use in the future."

Jorge changed gears. "When it comes to personal behavior, our belief is that if we are clear about the boundaries of good behavior, then we'll have a lot fewer problems. As Jim says, we go out of our way to hire self-disciplined people. We expect them to conduct themselves in disciplined ways, because when they do, we all avoid a lot of time and resource-sucking bureaucracy. I can say that, here in Oakland, that expectation has certainly proven to be true."

"Agreed," chimed in Don.

George got Jorge's attention. "You've made a point of discussing discipline quite a bit. I don't mean to be the skunk at the garden party, but are you as militant as that sounds? Do you keep your boot on the neck of your employees?"

"Oh boy, George, if that's the impression I gave, I've given you a very wrong idea of what Friedman is like. The point I was trying to make is that, because we have self-disciplined employees, we *avoid* a lot of disciplinary problems. We make the fences clear and rely on our people to navigate safely within them. They pretty much always do, with very rare exception."

Jorge waited to see if there were any questions. When none arose, he continued. "In addition to pushing subordinates out front, leaders support those who report to them. You'll note Gavin was right there with Jennifer. If she'd gotten pushback from the supplier, Gavin would have ensured that the supplier would be left with no question that dealing with Jennifer was dealing with Friedman's official representative. Failing that, the supplier's representatives would be escorted out. That's how much we believe in our people.

"Gavin's job, the job of any Friedman leader, is to use the full weight of their position to support their people. If a subordinate runs into an obstacle, Gavin's job is to eliminate it or to quickly elevate it to the level that can eliminate it. For instance, Gavin was the one who arranged for the SMC supplier to be here today. He went to our procurement group and asked the commodity specialist who handles SMC to bring this supplier in."

Jorge waited to make sure everyone was following and that there were no questions.

"Finally," he began again, "the role of a leader is to blaze a trail. That means they are to look as far into the future of their discipline as possible, and to help us define where we'll need to position ourselves to stay ahead of the industry.

"We encourage our people to read industry periodicals that pertain to their field of expertise. We also provide a pretty extensive library of business books and pay for at least one industry conference or symposium per leader per year. We want our leaders to be as knowledgeable as possible. Truth is, most of our leaders become well-known in their discipline outside of Friedman. In short, we want them to lead and not just *oversee* their subordinates.

"Recapping, the four roles of leaders here at Friedman are:

1. Set expectations; define 'good.'
2. Hold accountable.
3. Support those who report to them.
4. Blaze a trail."

Jorge looked at his guests to see if he'd lost them. George and Jack were both silent but attentive.

"Seems to me," George opined, "you must lose a lot of people after investing so much in them. I'd think your competition would be lining up outside your door to snag the folks you've invested so much in."

"Boy, I'm glad you said that, George," Jorge replied. "As I already stated, our attrition is very low. Part of the reason for that is that our HR people monitor industry salaries. We don't try to lead that pack, but we want to stay competitive. As a result, we adjust our incomes once a year to match increases in the Labor Department's Consumer Price Index. We post CPI values publicly, so our people have a pretty good sense of what they'll make in the coming year. In short, we try to remove 'higher income' from the list of reasons people leave.

"Nonetheless, we all know that people leave for reasons other than pay. That's part of our motivation in growing our people. We make their growth opportunities clear to them. Once they can perform all the skills on their skills matrix and they decide on the career path they want to pursue, we match them with a mentor who will work with them to *grow* them into a new position. When people with that job title plan vacation or are out sick, we give their understudies an opportunity to function in their role. After each opportunity, the understudy is assessed, and that assessment is reviewed with them. Afterwards, it's added to their annual performance review. When the position opens, we've already done all the groundwork. We move the most qualified candidate into the slot."

This time Jack asked Jorge, "What's a skills matrix?"

"Great question," Jorge said, complimenting him. "Let's go to my office and I'll show you how they work."

Jorge led the group to his office, where he quickly sketched an empty lattice on his whiteboard. "Suppose," he started, "you own a restaurant dedicated to fast food. You sit down with your managers and develop a list of skills entry-level employees need to be able to perform." Jorge quickly created a list.

Expected Skills: Burger Flipper 1

---

1   Can clean dirty dishes
2   Can empty trash containers
3   Can clean equipment
4   Can cook French fries
5   Can cook burgers
6   Can stage components (cheese, buns, lettuce, etc.)
7   Can deliver food
8   Can run cash register
9   Can make drinks

"Now," he continued, "you agree with your managers that you'll give new employees 30 days to demonstrate their ability to routinely perform all those skills. Because these are high-turnover jobs, you instruct your managers to test each employee each week until they can perform all the skills or the 30 days elapse.

"When an employee can perform a skill, the supervisor puts a '1' in the cell adjacent to the skill. A blank cell means they cannot yet perform the skill. My teams conditionally format[1] the cells so that, if the value is above '0,' the cell turns green."

			Strengths					
			Stew	Karen	Lou	Stacy	Francine	Gail
	Expected Skills: Burger Flipper 1							
1	Can clean dirty dishes	X	1	1	1	1	1	1
2	Can empty trash containers	X	1	1	1		1	
3	Can clean equipment	X	1		1		1	
4	Can cook French fries	X	1	1	1	1	1	
5	Can cook burgers	X	1		1	1	1	
6	Can stage components (cheese, buns, lettuce, etc.)	X	1			1	1	
7	Can deliver food	X	1	1			1	
8	Can run cash register	X	1			1	1	1
9	Can make drinks	X					1	
	Promotional Skills: Burger Flipper 1							
10	Can run take out window	0						
11	Can supervise shift	0						
			8	4	5	5	9	2

"Back at Burger Haven, you and your supervisors decide that you'll give your employees an additional target to shoot for. When they can perform all the skills of Burger Flipper 1, they are encouraged to develop the skills of a Burger Flipper 2. We'll call those 'Promotional Skills' for a Burger Flipper 1.

"The next week, your managers begin evaluating their peoples' skills. You'll note that only one employee, Francine, can perform all nine skills. She is now eligible to practice the *Promotional* Skills of a Burger Flipper 1. When she can perform those, too, she'll be promoted to a Burger Flipper 2 and receive a $1.00 per hour raise.

"Because a Burger Flipper 2 can perform more skills, they are more valuable to the firm, so the supervisors encourage them toward the higher-skill group.

"By the second week, your supervisors note that several employees all lack the same skills. They suggest a second matrix that shows where shift weaknesses and skills gaps exist. You create the following *weakness* section."

			Strengths						Weaknesses						Group
			Stew	Karen	Lou	Stacy	Francine	Gail	Stew	Karen	Lou	Stacy	Francine	Gail	
	Expected Skills: Burger Flipper 1														
1	Can clean dirty dishes	X	1	1	1	1	1	1							0
2	Can empty trash containers	X	1	1	1		1					1		1	2
3	Can clean equipment	X	1		1		1		1		1			1	3
4	Can cook French fries	X	1	1	1	1	1							1	1
5	Can cook burgers	X	1		1	1	1			1				1	2
6	Can stage components (cheese, buns, lettuce, etc.)	X	1			1	1			1	1			1	3
7	Can deliver food	X	1	1			1				1	1		1	3
8	Can run cash register	X	1			1	1	1		1	1				2
9	Can make drinks	X					1		1	1	1	1		1	5
	Promotional Skills: Burger Flipper 1														
10	Can run take out window	0													
11	Can supervise shift	0													
12	Can manage store	0													
13			8	4	5	5	9	2	1	(5)	4	4	0	(7)	

"If a cell is vacant in the 'Strengths' part of the matrix, it auto-populates as a '1' in the 'Weakness' section. Again, cells there have been conditionally formatted to turn red if there is a '1' in a weakness cell. On the far right, in the 'Group' column, you sum the number of employees who can't perform that skill. Now it becomes evident that 50% of your employees can't perform functions #6 or #7. Moreover, five of six employees cannot make drinks: skill #9.

"Viewed this way, it quickly becomes *visible* that you have two employees that are extremely weak. You also discover that there are three skills that employees seem to be having difficulties learning and that right now, only one of your employees can make drinks. That's a major concern. If you were to lose Francine, you'd have no one who could make drinks.

"Admittedly, this is a fictitious company, but the example is not all that unique. Most organizations never perform an analysis of their employees' skills. As long as all the work gets done, leaders rarely take time to acknowledge who is actually doing it. Only after a key person leaves do they realize how critical that person was.

"It's not uncommon for exceptional employees to perform far more than their peers who are being paid exactly the same. Without being recognized for their contributions with either praise or pay, exceptional employees often leave in search of an organization that will acknowledge their worth.

"Rather than take action to prevent other good employees from leaving, some managers focus on the task at hand: replacing the one that just left. When that fire's out, they go on to the next fire, and the next, and the next. Turns out, if you never remove the fuel from the forest, or eliminate the root cause of the problem, there's always a fire to put out, so it's not uncommon for some managers to never *have* the time to actually solve the root cause of problems. The ironic thing is that, never dealing with the root cause almost assures an endless supply of fires to put out. It's a never-ending loop."

Jorge fell silent and let his last statement sink in.

"Guys," he said at last, "Friedman is leading our industry in the use of new technology and in developing new processes, but at the end of the day, technology and processes don't satisfy our customers. Our people do. Friedman knows that our employees really are our most important asset, and we do everything we can to help them know that we know."

Again, he let the silence build before returning to the Skills Matrix.

"Note," Jorge pointed out, "this system is visual, and it's all based on an objective test, not a subjective opinion. This system assures you that if you end up promoting people or letting people go, your decision won't be based on popularity. Moreover, if, in addition to a master Skills Matrix form, you create an individual form for each employee, you can have them sign it each time they're reviewed. Their signature acknowledges their score. You can even take notes on the individual form indicating what instructions you gave the employee and any plans for improvement they commit to. You can have them initial those notes to acknowledge the coaching they received. If you end up having to defend your decisions regarding that employee, you'll have clear evidence that you'd been coaching them well before you made decisions to promote or discipline them."

Jorge paused. "Any questions?" he asked. It was quiet for a second before Jack confessed, "That's amazing. Do you have one of those matrices covering all of your skills groups?"

"We do," admitted Jorge. "Every skill; every employee. By the way, it's probably intuitive, but let me point out that the supervisor is able to accurately assess each employee's successful performance of their skills because each skill is covered by Standard Work: a document that spells out the step-by-step instructions for performing that skill correctly."

Switching gears, Jorge said, "We're here to talk about Culture, so let me tie this discussion into that topic. The use of a skills matrix in making hiring, firing, and promotional decisions levels the playing field. It makes clear to your employees that success is the result of hard work, not favoritism. That sends a very strong subliminal message to your people: they can trust you."

Jorge paused before adding, "Gentlemen, *continuous improvement only takes place in an atmosphere of respect and trust.* If our people don't feel they are respected or that their leaders can be trusted, they will not come to us with their improvement ideas. I can assure you that Jennifer and her peers come to Gavin with numerous improvement ideas. As a matter of fact …"

Jorge led them to Gavin's KPI board. On it was a Key Performance Indicator that simply read *Implemented Suggestions.* The metric was cumulative. The goal reflected that Gavin's 10 subordinates were expected to provide a minimum of 5 *implemented* suggestions per month for a total of 60 per year. The press team was already ahead of their goal by two for the year. "By comparison," Jorge stated, "last I checked Toyota in Georgetown, Kentucky, was averaging about 11 implemented suggestions per employee per year. We have a long way to go, but at least we're in pursuit.

"One last thing," Jorge stated. "I've already admitted that turnover in this plant is at 3%. That means that the total percent of our population that has left in the last 12 months averages 3%. That number includes layoffs, disciplinary discharges, voluntary resignations, and retirements."

"Wait!" Jack interjected. "You conduct layoffs?"

That got a good-natured laugh from Jorge. "I wondered if you'd catch that. No, we haven't had a layoff in over eight years; not since Jim became VP of Global Operations. But if we did, it would get counted in this number."

George and Jack looked at each other. That number struck a chord. Theirs was over eight times that number.

"Don," Jorge asked, "isn't yours even lower than mine?"

Don took the cue. "We're currently at a little over one and a half percent," he stated, "but I can still remember the days when it was closer to 25%.

"Cost of living in the South is much lower than here in California, so we always made sure we were among the highest-paying employers in the Charleston area. What we discovered, only after Jim took me down a peg or two," he said, smiling at his boss, "was that my inferior staff was driving good people away. In addition, because I kept people in leadership roles that I knew I could control, those positions never opened up. Employees with any gumption left in their first year.

"Now we try to behave like a meritocracy, promoting the best of the best and giving hope to those who didn't get selected this time. We take succession planning seriously. We have a whole list of *forward promotable* people who are waiting for leadership jobs to open up. As our workforce ages, we expect to see more and more openings. Our HR department keeps track of who is thinking of retiring and when. We make sure we have at least a couple of qualified people to backfill every potential opening."

Jorge looked at his watch. "I have a panel of employees to speak with you after lunch," he said. "Why don't we run for a quick bite so we can beat the lunch crowd?"

Over lunch, Jorge explained that he'd asked members of his accounting, sales, contracts, and procurement organizations to meet with George and Jack. "I figured those occupations would be the closest to yours, so you can see that, just because we manufacture a product, our behaviors aren't just practiced in our manufacturing areas.

"By the way," Jorge continued, "none of us"—he pointed to Jim and Don—"will be in the room. That way you will be getting unfiltered responses directly from our people. In fact, there will be no supervisors in the group at all."

The panel discussion proved to be a real triumph. Jack and George learned that the office personnel at Friedman (Oakland) respected their leaders immensely. There was a bit of hero worship of Jorge, but leaders in general were revered for their knowledge and support. "Honestly," one woman had told them, "if I didn't like to live indoors, I'd work here for free." That got a chuckle from the group, but the sentiment seemed to be shared by other panelists.

"Some of my best friends work here," said another woman. "Honestly, of my four best friends, three of them work here. The fourth goes all the way back to kindergarten. We build deep ties with our workmates," she explained. "We're more a family than a workforce. We work to make a living, but we work hard because we don't want to let our colleagues down."

After the panel discussion, Jack brought a question back to Jorge. "When I asked the panel members about their culture, the panelists looked at each other in confusion. They couldn't answer our question. Why was that?"

Jorge laughed his good-natured laugh. "It's both an honest question and response," he stated. "Let me see if I can explain the confusion. Years ago, I'd asked the same question of a colleague at Toyota. My colleague told me that, much of what we consider their *culture* is just a part of daily life at Toyota. Their employees don't even think about it. It's not that they don't think of it as unusual; they honestly don't think about it at all. 'It's like water to a fish,' my friend had told me. 'Unless they're removed from it, they aren't even aware of its existence.'"

Jorge's explanation made a lot of sense to both Jack and George. It put the confusion of the panel in proper perspective. Thinking back, the men realized that the panel hadn't refused to answer or avoided answering; they honestly didn't know the answer.

It was a little after 3 PM when Jim looked at his watch. He could tell both Copper-Bottom men were in overload. "It's been a full day," he said, speaking for the first time since his earlier monolog on hiring. "Let's retire to our hotel and meet back in your lobby at 5:30 PM. Dress in casual attire. Jeans are appropriate if you have them. Jorge and his family will be meeting us for a street festival. We'll be eating from food trucks and street stalls, so you'll want to have cash for meals and any souvenirs you might want. I've already checked and there's an ATM in your lobby," he said with a smile.

Principle #16: An organization's future starts with hiring the right people. Hire candidates who are self-disciplined; then teach them how to engage in disciplined thought and take disciplined action.

Corollary #16–1: Hire for attitude and train skills. Look for people with positive, can-do attitudes, people who habitually see the glass as half-full and are eager to do their part to raise the level.

Corollary #16–2: To lead the market, employees need to help their firm constantly reinvent itself.

Corollary #16–3: Grow talent from within, so most openings are at entry-level.

Corollary #16–4: Create step-by-step instructions (Standard Work) for all our jobs.

Corollary #16–5: One of the most important roles of a leader is to be prepared to use the full weight of their position to support their people.

Principle #17: Continuous improvement only takes place in an atmosphere of RESPECT and TRUST.

NOTE

1 Conditional formatting is a method of altering the formatting of a spreadsheet cell. In this case, the condition is that, *if the value of the cell is >0, then the cell turns green.*

19

Another Bite of the Apple

Food trucks and stalls lined the street, with picnic tables arranged down the center. There were also a couple of beverage tents and a street band. Because the festival was only a half-dozen blocks from the hotel, no one felt concerned about having a second beer. It was a warm evening with gentle breezes and a starlit sky. The setting had been halcyon.

Jorge's family proved to be a delight. His oldest child, Al, was getting his master's in economics from Cal State Berkley. Al had been recruited into Stanford as an undergrad on a basketball scholarship. He had played all four years, but his passion was business. When Berkley offered him an academic scholarship, he readily accepted. Al was sharp, funny, and as unassuming as his dad.

Marie, Jorge's daughter, had also been recruited out of high school. In her case, it was for her musical skills. She played the flute and had played in the California All-State Band for years before going off to college. While she'd also been recruited by Juilliard, she'd ultimately chosen the Eastman School of Music in Rochester, New York. Although it wasn't as well known, she liked the atmosphere of the school and Rochester in general. "Did you know," she asked the men, "that Rochester has the highest per capita education level in the United States? It's home to Eastman Kodak, Bausch & Lomb, Xerox, and a host of very high-tech companies. Besides, I kind of like the bohemian feel of the downtown culture," she added.

Maria Castanza, Jorge's wife, beamed with pride to hear her kids talk about their lives. She seemed diminutive and unassuming as she listened to the ebb and flow of conversation around her. Had Jim not told the men in advance, no one would have ever guessed that she had a PhD from Berkley or that she was the corporate VP of HR for a global pharmaceutical company.

DOI: 10.4324/9781003336051-20

Before arriving at the festival, Jim had also told the men that Jorge's family were second-generation Americans and that Jorge, his wife, and two kids lived in a modest home in a Bay Area suburb on the "north side of the bridge," meaning the Golden Gate. Jim had conveyed this information in a very reverential manner, indicating how hard Jorge and Maria Castanza—both of whom were the children of migrant workers—had worked to get where they were.

Still finding Jorge's background remarkable, Don, who had now known Jorge for years, was more in awe of him for the degree of advancement his organization had achieved during his tenure as General Manager. Without a doubt, the Oakland facility was the go-to place for new leaders to visit when embracing the Friedman culture, and Jorge was the odds-on favorite to replace Jim when he promoted or retired.

It came as a total surprise when Jorge started telling the table about all that Don's plant had achieved in the last few years. How Don's had been the first Friedman facility to introduce plastic cabinets to the electrical industry. How his plant had transformed a dilapidated paint system into a state-of-the-art system that rivaled any in the auto industry. "And," Jorge had gone on to say, "Don did all that while making double-digit improvements on almost every measure of his plant's performance."

Don was actually blushing when Jorge finished and was glad that the accolades had ended. In his mind, Don knew he was just doing his job and felt he had so much farther to go to achieve the level of perfection that existed in Oakland.

After a short silence, during which they all sipped their beers, Jim began to speak.

"When I first met Don," he began, "it wasn't under the most favorable conditions." He looked at Don with a knowing smile. "I had been thrust into my position a few years earlier and had my hands full with underperforming operations around the United States. For the first couple of years, Charleston's performance was good enough to stay off my *naughty* list, but then, as other plants started employing Lean in earnest, Charleston's numbers started to look anemic by comparison. I went to look.

"When I arrived at the plant, I found that Don had met the letter of the law I'd established, but that's it. His people couldn't explain what they were being asked to do or why. As a matter of fact, few of his direct reports could really perform their jobs. When it came to decisions, everyone

I interviewed deferred to Don. It became evident that they just executed what he told them to do.

"As Don has already stated, new talent fled Don's facility. The old guard, with whom Don had surrounded himself, was made up of all 'yes men,' and I mean that literally. Not only did they do as Don instructed them, but each was a man. Not one sought, or accepted, input from those below them. They were ingratiated to Don, knowing in their hearts that he alone kept them in their jobs.

"Like a puppeteer, Don pulled every string in the plant through his staff. He'd done a masterful job for year, but now couldn't compete with the facilities that had recently converted to Lean. Those facilities had hundreds of people making good decisions and making daily improvements. As good as Don was, he'd never be able to compete.

"I don't think I'm telling stories out of school when I say that we clashed. We finally reached the moment in which I gave Don an ultimatum: do business using Lean, or be terminated.

"I knew Don was extremely sharp and had tons of potential. I didn't want to see him going to a competitor, but I also couldn't have him ignoring my directives. We needed to be clear about who was in charge. There was only one way for Friedman managers to lead: the Friedman way."

Jim stopped. "Don, the rest is your story. You should tell it."

Don was caught off-guard and waited a beat or two before picking the story back up.

"Jim politely left me to explain what happened when he offered me a choice between using Lean or him firing me. He was emphatic: I was going to have to use this Lean stuff or leave.

"Now understand, my family's been in Charleston for generations. I wasn't about to leave Charleston, and there weren't many opportunities like the one I already had. I decided to comply until I could figure out an alternative."

What Don hadn't said was that his ancestors had received a land grant from the King Charles II of England back in the 1600s. The plantation he'd inherited was a fraction of the original grant, but without a doubt he was considered Charleston aristocracy.

Don continued. "What happened next was quintessential, Jim. He let me save face by sending me to Oakland to see some general manager out there. Meeting Jorge"—Don shot him an admiring glance—"was like turning the cereal box upside down to discover the prize at the bottom. Jorge wasn't just a world-class GM; he was a gracious host who opened his business, home, and family to me.

"You've seen his plant and his people. Jorge recognizes the dignity and strength of each of his employees. He knows them all by name and most of their extended families, too. They revere the ground he walks on and would wade through molten lava to help him. That's because they've seen him do the same for them.

"Allow me one more diversion," Don asked the group.

Never mentioning that he was a West Point graduate with a distinguished military career, Don said, "I left the Army with a clear grasp of the *Command-&-Control* leadership model: tell subordinates what to do and when to do it. If they fail, discipline them. If you find yourself disciplining them too often, get rid of them. Jorge and Jim have taught me what it means to respect your people and to call forth the best from them. We at Friedman call that process *Coaching*.

"Let me say that a different way. I now know the culture at Friedman in Charleston was extremely sick when Jim first visited us. Between the way Jim handled me and the way I watched Jorge lead, I realized that my organization was sick because of me, because of the model I was using. Don't get me wrong: it worked. It got the results I wanted, but it could never get better than me. Friedman Charleston was only going to be as good as me, and I was running out of bandwidth. Using the Friedman model, leaders grow their people and, as their people get better, leaders get better results. That way, the entire organization grows and gets continuously better."

Don looked at George and Jack. "I guess what I'm saying is that the coaching model works. Before, when I was the one calling all the shots, I got the results I wanted. Now, I still get the best results, but we're growing our organization by growing our people. Each month we do that, our performance gets a little bit stronger."

Principle #18: Grow your people, and as they get better, you get ever-better results.

Corollary #18–1: As results get better, your entire organization grows. Like a sapling, each round of growth makes the organization stronger and more resilient.

20

A Lot to Cogitate

The following morning the group met for a leisurely breakfast. Although they'd left time before their flight to return to the plant, neither George nor Jack felt the need. "May I make a suggestion?" Jim asked.

George nodded.

"Would it make sense to have a debrief of yesterday?"

"Brilliant idea," agreed George. "I was thinking the same thing, but I hoped you'd lead us."

Jim thought for a moment. "Okay," he began, "tell me what you saw in Jorge's plant yesterday."

George and Jack looked at each other. George deferred to Jack with a subtle hand gesture.

"Well, the first thing I remember noticing was how clean everything was. Then I noticed the degree of organization. Things weren't just tidy. It was easy to see that everything clearly had a set location. There appeared to be little excess."

Jack paused for a moment, then added, "Something else I noticed was that things were labeled and shadowed: hand tools, cleaning equipment, test stands, WIP Carts. Even machines were outlined."

"What I noticed," George chimed in, "was that everyone seemed to know exactly what was required of them and seemed to be self-governing. I remember that press operator telling the supplier what was wrong with their product and what would be needed to fix it."

Jack laughed and said, "The hype about Jorge's kitchen table was spot-on. And not just that he had one, but that it was clear that he used his office to build relationships, not to intimidate."

"Good point," George agreed, "and that leads me to remember that Jorge's people all knew what was expected of them and that none of his leaders were hounding them. As I said earlier, the workers seemed to be self-governing. Now that I think of it, I can remember Jorge pointing out his supervisors and managers when we were on the floor. They seemed oblivious to us, so I don't think their presence was to impress us, but they seemed to be taking an active interest in what their people were doing. They appeared to have their finger on the pulse of their organization without being all over their people."

Jim interrupted. "That's because every day, every worker is given the list of what will be expected of them. They know it's their job to make that happen. They don't need someone to play the adult and remind them. If they need help, they can call their boss at any time, but every supervisor has established how much authority each worker has to solve their own problems. It's rare that employees need more. When they do, their boss gets them that help.

"Recall," Jim continued, "the situation with the supplier that we observed. The press operator handled matters, but her supervisor was there to show his support, implying that the weight of his office was behind everything she said."

"I guess," George said, picking back up, "that's what I noticed the most. People knew what they were doing and didn't need someone standing over them to make sure it happened. Leaders seemed to be *available* but not underfoot. They seemed to run interference and to remove obstacles, rather than constantly demanding things." He stopped.

"To be honest," he continued after a pause, "I was awed and a bit envious. I'd heard stories of organizations that operated like Jorge's shop, but I thought those stories were apocryphal. If I'm honest with myself, I'd admit that I'd secretly thought I'd want to lead that way: with no one waiting (or needing) to be told what to do. They'd already know what was needed and would be moving to make it happen. Like I said, I was impressed."

Jack picked up. "Contributing to what George just said, I was amazed by Jorge. He spent most of his time with us, but nothing in his plant seemed to stop or even slow down because he wasn't overseeing everything. Even the press operator's boss deferred to her, acknowledging that she was the expert when it came to using that material. It was impressive."

"Great observations," Jim said when both men fell quiet. "It's clear that you were paying attention. That's deep observation. Lean leaders use it as a way of understanding what's *really* going on. Those skills will stand you in good stead when you Gemba walk." Jim then remained silent for several seconds.

"I'll leave you with one other thought," he said at last. "Cultural change involves changing the people in that culture. People change slowly in general, but the more rank an employee has or the older they are, the more resistance to change they tend to exhibit. I tell you that because, if you follow our way—really, the Toyota way—you'll find that you're in a marathon, not a sprint.

"People change at different rates. Your job is to create the expectations, set the pace and hold fast. Do your part, including setting the standard and holding subordinates accountable, and your organization will slowly transform.

"Cultural change is usually glacial. Be patient. Stay the course."

He paused for a second before adding, "What I'm about to share is counterintuitive, but the fastest way to change your culture is to change yourself. The reason I say that is that your people will all be watching you. If they see their leaders trying something new and spending time working through the details, they'll want to be part of it. When the time comes, they'll consider it an honor to be invited to participate. If, on the other hand, you go in with guns blazing and try to *make* them change, they'll resist. You'll have an uphill battle.

"Don," Jim asked, "would you agree?"

Without hesitation, Don said, "One thousand percent, Jim. As you've already said, people resist change they feel *forced* into, but if they feel they are being excluded from something important, human nature is to want that thing."

Jim picked back up. "Jack, in the beginning, focus your leadership team's attention on Key Performance Indicators. Roll them out one management layer at a time. Make it a point to visit KPI boards and ask questions. Don't just ask your direct reports. Ask anyone who reports to that board's owner. If they don't know the answer to the question, I guarantee you they'll go in search of it. They won't want to look dumb a second time. Besides, you want everybody to understand what's going on. Later, when you visit lower-tier KPI huddles, seek the opinions of all those employees. That will throw them off-guard," Jim said with another laugh. "They're used to being told, not asked."

Jim offered, "Be patient; like spring after a long winter, change will come, and it will be change that you'll be leading." There was a pause as the Copper-Bottom leaders reflected on what Jim had said.

"Since I'm giving advice so freely," Jim added with another laugh. "Just as you'll be doing, focus your subordinates' efforts on changing themselves. Use Don and his people to answer questions or give advice. Remind your subordinates that employees will do what they're told, but that won't change them. People will only change when they see their leaders using these new behaviors and succeeding. *That,*" he concluded, "will earn you their respect and they will follow where you lead.

"In short: lead first and others will follow. When there's a strong enough body of followers, the tide will turn. Don't exhort, and absolutely don't push. Just lead by doing and coaching."

Jim fell silent for a beat, then asked the question they'd all been circling: "Could any of this work at Copper-Bottom?"

There was a long silence as both George and Jack thought. When neither spoke, Jim said. "Maybe that's a question to think about on the plane. We probably should be getting you to the airport. Traffic here is brutal."

The moment for advice had passed and the men shook hands all around before Don, Jack, and George got into their ride to the airport. They were soon just a yellow dot in traffic.

Principle #19: Cultural change involves changing the people in the culture; people change slowly.

Corollary #19–1: The more rank an employee has, the more resistance to change they tend to exhibit.

Corollary #19–2: The older a person is, the more resistant to change they have a tendency to be.

Principle #20: The fastest way to change your culture is to change yourself. The example you set is the one others will follow.

21

Thursday: Drilling Deeper

When Jack arrived back in Charleston late Wednesday night, his head was still spinning. During the long flight, he'd wondered again if what he'd witnessed in Jorge's plant could work at Copper-Bottom. At first his mind was flooded with all the reasons it couldn't. Friedman, after all, was a manufacturing company with a physical product; Copper-Bottom was a service company with no product. Copper-Bottom didn't have high volume products in physical cells, or machines, or a factory or … The *reasons* it couldn't work spun out of control until he realized that none of the things Jorge had shown them had anything to do with the fact Friedman was a manufacturer. What they'd seen was the difference in the way Friedman leaders led.

KPIs, for instance, were a leadership tool. Leaders, top to bottom, set clear expectations and monitored performance against them. Performance told them how their subordinates were doing. If performance was flagging, leaders asked questions intended to get the subordinate to think through the root cause of the problem if they hadn't already done so. Together, they'd discuss how to get performance back on track. Not only did it sharpen the subordinate's skills, but it deepened the bond between leaders and subordinates.

Jorge had made it clear that leaders were expected to clear obstacles from the paths of their personnel; to use the full power of their position to allow subordinates to make the total satisfaction of Friedman's customers possible. That built confidence, pride, and created a "we" mentality.

Friedman's leaders also supported their people's growth opportunities. Skills were made clear by Standard Work: the single best way to perform that skill known today. Standard Work was documented, usually pictorially, so evaluating an employee's level of skill was totally objective.

DOI: 10.4324/9781003336051-22

Since performance reviews were based on the employee's skills in performing their current job, the use of Skills Metrics made that part of the performance review quick. If the employee didn't meet all the expectations of their current job, the two talked about a plan to eliminate any deficiencies. If the employee met all expectations, the supervisor and employee used the time to explore growth interests and opportunities. Once chosen, they laid out a plan to seize that opportunity. Either way, the employee left the interaction with a plan that would be discussed at their next review. Something that had really surprised Jack was that growing their subordinates seemed to be one of the highest expectations of Friedman's leaders.

Another surprise: failure wasn't met with reproof but with listening and coaching. Friedman leaders had been trained to understand that change involved risk. Employees were encouraged to take calculated risks within their field of expertise. Risk-taking made periodic failure a foregone conclusion. When a failure occurred, Friedman leaders operated under the belief that their people all meant well and gave their best, even when their results were not what they desired. Like a caring coach, leaders walked their employees back through what they'd done and asked what they'd do differently next time. If experience had taught the leader that the proposed solution wouldn't work, they shared their experience and acted as a coach, working the subordinate through the problem's resolution. Although they hadn't seen it, they'd been told that "telling" the employee the answer was only used as a last resort.

Jack had wondered aloud how Friedman leaders had time to coach their people. He knew from personal experience that coaching took a lot of time; time leaders he knew rarely had. Jorge's response caught him off-guard.

"Jack, first, our leaders don't spend their days in front of a monitor. Easily 60% of their day is spent in the presence of their people. In addition to that, we train our leaders to delegate a lot of their rote activities. To do that, they have to create Standard Work for the activity. The subordinate is trained in the Standard and evaluated until they can perform it flawlessly. As much as possible, we make performance standards visual: good performance = green; nonconforming performance = red, that kind of a thing. As with all Standard Work, the leader follows up periodically to ensure performance hasn't drifted, but the end result is more time for the leader to rise above the mundane and focus on the future of their people, their processes, and their product."

To a person, Friedman personnel operated with a clear understanding of both their jobs and the expectations placed on them. What they'd seen were employees who knew their jobs and did them flawlessly.

Before he stepped back into the fray of daily activities at Copper-Bottom, Jack wrote down his thoughts. He suspected that he'd quickly reach a point where he'd be so invested in killing alligators again that he'd forget what he'd learned. With that done, he went in search of his staff. He found them in the conference room just as Tim was releasing them on a 10-minute break. Jack caught up with Sharon to see how things had run in his absence.

When everyone returned from a break, Tim said, "Jerry, I want to start with your department, so you get a sense of what we'll be doing. That way, you can give us help as we move forward with other organizations."

Jerry nodded.

"First question," Tim stated. "Do you refer to your organization as Finance or Accounting?"

"Accounting," Jerry replied.

"Great," Tim responded, writing "Accounting" on the whiteboard. "So, what would we measure if we wanted to know how Accounting supported the Copper-Bottom metric of *Margin*?"

Jerry thought for a minute. "I don't see that we do anything to support that."

Tim feared that they were going to have a repeat of Jerry's earlier obstructive behavior, but before he could worry about it for long, Jack jumped in.

"Jerry, your organization provides the margin data for individual accounts, as well as the aggregate margin. That is central to our being able to report on time."

"Well," Jerry responded, "put that way, I see what you mean. In that case, maintaining accuracy of the data and providing the monthly statistics in a timely fashion are two things that we do to support the company's *Margins* metric."

"Perfect!" complimented Tim. "Okay, if accuracy and timeliness of margin metrics are what you provide, how would you measure yourself on providing them?"

Sharon asked, "May I offer a suggestion?"

Jerry looked at her but made no comment.

"It would be great if we could have them all by the third day of each new business month."

"Is that possible?" Tim asked Jerry.

Jerry seemed to ponder the recommendation. "I think we could do that, but it would mean pushing some other reports out. May I talk with Jack about that and get back to you?" He hesitated, then said, "In the meantime, go ahead and use it."

"Good," said Tim, writing the metric in the appropriate box in the table. "How about accuracy?"

Accounting Metrics		
Metric	**Goal**	**Origin**
Margin Data	≤ 3 day of EOM	Mission & Cost
Margin Data	100% Accuracy	Mission & Cost

"That's going to be a little tougher," replied Jerry. "I mean, I think we're pretty accurate now, but then we have the luxury of taking as long as it takes to get it right.

"Having margin data accurate and delivered within three days is going to be a challenge. Some contract managers don't report on time. They'll sometimes wait to hear from new clients to see if the client has accepted a proposed contract, or if they'll have to negotiate further."

"I won't deny that happens sometimes," Jack stated, "but don't you feel that's the exception rather than the rule?"

"True," replied Jerry. "You know us accountants," he said with a smile, "we're a conservative lot. Let's give 100% accuracy a try and we'll see if we need to modify it downward later."

"That's the spirit," said Tim. "How about answering client questions? Anything there?"

"Tim," interrupted Jack. "If I could?"

Tim nodded his assent.

"Jerry, let's make the timely closing of the books the subject of a meeting with Jennifer's program managers. Let's make the need to snap the line at the end of the calendar month a firm expectation, regardless of the state of the contract."

Jerry nodded, and Jack indicated that Tim could proceed.

Tim asked again, "Jerry, how does accounting impact Copper-Bottom's ability to answer customer calls in a single call?"

"Actually," responded Jerry, "if a client has a question about billing, my folks field those, so, yeah, that will need to be one of our metrics, too. I'm not sure," he continued, "whether we can do it in one call, though."

"Good point," Tim acknowledged. "Here's the thing. If you aren't already at optimum, if you don't set a goal that you can't currently meet, it's unlikely that you'll ever get better.

"Let me ask you," Tim continued, "why can't you answer it in one call?"

"Simple," came Jerry's response. "We need to research the charges and get back to the client."

"Why do you need to get back? Can't you research the charges while the customer is on the line?" asked Tim.

"What's in the system is not always accurate," Jerry responded.

"Why aren't data accurate in the system?" asked Tim.

"All financial data goes through our corporate headquarters. They post all payments and all charges. We don't see the results for 24 to 36 hours after the transaction is received at HQ."

"Okay," Tim acknowledged. "Why does it take them so long?"

"Two reasons. First, the inputters often don't get the transaction for 24 hours. They get a daily queue that is built the night before. Second, the transactions aren't in real time. The system updates overnight, so even though a payment was input today, field offices like Charleston can't see them until tomorrow; however, if we call HQ, they can give us real-time info."

Tim smiled. "I'm not surprised by your responses, but let me pursue the same line of questioning a little further."

"So, why are the postings not in real time?"

"Ah, that's the $64,000 question," Jerry responded. "The answer is the same reason that our software is so archaic: the company is dragging its feet implementing a system upgrade that will be real time."

Tim pursued the line of questioning. "Not to be impertinent, but why is the company dragging its feet?"

"I can only give you my opinion," stated Jerry, looking nervously at Jack, "but I believe it's because every time they test it, they run into problems and that postpones its implementation. Don't get me wrong, I'm not in a rush to get a bad system, but I can't understand why they are taking so long."

Skip, who had been quiet all this time, cleared his throat to speak. "I think I can help a little there. The original contractor went bankrupt about three-quarters of the way through the creation of the new system. Corporate had to shop the design out again, and that took time. Then there were months during which corporate and the new contractor debated whether to start with a clean slate or try to reuse what they had. Because the previous contractor had been so far into the development, Corporate opted for the latter. They were also told it would be faster.

"Unfortunately, the new developer keeps finding bugs in the original code. The software is so complex that every fix touches other features that need to be updated, and those updates touch other features, and on and on. It's been a nightmare."

For the first time, everyone in the room understood what was going on and why. It made so much sense, but even though it was on everyone's mind, Nadine was the only one to ask, "Why didn't they just tell us?"

Skip offered, "I don't know the real answer, but I'd guess that HQ is both embarrassed and aware they have little control over the process at this point. The implementation just keeps slipping to the right and they seem powerless to get it back on track."

When Jack finally responded, it was to say: "Interesting. It all makes sense now. I think I'll talk with the other VPs and see if we can't push for a phased implementation. That way they can send updates as they work out the bugs, but meanwhile, we'll all be able to use what already works."

"Jerry, let's talk offline and you can give me your preferred order of implementation."

"Thanks for the explanation, Skip," said Jerry with a newfound respect.

"Good dialog, everyone," Tim said, praising the group. "Earlier, when I was winding Jerry through the reason his people can't answer questions in a single call, I used a form of problem-solving called *the 5 Whys*. It's a quick and easy way to get to the root cause of a problem. If you noticed, each answer Jerry gave me led to another '*why?*' question, until we finally got to the root cause.

"Keep that in mind moving forward," Tim encouraged them. "It's especially useful when you have people who aren't aware that they know the root cause until you walk them backwards through the 5 Whys process.

"All right, let's get back to the original question: Does answering customer questions in a single call seem like an attainable goal?" Tim asked.

"Not today," answered Jerry, "but I'm willing to be measured against that target until we can."

"Great response!" encouraged Tim. "Let me ask you, though. Should you just count the number of calls answered, or should it be the average number of calls it takes to answer customers' questions?"

"Good point," replied Jerry. "Simply counting the number of calls won't really give us anything to work with. It needs to be the average number of calls, incoming and outgoing, during each measurement period, divided by the number of customers who called in. That way we'll be able to see if the trend is getting better or not."

Tim wrote the goal in the table.

"Next!" Tim was on a roll. "How does Accounting support the company mission of Schedule?"

Jerry thought for a second. "Well, getting the margin data in less than three days is one way, but I take it you mean something else?"

"Right," said Tim.

"Hmm. Well, there's the fact that we close the books in a week or less."

"That *is* helpful," commented Sharon.

"Tell us how that enables mission accomplishment?" asked Tim.

"Well, first off, it forces us to keep our accounts current. That is helpful throughout the month, but closing swiftly at the end of the month lets us know where we are, how our division is performing, and whether we are ahead of or behind our target."

"What do you think?" Tim asked the group. "Is this the best way to measure Accounting's support of the Schedule part of your mission?"

"I have to say," Jack began, "it is helpful to know where we are at all times."

Getting no pushback, Tim asked, "Jerry, should you also be reporting on revenue and expenses?"

Jerry thought for a second. "Well, as you know, to calculate Margin we first have to calculate those two. However," he continued, "if all we look at is Margin, we don't know if we achieved it by bringing in more revenue or by expending less."

Turning to Jack, Jerry asked, "Would you want to see expenses, revenue, just margin, a combination of any two, or even all three?"

It was Jack's turn to think. "All three," he said at length. "I need to report margin, but what matters most to the directors are revenue and expenses."

"Consider it done," Jerry responded.

"Back to your measure of schedule, are you sticking with closing within three days from the end of the previous fiscal month?" Tim asked.

"I do think that makes the most sense," Jerry stated.

"Last up," announced Tim. "Safety. What do you think, Jerry?"

"I think that, if we're using audit results to measure the overall organization, we ought to use them in every department. I mean, it's not like we've got the kinds of hazards you'd have in a factory."

"I think that should become the universal measure of safety for the entire organization," Nadine agreed.

The other staff members concurred.

"Then that completes Accounting," Tim said. "Let's take a break."

Accounting Metrics		
Metric	Goal	Origin
Safety Audit	TBD	Safety
Margin Data	≤ 3 day of EOM	Mission & Cost
Revenue Data	≤ 3 day of EOM	Mission & Cost
Expense Data	≤ 3 day of EOM	Mission & Cost
Answer Client Questions	1 phone call	Quality
Time to Close	≤ 3 day of EOM	Schedule

The rest of the afternoon was more of the same. Department by department, they struggled through the measures of mission success. As they got the hang of things, Jerry took over recording the metrics on the white board, and Tim kept the electronic version on his laptop.

By 3:45, the team was worn out.

"Bad news," announced Tim. "Tomorrow, we go down to the next layer. If there are organizations that have supervisors or lead people, we'll need to continue down to that level.

"Back in here by 7:55 tomorrow morning," Tim concluded.

To everyone's relief, they knocked out the other metrics by mid-afternoon on Friday. By then, Jack and his staff were mentally fatigued.

Sharon announced that she was ready to get back to her real job.

"Hold on," cautioned Tim. "This *is* your real job. From now on, following your organization's performance against these metrics will offer you two new opportunities.

"First, you're going to know how you're doing much faster than waiting until the end of month, or even the end of the week, for feedback.

"Second, these metrics will become the basis of a new relationship you're going to forge with your employees. We'll get into that next week.

"See you next Monday," Tim concluded. "By then, I'll need the first copies of your metrics on these walls on 8.5 × 11-inch paper, printed in landscape mode. Remember, we're going to want to monitor progress using run charts, so do your best to go back at least two months and create the performance line. You'll also want the charts to possess your goal lines and the arrows that show the direction of good.

"We good?" Tim asked the bone-weary group.

There was mumbled agreement as people gathered their belongings.

"All right, have a great weekend." Tim said brightly, although he felt totally exhausted.

As Jack's staff filed out, one might have gotten the impression that they were emotionally beaten down, but that wasn't the case. Each held a growing belief that the last week would indeed change the culture at Copper-Bottom.

It wasn't so much that they didn't want to lose their jobs—they were too exhausted to think that far ahead—it was more that everyone was tired of the way they'd felt in the old culture.

In short, for the first time in years, they felt *hope*. It wouldn't take long before their hope would be vindicated.

Principle #21: A huge part of the difference between healthy and unhealthy cultures has to do with the way their leaders lead.

Principle #22: Growing their subordinates is one of the highest expectations of leaders.

Principle #23: Change involves risk. Employees need to be encouraged to take calculated risks within their field of expertise. Risk-taking makes periodic failure a foregone conclusion.

Principle #24: Leaders need to rise above the mundane and focus on the future of their people, their processes, and their product.

22

Out of the Blue

It had been a long week for Tim as well. On Saturday, he took a break from his usual chores and drove to the beach. He didn't go to tan or swim. He just wanted to lay in the warm air and read. There was a growing pile of books beside his bed that he intended to read. He saw today as the perfect time to begin that process. The morning weather was glorious and the beach surprisingly empty.

As fate would have it, he would prove unsuccessful in finishing his book, but there was a serendipitous event awaiting him at the beach.

Tim always found that when he had time to let his mind coast, he came to new and often deeper understandings of the concepts he practiced. Downtime, however, was at a premium these days. Besides his work at Copper-Bottom, he had a team of three that he guided back at Friedman. Each of them had their own Lean projects and Kaizen events. Plus, he sat in on the Lean Council at Friedman and often guided it as well. Achieving all his Friedman tasks each week usually took a full day: a full day he had to fight to withhold from his work at Copper-Bottom. He'd missed working with his own team these past few weeks and looked forward to catching up with them on Monday afternoon.

A few years ago, Tim had been a supervisor at Friedman. Jim had informed Don that he'd need a full-time Continuous Improvement Director. He'd also told Don that it was preferred that he promote someone within his own organization. Don had reached out and asked him to assume that role. Because all of Don's staff were new, no one knew about Tim's rapid promotion. They watched his work and easily accepted him as their full peer. The two-pay-grade promotion had been a shock to Tim, but he quickly acclimated to the role. At Jim's recommendation, Don had sent

DOI: 10.4324/9781003336051-23

Tim to a sister plant where he understudied another CI Director for two weeks as he learned the intricacies of his new job.

Word at the time was that Don himself was perilously close to being terminated, but that he'd seen the value in what Jim was asking him to embrace. It had changed the way he managed forever. As he had with Copper-Bottom, Don was now quick to tell his peers about his epiphany and the difference it had made in him and his organization.

Tim had been practicing Lean for several years by the time Don chose him, albeit only within operations. He fervently believed in the value of Lean and didn't need to be asked twice. Not knowing that there was a promotion attached, he readily accepted the offer and, within weeks, began applying the same skills he'd developed in operations to the greater Charleston campus of Friedman Electronics. Now he was responsible for an entire team of full-time practitioners and for implementing Lean throughout the entire plant. He'd even appointed one of his team members to start working exclusively with their local suppliers who had problems meeting Friedman's quality, on-time delivery and cost requirements, or combinations of all three.

But today Tim was on the beach and deeply engrossed in a book when a shadow spilled over him, and he heard someone saying his name. He looked up to see Patty Purcell standing nearby with a young boy. She was wearing a swimsuit, and Tim realized that she looked extremely good in it.

"Ms. Purcell?" he asked.

"Patty, please," she corrected him. "I'm so sorry," she began, "I don't mean to interrupt your study. I was just surprised to see you here. Do you often come to this beach?"

"No," Tim admitted, standing to address her. "I rarely get to the beach these days," he said. "Who is this big guy?" he asked, holding his hand out to shake the boy's hand.

"Tim, this is my son, Scott. He'll be seven in a week."

"Well, hello, Scott," said Tim.

Turning back to Patty, he asked awkwardly, "So what brings you to this beach? Do you come here often?"

Patty admitted she did. "Since the run-in with Mr. Corn, I lost a lot of weight and got pretty sick. I used some of my settlement money to hire a life coach, and she's been working on my mind and body. One of the things she's told me is that a tan goes a long way toward making you look and feel healthy. Of course, she has also been working on meals and exercise. The combination of those has made Scott"—she looked at her son—"and me feel so much better. Don't you think so, son?"

The boy nodded vigorously but said nothing. He'd continued to cling to Patty's waist since being introduced. Tim was amazed at how open she'd been about the lawsuit and even more amazed that she even knew who he was.

"I know this must seem very forward," Patty stated, "but I wonder if we could join you?" She leaned in to whisper in Tim's ear. He could feel her warmth and smell the light fragrance she wore. "Scott could really use a male influence," she whispered. Then, as an afterthought, she asked, "You're not here with someone, are you?" Realizing for the first time that she may have interrupted a date, Patty blushed furiously.

Tim barked a laugh. "No, ma'am," he said. "Just me and my book."

"Phew. I don't want you to think I'm forcing us on you. If you have other plans ..."

"No. Quite all right. I was mostly just here to get some sun and soak time."

"Soak time?" Patty asked.

"Time to disengage from the rest of my life and gain some perspective while letting what I've learned soak in."

"Ah," Patty acknowledged, smiling broadly. Tim realized what a pretty smile she had.

She had wheeled Scott's plastic wagon full of beach toys up to Tim's blanket and now spread her own blanket next to his.

"Scott," she inquired, "would you like to go down and dig at the water's edge?"

Tim could see the child's face light up. He headed to his wagon, where he retrieved a shovel and bucket. He quickly set them down and whispered in his mom's ear.

"Scott wants to know if you'd like to join him," Patty asked.

It had been a long time since Tim had *played* at the beach. Truth was, he really did enjoy it.

"Sure," he agreed, and the two headed off to the ocean's edge.

About an hour later, Patty came down to tell them that lunch was ready. Tim had planned to be gone by noon but had lost track of time. He and Scott had built a large sandcastle and dug a shallow moat around it. Now they were building a small village on the other side of the moat.

Patty took photos of the castle, and then of Scott and Tim with their tools. They all laughed.

Tim had the foresight to take a photo of Scott and Patty as well. It was all very spur of the moment, but he suspected he'd enjoy having a photo of them later. He took a couple more back at their blankets. He had hopes of using the photos as an excuse to get Patty's phone number so he could text them to her.

As they walked back to the blankets, Patty said, "I noticed that you didn't bring any food. We have plenty. Would you join us? It's nothing fancy," she admitted, "but it's healthy."

Lunch turned out to be crunchy peanut butter and honey on flatbread, celery sticks with hummus, and apple slices. Not exactly the burger and fries that Tim had planned on, but the company was much better. He had to admit he liked Patty. One would never guess what she'd been through from the way she behaved. She seemed to have an easy grace. He wondered if he dared to talk about it, but decided against it. Why ruin a nice day at the beach with a beautiful woman?

"You're starting to get pretty red on your neck and shoulders," she said. "May I put some sunscreen on you?"

"I hadn't planned to be here this long," he admitted, "but it's not every day that I get to build sandcastles with a great builder like Scott," he said, giving the boy a playful punch in the arm.

Patty rubbed the sunscreen on his back, shoulders, and neck. The fragrance was what he'd smelled on her earlier. Her hand felt good gliding across his skin.

Patty had brought a deck of cards and, after applying the same sunscreen to herself and Scott, the trio played several hands of Go Fish! There was a lot of laughing and joking. Scott allowed himself to be a child and enjoyed the time just playing with his mom and Tim.

When the day ended, Tim walked Patty and Scott back to their car. They'd stopped at an outdoor shower to wash the wagon and tools down. When they arrived at Patty's car, Tim noted that it was clean and neat but several years old. He helped load the wagon and tools into the hatchback. He shook Scott's hand again and Patty gave him a chaste hug.

"Thanks for spending the day with us," she said. "I'm sure you had your own plans for the day, but it was just nice getting to know you."

"Funny," Tim confessed, "those were going to be my words. Besides," he admitted, "I enjoyed you both." He could see Patty's face brighten, as if, despite her calm and peaceful demeanor, she was secretly worried about disappointing.

After Patty buckled Scott in his child's seat, Tim walked her to the driver's side of the car and opened the door for her. Just as she was about to get in, she spontaneously gave him another hug, this one not as chaste as the last. "Thank you," she whispered.

The car fired up immediately and she rolled down the electric windows to let the afternoon's heat out. "I'd invite you to supper," she said, "but I'm afraid I'm unprepared and Scott has homework." There was a second or two pause before she asked, "Another time?"

Tim realized he'd really like to see Patty again. "Absolutely!" he stated enthusiastically. "How about I give you a call and we set something up?"

Patty smiled. "I'd like that," she agreed.

There was a pause before Tim asked awkwardly, "May I have your number?"

Patty blushed bright red and said, "Oh, my. What a silly I am." She opened the console between the seats and withdrew a pen and small pad. She carefully printed her number on the pad along with her name. Tim noticed that she had beautiful handwriting.

Patty handed the slip to Tim. He took it, then momentarily laid his hand on her arm, which was now resting on the window opening. "Thanks again," he said. He bent down and waved goodbye to Scott through Patty's window. He squeezed her arm, then walked back to his own car before driving home. On the drive home, Tim realized he felt a hollowness in his chest. He hadn't felt that way in a long time.

23

Dialog as a Way of Coaching

The weekend had been a welcome respite for all. When they met on Monday morning, everyone was much more energized than when they'd filed out on Friday. This meeting was short compared to those the previous week.

Jack had supplied bagels, cream cheese, fresh fruit, and coffee out of his own pocket. As colleagues bantered about their weekend exploits, there was an air of mirth and hopeful expectation in the room.

At 8 AM, Tim brought the group to order. He explained that they'd be discussing two things: KPI Boards and Coaching.

"Before you ask, KPI stands for Key Performance Indicator. The metrics we created last week are just that, Key Performance Indicators. A KPI board is where you will display the KPIs for a specific group.

"For instance," Tim continued, "you have top-level KPIs, the ones that you derived directly from the Mission Statement." He pointed to the graphs neatly taped to the conference room wall. "Those are the KPIs for this group. Each of you will need to have your own board somewhere in a prominent place. Many organizations put the top-level KPI board in a main hall or outside the cafeteria. They put their director-level boards outside the director offices, or in a central location within their organization.

"A quick sidebar: Company-sensitive data, like your margins, needs to be shared privately, perhaps on a shared drive with limited access, but everything else needs to be posted publicly. You want your people to see how you're doing. Not only does your KPI board inform; it also builds a sense of camaraderie, a sense of 'we're all in this together.' As you already know, every discipline is going to be measured using the KPIs we developed last week.

DOI: 10.4324/9781003336051-24

"Because their KPIs are derivatives of the company's KPIs, employees will not only be able to see how they're doing, but also how their jobs impact the greater company and its Mission. That creates organizational alignment: everyone pulling in the same direction.

"Let me digress a minute longer," Tim continued. "You may ask, 'Why are we going to make our metrics so public?' Or 'Why are we going to place our performance metrics where not only employees, but suppliers and customers can see them?'

"The answer is that your performance is not only a measure of this leadership group but of your entire organization. Posting it publicly is a form of self-accountability." He paused. "And a form of *leadership*. 'Leadership?' you ask. 'How can posting our performance be an act of leadership?' The answer is that you will be asking subordinates to post their performance as well. By posting yours first, you are leading by example.

"You may think that leading by example makes for a quaint aphorism but it has little practical value. Quite the contrary! True leaders lead from the front. They practice what they preach, and are almost always the first to do so.

"I suspect some of you saw the Mel Gibson movie *We Were Soldiers*. It's the true-life story of Lieutenant Colonel Hal Moore during the first American battle of the Vietnam War. Before the battle, LTC Moore told his troops: 'When we go into battle, I will be the first to set foot on the field, and I will be the last to step off.' That's leading by example.

"Leading by example is going to be one of the most powerful tools that you are going to use to change your culture.

"Now, as I've already said, each of you will also need to have a KPI board for your department. It needs to be labeled with the department name and located in a prominent location where *all* your employees can see it. Also, as I said earlier, outside your office seems to be the optimal place.

"Questions?" Tim asked.

The room was quiet for long seconds. Tim drank from a bottle of water, seemingly oblivious to the silence. In fact, he was weighing how much pushback he was going to get on the topic. When he didn't get any, he continued with his monolog but fully expected to hear more on the topic later.

"Okay, how are you going to display your performance? This is going to be important. As I said earlier, every organization is going to display every metric using a run chart. Why a run chart? Because a run chart displays a *trend over time.* By that I mean that the viewer will not only be able to see the most current performance, but each preceding period's performance at the same time. And they are going to see that *trend* as it compares to your goal. An example would help."

Tim went to the whiteboard and drew the following:

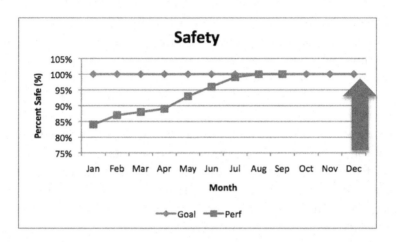

Looking for feedback, he called on Nadine. "So, Nadine, what does this chart tell you? First, are we getting better, worse, or stagnating?"

Nadine looked at the chart for several seconds before hesitantly saying, "It looks to me like we've been getting better over time, but that we've plateaued at peak performance."

"I'm not arguing," Tim said, "but what makes you say we were getting better?"

"Well," began Nadine, "we were at about 85% in January and have gotten progressively higher ratings each month over the last"—she counted the postings—"nine months."

"Again," said Tim, "I'm not disagreeing, but what tells you that you've gotten better?"

Nadine thought for a moment. "The fact that we got closer and closer to our goal," she responded.

"Good!" Tim praised her. "Here's the takeaway. Every chart must—I mean that literally—have the goal line posted on the chart. There is a famous Toyota leader named Taiichi Ohno, who stated 'Where there is no standard, there can be no Kaizen' (change for the better). The chart's goal is the chart's *standard*, and it's a critical part of every chart. It's the yardstick against which you measure progress. In addition," he continued, "you'll also want to have an arrow showing the direction of good.

"Because you're using run charts, the timeline is always displayed along the bottom. If you are at a senior level, like Jack, you'll measure your performance monthly, whereas all of you, Jack's direct reports, should probably measure your performance weekly. Your direct reports, managers, will probably measure theirs weekly. If you have supervisors, they'll measure daily, and your worker teams will measure their performance hourly.

"So," he recapped, "we always display some measure of time along the bottom axis and the time gap between measurements gets smaller as you go down through your organization.

"Many of you will find your vertical axes will be in units of percent. That's not a requirement; it just provides a convenient measure of relative performance. Again, in our factories, our hourly folks measure their performance in 'units per hour,' because that's the critical measure of their performance. This body will be the one to determine those units of measure and the frequency with which they are posted."

Copper-Bottom Health Solutions			
Metric	Goal	Origin	Owner
Margin	≥ 40%	Mission & Cost	Accounting
Answer Client Questions	1 phone call	Quality	Operations
Respond to Mail	≤ 48 hours	Schedule	Operations
Biweekly Safety Survey	100%	Safety	Human Resources

"Let's take a second and figure out how frequently you'll be posting your metrics and what units of measure you'll use along the vertical axis of each.

"Jerry, looks like you'll be providing the first metric: Margin. How frequently and what will be the units of measure?"

"I surmise the top-level frequency will be monthly," Jerry began.

"Correct," Tim affirmed.

"And I would imagine we'll report that as *Margin as a Percent of Total Sales*. That will make percent the unit of measure."

"Makes sense," agreed Tim. "Jack, you good with that?"

"That's certainly what I want to see," Jack stated.

"Okay. That concludes your Margin metric. Let's move to the next: Answering client questions. Who will own this metric?" Tim asked.

"Operations. I think that will be me," responded Sharon. "In fact, I own that one and the next. And let's see, frequency on the first one will be daily, and units of measure will be calls per day."

"Ah," Tim intervened. "Frequency at the Lean Council level will always be monthly. How does that change your units of measure?"

Sharon thought for a second. "I'm not sure," she admitted.

"Quite all right," Tim stated. "That's why we're doing this in here."

"I would guess that you are going to want to know how many calls a client needs to make to get an answer to their question. Is that right?" Tim asked.

Sharon nodded.

"If a client has multiple questions, do you count each one?" Skip asked.

Sharon thought out loud. "If we count every question and, say, we routinely answer multiple questions on a single call, it's possible that we could actually end up with a *questions answered per call* value greater than one. I think that takes us in a wrong direction.

"If, on the other hand, we only count the number of calls from a client, we may still answer multiple questions but only get credit for answering the questions of the initial call. If it takes multiple calls to answer all their initial questions, then it will reflect as if it took us multiple calls to answer one question."

"What's the intent of this metric?" asked Tim.

"To prevent clients from having to call us multiple times in order to get their questions answered. Our goal is to answer all their questions in a single call."

"In that case," Tim asked, "wouldn't you want to measure the number of calls from a customer within a given window, say, three days?"

"Let's see," Sharon pondered the question. After a few seconds she said, "If the goal is to answer all their questions in a single call, then that would work."

"Good," Tim praised her. "This is your metric, but what I'd suggest you measure is *Average Calls per Customer within a Three-Day Period*. How does that sound?"

"I like it," replied Sharon.

"Just curious," Tim queried. "If you rated yourself against that goal today, where do you think you'd land?"

"Oh, boy," Sharon responded. "Monthly average of calls per customer? I'd guess somewhere between 1.75 and 3.25 calls per client, if measured within a three-day window."

"What happens if your people report that?" Tim asked.

"Well, if you're asking will I post that, the answer is 'Yes.' If you're asking if I will be happy with it? Hmm." Sharon again took a second to think. "What is it you say, Tim?" she asked. "Isn't it something like 'It's just data and it is what it is'? In the beginning, I guess I'd have to accept it as fact," she continued, "but I'd sure want to improve it."

"That's the perfect answer," Tim replied. "Now," he continued "that drives to the heart of the issue we're facing: culture. You see, if your people fear the result of reporting the truth, what will they do?"

"Good point," acknowledged Sharon. "They'll hide it."

"Knowing that, what behavior should that invite from leaders?" Tim asked.

"To not want them to fear telling the truth, I guess," Sharon replied.

"Absolutely correct," Tim said. "And how can you do that?"

Sharon looked stumped.

"Anyone?" Tim asked.

When no one responded, Tim answered his own question. "It implies that you should find ways to reward, if only in words, the reporting of the truth. Do you remember the movie *A Few Good Men*?" he asked.

There were nods and around the table.

"What was Jack Nicholson's character's iconic quote in that movie?"

"'You can't handle the truth!'" Jerry responded for the group.

"Very good," Tim said. "Well, you need to be able to handle the truth. You need to be willing to hear what really happened, not just what you want to hear or what you assume you should hear.

"Last week, Don said that Sharon was the kind of employee with whom he likes to surround himself. That's because she told a hard truth when there was a strong possibility of adverse consequences. I'd encourage you to take on the same attitude. Reward truth-tellers, especially when telling the truth could otherwise result in ridicule or even termination.

"When you show your people that you can do that, you'll start to hear the truth all the time. Moreover, you'll earn their trust.

"By the way," Tim offered offhandedly, "works for kids, too." That drew a ripple of laughter.

"At the risk of restating the obvious, if you begin the problem-solving process with anything but the truth, should it surprise you if you get an answer that doesn't solve the problem or is unworkable? The truth is going to be critical not only to your organizational welfare but to your commercial success in the future.

"So how do you get it? How do you get the truth?" Tim asked.

Sharon answered. "First, you ask for it. Next, when you get it, you simply accept it as a statement of fact—neither the *answer* nor the *respondent* is bad. They are both neutral. And," she continued, "the truth is just a starting place. From the truth, you can begin your journey to improvement."

"Wow!" Tim stated admiringly. "Very good, Sharon." She blushed, but he could tell she was pleased to have been recognized for her good response.

He continued, "Once your people realize they can trust you with the truth, they will start to offer you their suggestions on how to improve those things under their control. They will also tell you about equipment and processes that don't work, or that don't work correctly, or about things that are going wrong, things you might never have discovered until too late.

"You won't be able to correct everything, but the fact that they tell you about problems is a sign that you're winning their trust.

"If you can't fix their concerns, tell them. Let them know what inhibits you—not blaming others, but sincerely telling them when finances are the issue, or when you lack control over the problem. Tell them you'll keep their concern in mind and pass it upward when the time is right.

"Okay," Tim concluded. "We good?" he asked, looking around the room. There were nods and 'Yeses' from everyone, so he continued.

"Can we move on?" he asked, glancing at Sharon, a look of mock frustration on his face. Everyone laughed, knowing that he, and not Sharon, had been the source of the delay as he made his point.

Without being asked, Sharon stated, "Respond to mail in less than 48 hours." There was a broad smile still on her face. "I guess that would be letters answered in less than 48 hours divided by total letters received.

"Oh, wait!" she said We'd be measuring in percent, because we'll be taking a monthly average."

"Very good," praised Tim.

"And, finally, the biweekly safety survey. Who will report on that?" Tim asked.

Nadine raised her hand. "That'll be me," she said. She bit her lower lip before beginning again. "I'm not sure what the survey looks like yet," she stated. "Can I tell you how we'll measure it later?"

"Good point," Tim acknowledged. "Let's talk it through. Similar surveys we've used look something like this," he said, drawing on the whiteboard again.

Question		Points					Score
	5	4	3	2	1	0	
1 Are there tripping hazards in area?	0	<3	(<5)	<7	<9	>9	3
2 Are there frayed wires in the area?	0					(>0)	0
~ Are there slipping hazards in the area?	0	<3	<5	(<7)	<9	>9	2
~							
50 Is the safety chart posted in area?	(Yes)					No	5
A Sum of Scores							65
B Total Points Available (50 x 5)							250
C Percent Score (A/B x 100)							26%

"The person conducting the survey examines the area, then circles the response that is appropriate. Let's say in the first case there were four lower filing cabinet drawers open, which are tripping hazards, a frayed lamp wire and paper on the floor in five cubicles, which are slipping hazards.

"Under *Tripping Hazards*, the auditor will circle the <5 box, since there are more than 3 but fewer than 5 total tripping hazards. Next, they'll write the corresponding number of points in the score box at the far right. In this case, the score is 3.

"Now, because frayed wires are potentially lethal, any occurrence results in a score of zero; hence, the next score is zero.

"After the entire survey is filled out, the auditor totals the points, and that is the area's raw score. Questions so far?"

There were no questions, so Tim continued. "Now, you'll try to design the form to have the raw score yield a whole percent when divided by the total number of available points and multiplied by 100. After you convert the raw score into percent, you'll plot that on a run chart."

Again, he went to the whiteboard and began drawing a chart, checked his watch, and turned to face the crowd. "This would be a great time to take a break. Be back in five." As folks exited, Tim continued to rough out the chart.

"Okay," he began when everyone was back. "Here's a typical chart. What can you tell me about it?" He waited.

Skip raised his hand.

"Go," Tim instructed the IT director.

"Well," Skip began, "the initial department's score is pretty pathetic, but I guess that's to be expected, right?"

"Go on." Tim smiled encouragingly.

"Well, I guess the big thing is that they continue to get better week after week, and the most recent week shows double-digit improvement."

"Excellent!" Tim praised. The latter smiled appreciatively.

"Some takeaways," Tim continued.

"First, the department is improving, as Skip said. That alone is good news. Keep in mind, it's not where an organization starts that matters, but where they finish, right?

"Second, you can plan on first scores being pretty anemic. It will take folks a while to figure out what's going on and how it all works. Give them time. Ask what you can do to help. Be supportive." Tim paused, then said, "That'll confuse them." He got a hearty laugh.

"They'll also be waiting you out," he continued. "If yours is like most organizations, your people will all have seen *flavor of the month* before, so they will do as little as necessary at first to see how serious you are. That's why it's so important to check their KPI boards faithfully.

"While you're there, ask the department personnel to tell you what's going on and what the charts are telling them. Two things will occur: first, they'll give you answers, some right, some wrong, but this is a priceless opportunity for dialog: time for you to get to know them and them you.

"The other thing that will be going on is that you'll be showing both your resolve in keeping these metrics alive and also in changing the nature of the conversation between you and them.

"Never forget," he summarized, "this is about neuroscience. The human brain can only assimilate so much change at a time, and it always does best when change becomes routine. Repetition and follow-through will become critical to your joint success.

"Okay," Tim asked, "what questions do you have?"

Jerry finally raised his hand. "Tim," he began, "you've talked about changing the nature of our relationship with our people. How exactly do you propose we go about doing that?"

Tim acted as if he hadn't heard Jerry and looked around the crowd, asking, "Anyone?" That got a laugh.

He looked back at Jerry. "Just picking on you, Jerry. Actually, that's a brilliant question. I had planned to talk about it later, but since you're interested, let's dive in.

"I personally hate role-playing, but I think that might be the best way to answer your question. You willing to play along?"

Jerry nodded apprehensively.

"Okay," Tim began, "let's assume that this is your organization's chart," he said pointing to the one he'd just drawn. "I come into your department on a weekly tour and stop at your KPI board. I wave to get your attention and ask, 'Jerry, explain this chart to me.'

"You approach, realize I'm pointing to your Safety chart, and say ..." Tim held out his hand, indicating that it was Jerry's turn to role-play.

Jerry looked momentarily confused, then took on a different persona. "Oh, hey, Tim. Let's see, that's our Safety chart. What do you want to know?"

"Excellent!" Tim praised him. "You're a natural." He then fell back into his persona and asked, "How come you're so far off goal?"

Jerry bobbed his head left and right as he thought of his response, then said, "It's actually a lot better than it looks, Tim. As you know, we've just started measuring safety and using this survey. Originally, it caught my people off-guard, but now they're getting the hang of it. As you can see, their scores are getting stronger every week."

"Good point," Tim agreed, still in persona. "Where are you facing your biggest problems, and how can I help?"

Jerry thought for a second and said, "I think it would really help if we could take my entire organization for a walk through the department and explain to them how the survey works, why it's important, and how they can improve their scores."

Still in character, Tim said, "Great recommendation. When would you like me here?"

"How about next Tuesday right after lunch?" Jerry asked.

Tim pulled out his phone and consulted its calendar. "I can do that," he said. "Want me to bring the forms, or will you?"

"Why don't you? It would make it a lot easier, if you don't mind."

"Consider it done," Tim replied, then dropped his role-play persona. "How did that work?" he asked the class.

"I see exactly what you've been saying," replied Jerry. "Now it makes sense."

"Anyone else?" Tim asked and waited.

"I'm not exactly sure how to ask this," Sharon said, "so be patient with me." Then, as if she had an epiphany, the words just tumbled out. "What happens if they start to backslide?"

"Great question," said Tim. "What do you *think* should happen?"

Sharon thought for a second. "I think there should be consequences, like some kind of disciplinary measure," she said.

"Like what?" Tim asked.

Again, Sharon thought before answering. "I guess there should be a letter of reprimand or something," she said at last.

"Okay," Tim acknowledged. "So let's think how their score could slide. Any ideas?"

"Inattention. Apathy," shot back Jerry.

Tim made no comment and wrote the words on the board.

"Anything else?"

"They didn't know what they could do to improve the score," offered Nadine.

Tim wrote, "Don't know how to improve," again without comment.

"Did the wrong thing," Jennifer, the Director of Sales, suggested.

Tim added her idea to his list.

When there were no further ideas, Tim asked, "Any chance they could be frightened of doing the wrong thing and of messing up further?" There were nods.

"So what could cause a backslide? Let's start with Jerry's suggestions: 'Inattention and apathy.' What could cause those?"

"They just don't give a rat's ... behind," replied Jerry.

"Why would they not care?" asked Tim, feigning puzzlement. "I mean, you did tell them this was coming and that you'd be checking up on them, right?"

A smile grew across Jerry's face. "I'm not saying *we've* done this, but I've heard of companies where they might not have followed through in the past."

Tim chuckled. "That's like telling a doctor that you have a friend who has certain symptoms and want to know what the physician would recommend to cure the friend."

Jerry smiled, but said nothing.

"Okay," Tim conceded, "so management might not have done its part in the past. Is that what I'm hearing?"

"I wouldn't have put it that way, but yeah," replied Jerry.

"So," concluded Tim, "how is that the employee's fault? Why should they have been disciplined?"

Silence.

"Any other reasons an employee might be inattentive or apathetic?"

"They never bought in," offered Sharon.

"So, whose job was it to know if they didn't buy in?" asked Tim.

Sharon thought for a moment. "You mean *we're* supposed to worry about whether they buy in or not? How does their behavior become management's problem?"

"Well," Tim queried, "whose idea was it to change things? Who is it that wants them to display new behaviors? Whose job is it to manage them, anyway?"

"Okay," she conceded. "I get your point."

Tim started in another box of his table.

"Okay, next up: Made a mistake. Whose fault is that?"

"Well," Jerry said slyly, "seems to me that the employee was the one to make the mistake. How can it not be their fault?"

"Let me pose a hypothetical," Tim began. "You've never been sailing. Your friend takes you out on his boat and tells you that he wants you to sail it. He demonstrates how to turn, how to trim the sails, how to handle strong wind, all the tricks, and then he promptly puts you in the helm, turns the boat over to you, and says, 'Sail!' Could you sail?"

Jerry didn't answer, but Sharon did. "I know I couldn't," she admitted. "I can't swim, so I wouldn't remember anything. I'd be scared witless about capsizing and drowning."

"Great point," agreed Tim. "Now, think of someone who never did well in school, especially in math. What do you think all this graphing stuff seems like to them?"

"Gotcha," Sharon conceded. "This is math to them, so they're afraid of capsizing and sinking."

"Bada-bing!" Tim shot back. "So, simply showing them how to sail one time isn't enough. I've got to go out with them, maybe several times, and work with them until sailing becomes second nature.

"Coming back to our table here," Tim said, pointing to the whiteboard. "If they didn't know how to graph, or what to do when the graph goes the wrong way, or took the wrong course of action to correct it and made things worse, who failed: them, or management?"

"Management" came the disgruntled response.

	Problem	Who Owns Problem?	
		Management	Employee
1	Inattentive or apathetic	X	
2	Made a mistake	X	
3	Don't know how to improve	X	
4			

Tim filled in another box in the table. "See where this is going?" he asked. There were nods around the table.

"Finally," Tim asked, "who is responsible for helping them to understand which courses of action corrects which problems?"

No one waited for the example. Almost in one voice they responded, "Management."

Tim completed the table.

"What's the takeaway?" he asked.

This time, Jennifer raised her hand. "That we shouldn't assume that the employee had control over the causes of their failure?" she asked. "That we need to start with the premise that the employee may have failed through no fault of their own and that we need to help them understand how to improve."

While she'd started her response with a question in her voice, the more she spoke, the more Tim could see her come to grips with an understanding of what she was saying. By the time she concluded, what had started as a question had become a statement.

"Great job, Jennifer," Tim praised her. "I couldn't have said it better myself.

"Here's what Dr. W. Edwards Deming said on the topic. He said that most problems originate from poor *systems* and that managers own all systems; hence, managers own the source of almost all of the problems in an organization. Think about that.

"My advice to you is to assume an employee's innocence from the start and go looking for the root cause or real problem. If you don't, you'll spend a lot of time chasing down phantoms. As you do, the problem will grow worse and you're very likely to alienate or eliminate good employees in the process."

Tim stopped, indicating he was switching gears. He took a sip from his water bottle and plowed ahead. "So what does that all mean?" he asked.

No one spoke for long seconds. Finally, Jennifer timidly raised her hand.

"Shoot!" Tim instructed her.

"Just guessing," she began, "but I sense that you think we should automatically presume our employees are always doing their best."

"Not a bad start," Tim complimented her, "but let me ask you, why wouldn't you assume that in the first place?"

This time Jerry spoke up. "Because they don't," he stated emphatically.

"What evidence of that do you have?" Tim asked.

"Let me see," Jerry shot back. "I have people who post journal entries to the wrong accounts. I have people who forget to pay invoices per the terms. I have people who overpay and underpay, who miscalculate payroll, who miscalculate expenses." He stopped. "Do I need to go on?"

Everyone in the room seemed to think that Jerry had had the last word but secretly hoped that Tim had a winning rebuttal.

"Jerry," Tim began, "I could be wrong, but my bet is that journal entries for the same thing change based on the circumstances. Am I right?"

"Well, sure," Jerry responded. "It all depends on a variety of things."

"Again, I could be wrong, but my bet is that you've felt those rules are too complex to reduce to writing, so you've encouraged employees to come to you to be told what account to post the entries to. Right?"

"Rather than mess the posting up? Absolutely!" Jerry replied emphatically.

"Going out on a limb here," Tim admitted, "but my bet is that the employees who post to the wrong journal are the ones who fail to come to you. Correct?"

"Again right," Jerry agreed.

Tim was quiet for a moment, lips pursed.

"Anyone else see a problem with that?" he asked at length.

The room fell deadly quiet, then Jack spoke up. "If every posting is *situational*, employees only have a 50/50 chance of making the right call unless they understand the rules pertaining to that situation. In essence, Jerry is building job security into his position," he said, winking at Jerry.

"Thanks for your analysis, Jack," Tim agreed. "Jerry, my bet is that you see no problem with that. Am I correct?"

Jerry was a bit taken aback by Jack's comment and wasn't sure how to respond now. "I don't have a problem with them making a decision," he began, "but they'd need to have a master's in accounting in order to understand how to do it," he concluded. "Hell, I don't like being bothered all the time with their"—he stopped himself—"constant questions."

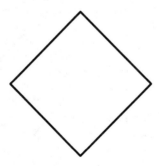

"You familiar with decision trees?" Tim asked.

"I don't know," Jerry replied a bit defensively. "What does one look like?"

Tim went to the board and drew a diamond. "What's the first question you ask yourself before assigning an entry to a particular account?" he asked.

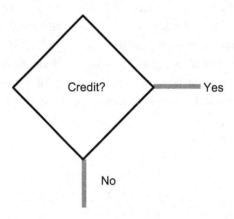

Jerry thought for a second. "I guess I'd ask if it's a credit or debit."

Tim wrote in the box:

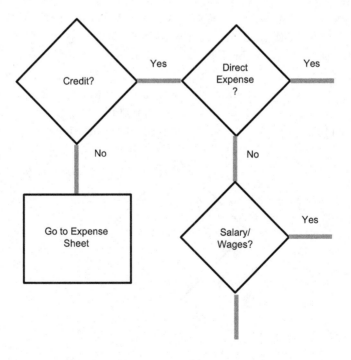

He then drew arrows from the right and bottom corners of the diamond and wrote "Yes" on the arrow facing right, and "No" on the arrow facing down. "Okay," Tim asked, "if the answer is 'Yes,' what happens?"

Jerry stated, "I'd ask if it's a *direct* expense or *indirect*?"

"Explain the difference," Tim asked.

"Well, a *direct* expense is one that we will charge to a particular customer's account. For instance, we frequently print instruction pamphlets for the employees of certain customers, so the employees know which things are covered by our insurance and which aren't. Those pamphlets are often specific to a particular customer, including their logo. We won't use those brochures with any other account, so we'll charge the full cost of printing them only to that account.

"An *indirect expense* is one that we incur as a part of doing business; for example, printing fees for our general marketing brochures. The brochures aren't for a particular client. They are a cost of doing business."

"Thanks," said Tim, continuing his decision tree. "Okay, so what happens if they're not a direct expense?"

"Then I ask if they are salaries or wages." Tim drew a new diamond on the board and wrote 'Salaries/Wages?' in it. He connected that diamond to the one labeled 'Direct Expense'?

"Do you see how this decision tree is working?" Tim asked Jerry.

"I think so," said Jerry. "It looks like a flow chart."

"That's exactly what it is," responded Tim. "We used these in our organic chemistry labs," he continued, feigning a shudder to show his disdain for the subject.

That drew a laugh.

"In essence, each question leads to a decision and each decision leads to reducing the number of options left. Decision by decision, the employee walks themselves into the answer."

"If you give your employees one of these decision trees and a little training, it does two things: (a) it lets them understand the logic behind what you've been doing for them, strengthening their own decision-making skills, and (b) it also gives you a tool when reeducating them if they make a mistake. In essence, a decision tree becomes what we call *Standard Work* for making accounting decisions. Now does it make sense?" Tim asked again.

"I haven't used flow charts, or decision trees as you call them, since college," Jerry stated. "I never would have believed they could be used to improve my employees' decision-making skills if you hadn't shown me." Jerry's response carried the beginnings of respect for Tim and Lean.

"You can do what you want," Tim told him, "but the more decisions your employees are able to make on their own, the more you can use *your* unique knowledge and skills to advance Copper-Bottom. I know that, if I were Jack, I'd want you looking forward to advise me of potential problems and unique opportunities that lie ahead."

"That's true," interjected Jack. "I think that with your help, we could make much better decisions regarding our sales and marketing approaches. You could show us how to make better use of data we already keep."

Tim picked the thread back up. "So, Nadine, coming full circle, can you see why I think you should presume your employee is innocent and go looking for the real cause of the problem?"

She nodded.

"Now," Tim asked, "if we stand way back from this discussion, what I've been doing is coaching you. Just like a volleyball coach, I have you look at the problems you're having and walk you through ways to improve your performance, only I don't *tell* you what to do. I ask you questions and let you *discover* the solution on your own. The only time I step in is if you suggest a solution that will get you or the company in trouble. Even then, I not only tell you the answer that I know will keep you out of trouble, but I'll also tell you *why.*

"Can you use that same technique in working with your subordinates?" he asked.

Principle 25: True leaders lead from the front. They practice what they preach and are almost always the first to undertake anything they'll later ask their subordinates to undertake.

Principle #26: Never discipline an employee for stating an unpopular truth. The truth is just a starting place. Only from the truth can you begin your journey to improvement.

Principle #27: Always start with the premise that the employee may have failed but through no fault of their own.

Principle #28: When monitoring performance, it's not where an organization starts that matters but where they finish.

24

A Slight Hiccup

Over the next week, Jack's staff started to inform their subordinates of the new metrics. Preceding that, Jack met with his staff and the layer of the organization below his staff. With them gathered around his wall of metrics, Jack said, "I need to come clean about something. About three weeks ago, I got a wake-up call. I learned from our CEO that a member of my organization had been put through a lot of mental anguish by a member of my staff. I'm ashamed to admit it took place right under my nose. I was given clear direction from the CEO that I had to change the culture here at Copper-Bottom.

"I'm not proud of the fact that I had to be told. I'm not proud of the incident that led to that directive or that a good employee suffered, but what I am glad about is the new course we're on.

"As you all know, another Charleston company has agreed to help us improve our culture. With their help, my staff opened up to me. They told me a lot of things that were painful to hear. We agreed to start over and to do a better job this time. We agreed to hold ourselves accountable to doing the right things for our business, for our customers and for our employees.

"Going all the way back to our Mission Statement, we developed a list of things that we'd need to measure to know if we are being successful. We set goals for ourselves and have posted those charts here in our entry hall.

"These charts" he said, pointing to the board, "are really important for several reasons that I'll get into in a second. Right now, let me take you through each of them."

With that, Jack launched into a brief explanation of each of the top-level metrics. He and his staff had chosen to mount their KPI board on a wall

DOI: 10.4324/9781003336051-25

on main entry hall. That location had been chosen because every employee passed this wall at least twice a day.

Since Safety was first, he stopped to ask why his team had chosen to measure that first. There were several wrong guesses before Jack said, "Our mentors taught us that if you," he pointed to the crowd, "aren't safe, then your leaders have failed you. It's our job to provide a safe working environment in which you can do your job. Make sense?"

No one spoke, but there were subtle nods and elbowing throughout the crowd. Jack knew that they were watching to see how long his new behavior would last. He laughed inwardly, thinking that Tim had told him that that would be their response.

The leadership team had gone back to the beginning of the year, so they had several months of data on each chart. As he introduced each KPI, Jack asked, "How are we doing?" No one responded at first, so he started calling employees by name. He could tell that the ones he called were surprised that he knew who they were. "I'm going to have to change that," he admonished himself.

When he finished introducing the metrics, Jack said, "These charts are important because they tell us how we're doing in real terms, not just whether we're making money. The truth is that money alone isn't a good indication of how we're doing. We need to know if we're meeting our customers' needs, if what we do is of good quality, and if we are providing it when our customers need it." He continued, "My staff and I can't achieve these goals without you, so I'm here to ask for your help.

"Each of your organizations performs tasks that contribute to Copper-Bottom's overall success. We will need you to measure your own performance by answering the question, 'How is our team doing?' My staff and I pledge to keep our information current, and we'll need you to do the same. It shouldn't be hard. Most of you already know the important measures, but we intend to make them public so we can all *see* how we're doing.

"Although we'll provide you the measures, each of your bosses will sit down with you to develop goals. Like we have, you'll put them on your charts so we can all see how you're doing. If you run into trouble, your charts will tell us, and we'll help you get back on track.

"The point is, if we all work together, we will not only improve our performance; we'll improve our relationships.

"Questions?" he asked.

There were no questions. Jack felt pretty sure that the jury was still out with this crew. They'd wait to see how these metrics were used, if his staff would really keep up with theirs, and if metrics would be turned on them and used to discipline them. "Time will tell," he thought.

That week, Jack's staff told each member of their own staff what the latter's metrics would be. Each was given a format and asked to create run charts to measure their performance. They were also told to meet with their supervisor to establish the target for each metric.

To no one's surprise, Sharon's crew of managers quickly agreed on their goals. Sharon told them where they needed to be by the end of the year but let them set their own pace.

One of her subordinates wanted to be much more aggressive than the others. Sharon advised against it, saying that it was better to under-commit and overperform than the reverse.

"Think of it this way," she encouraged. "If you consistently outperform your target, then you'll simply set a new, more aggressive target and shoot for it. When that time comes, you and I will sit down again, and we'll agree on a more aggressive goal we can both live with. Sound fair?" The employee had seen the logic in her argument.

In the end, the manager elected to do it Sharon's way, later telling her how glad she was. "I've consistently been ahead of goal," the manager told her. "Had I done it my way, I'd still be behind. Thanks."

Sharon stayed on top of her managers' charts. She visited them weekly and signed each one for weeks. In the beginning, Sharon asked the managers to meet her at their KPI board and walk her through each of their charts.

Accustomed to Henry Corn, her subordinates were expecting a brow-beating at their boards. What they found was just the opposite. Because of Tim's coaching, Sharon asked probing questions, trying to get to what she called the *root cause* of problems. Remembering Tim's behavior, she used *the 5 Whys* more than once.

Sharon's "board talks," as they came to be known, didn't end there. If a subordinate's performance was flagging, Sharon asked them how they were going to improve it. When the subordinate articulated their action plan, she made them write it down on the Action Item List below that chart. If they didn't know how, she walked them through the process of developing an action plan.

Her subordinates quickly learned that each action plan had to include a date by which the action would be complete and the name of the person accountable for making it happen.

At first, that kind of accountability was intimidating to her subordinates, but as they began to see improvements, they came to respect Sharon's methodology. What they didn't know was that Sharon had learned this methodology from Tim.

Action Item List

Item #	Date	Problem	Description	Responsible (Name)	Due Date	Status	Comments
1							
2							
3							
4							
5							
6							
7							
8							
9							
10							
11							
12							

In cases when a subordinate was befuddled and didn't have a solution, Sharon would ask Tim to help them past their stuck point. This often resulted in what Tim called a Kaizen event. To Sharon's untrained eye, a Kaizen event was just a bunch of employees getting together to develop and test potential solutions.

The process was more methodical than that, but in the end, the team of employees developed and executed an action plan in a week or less. The plan either broke through the obstacle or dramatically improved their performance. No matter what you called it, Sharon definitely liked the outcome.

After a month of daily *board talks* with her subordinate managers, Sharon asked them to start bringing their subordinate supervisors to the briefings. She'd ask each of those supervisors questions about their bosses' charts and made it clear that, in a few weeks, she and their boss would help each of them to create and post their own charts.

To Sharon's surprise, many started pinning their own charts to the outside walls of their cubicles well ahead of schedule.

Tim had guided a Copper-Bottom team through the design of KPI boards for each level, and Sharon purchased one for each supervisor. She let them decide on the best spot in their area to install their board. After that, all supervisors posted their charts on their boards daily.

Next, she asked her managers to meet her at their boards. After quickly briefing her on their own performance, she'd have them take her to each of their subordinates' boards. There, each subordinate briefed their manager and Sharon on their performance. This process worked smoothly in Operations but not everywhere.

Jack had given each of his directors a couple of weeks to post their metrics and work out the bugs, then he started visiting their boards. All had gone well. Next, he'd asked his directors to meet with their managers to give them their metrics and work through the establishment of their goals. This is where things fell apart.

Jerry had posted his own metrics on time, but when Jack came to inspect his department, none of Jerry's managers had posted theirs.

Jack went in search of Jerry. "How come none of your managers have their charts on their KPI boards?" he asked.

"Oh, boss," Jerry lamented. "First, we had month-end with all of those postings; then we closed for both the month and the quarter. Keeping up with these metrics is going to be a lot harder than we thought."

Jack almost lost his temper. This was *old* Jerry behavior. He always had an excuse for not following through.

"Jerry," Jack asked patiently, "have you met with your subordinates and given them their metrics?"

"Yes."

"Have you asked them to track their performance?"

"No," Jerry answered promptly. "Boss, they've been so busy with their real jobs, I haven't wanted to add ..."

Jack cut him off and closed the door to Jerry's office. Now he was steamed. "Jerry," he said as calmly as possible, "this *is* their real job!" He stopped.

"Jerry, why are we using charts?"

Without hesitation, Jerry said, "Because you want to know how we're doing. You want to be able to keep our performance on track, but, boss, we're already ..."

Again, Jack cut him off.

"No, Jerry," he said emphatically. "We're doing this because we are trying to change our culture. These charts are a means to that end. The charts become the way we change the conversation with our employees.

"Look," Jack continued, "your organization is ground zero for the incident that led to all this. It was ground zero because you treat your employees like vassals: you don't back them; you don't relate to them; you give them assignments and expect them to perform without ever giving them any feedback. That's a failed practice.

"These charts," Jack said, "will give them feedback. You talking to them about their charts, learning what their problems are, and helping them to resolve them, *that* is how we change the conversation. That is how we change our culture."

Remembering that Jerry was still on probation, Jack tried another tact.

"Perhaps you're the wrong person for this job. Should I be looking for someone else?"

Jerry stood speechless for a second before stammering, "No. NO!"

"Then, Jerry, stop finding excuses and behave as you agreed to. Can you do that?"

"Yes. YES!" Jerry repeated for emphasis.

Jack decided to see if Jerry had really been listening. "So, what are you going to do, Jerry?"

Jerry looked down and then recited, "I'm going to give my people their metrics and goals, ask them to post their performance, and use their boards as a way of coaching them."

"What do you mean when you say you'll coach them, Jerry? What will that look like?"

"I'll ..." Jerry stopped.

"Here's what I want you to do," Jack instructed him. "I want you to shadow Sharon as she visits her KPI boards. Not one or two, all of them. Then I want you to write a report on how she treats her subordinates and what she expects from them. Finally, I want you to review that report with me in person."

Jerry looked at him, fear in his eyes.

"Do you understand your assignment?" Jack asked quietly.

Jerry nodded.

"I want it by this Friday" was Jack's final instruction.

Truthfully, Jack wanted to fire Jerry. He was tired of Jerry's failure to support his people. He was tired of Jerry's failure to get on board with the culture change. He was angry that Jerry was as responsible as Henry for the lawsuit. Frankly, he was just plain angry at Jerry.

As much as he wanted to fire Jerry, though, Jack remembered something that Don Spears had told him early on.

"Jack, it's easy to get rid of people. It's even cathartic in the short term, but you've got a mature organization. Everyone you let go is well-known and part of your culture. They understand your policies and procedures. They understand how things work. They understand your people and are part of the fabric of your organization. That experience is hard to replace."

"Oh, you can replace the skill and the body, but it's not the same. As John Donne states in the poem "For Whom the Bell Tolls":

No man is an island, Entire of itself.
Each is a piece of the continent, A part of the main.
If a clod be washed away by the sea, Europe is the less.

"So," Don continued, "when you let someone go, your organization is the less.

"My point?" Don had asked. "Make sure you deliberate long and hard before letting people go. When you do, do it because they no longer support you or the pursuit of your firm's mission."

Jack knew the advice was right and that Jerry was an important part of his organization. "BUT," he reminded himself, "Jerry was also at the epicenter of what ailed the culture of Copper-Bottom in Charleston." Somehow, he needed to end Jerry's old behaviors, but how?

For once, Jack didn't try to solve the problem himself. He let it be while he focused on his other work. Meanwhile, Jerry had his marching orders. The burden had been shifted fully to him. Time would tell.

25

Closings and Coaching

Jerry had been in Jack's office early on Friday afternoon. Jack later found out that Jerry had been up all night working on his report and that he had been a nervous wreck since their last meeting.

Jack listened patiently as Jerry read through his own copy of the report. When Jerry was finished, Jack said, "Let's take a walk. I want to see the boards in your department."

Jerry took Jack to his subordinates' boards. Each had the proper charts and Action Item Lists. Although they'd only recently been posted, the charts had multiple weeks of data on them. Each chart had a goal line on it and each *Action Item List* had names, dates, and actions recorded. It was clear from the Action Item Lists that the right things were happening.

Jack gave Jerry a grudging "very good." He then asked Jerry what day his subordinates briefed him. "Tuesday," Jerry replied.

"What time?" Jack asked.

"They start at 1:15," Jerry responded.

"Then next Tuesday, I'll meet you at your board at 1:00. I'll want all your subordinates there, too."

Jack was not about to let Jerry off the hook. It was clear that Jerry had intentionally procrastinated in adopting the new methodology. Jack now realized that Jerry was either secretly hoping it would all go away or that Jack wouldn't follow up. Either way, Jerry hadn't been on board, and that was unacceptable.

Jack made a mental note to stay on top of Jerry's performance until he proved to be either on board or off the team altogether.

The following Tuesday, Jack listened patiently as Jerry briefed his subordinates. When Jerry asked for questions, Jack turned to one of Jerry's subordinates and asked them, "What's going on in this chart? Performance is well below goal." It was a trick question, but Jack wanted to see how much Jerry's people knew about what was going on in the department.

The woman that Jack had asked shot Jerry a quick glance before starting her response. "Mr. Simpson," she began, "that chart actually measures days to deliver financial data to our customers. Being below goal is a good thing."

"Very good," Jack congratulated her. "And this chart," he said, indicating the "Time to Close the Books" chart. "Why did it take longer this month than last?" Jack pointed to another woman.

This was another softball.

"We had a double closing this month," the respondent stated. "Actually, it was a record best for the department," she went on to say.

"Can't you forecast when you are going to do a double closing? Why didn't your goal line reflect it?"

The woman looked quickly at her colleagues for moral support and plunged ahead. "Actually," she confided, "there was a lot of debate in the department about that. Several of us thought the line should be adapted to reflect months of double closings, but in the end, we agreed that if we left the goal the same, it would force us to improve the closing process." Jack noticed nods from the others.

"Very good," Jack commended the group. "Let's go visit your boards, and I'll listen in as you brief Mr. Falstaff."

By the end of the last briefing, it was clear that Jerry's people had bought into the new metrics and understood their importance. His esteem for Jerry Falstaff rose.

Jack made a mental note to thank Tim Stark for all the help he'd given the directors and their staffs in setting up the KPI boards and in rolling out the metrics. He realized that he'd seen Tim in the Copper-Bottom offices almost every day since the kickoff. He made a second mental note to thank Don for making Tim available. It was clear that Friedman Electronics was doing everything they'd promised and more. He owed them a deep debt of gratitude.

26

Change at Last

The week after his boss agreed to extend his probation to six months, Jack allowed Friedman's personnel to conduct the first morale survey. As expected, the score was extremely poor, but per his commitment, he sent the results to George. Because of Jim's counsel, George understood these scores were only the baseline and did not take issue. What he did comment on was when, by the second month, the scores started to nudge upward. He made note of that fact in an email to Jack and wished him luck in continuing to improve. "Ya need anything?" he'd asked in a later phone call.

Jack had sent him photos of his own wall and of a handful of populated KPI boards. He made a mental note to try to send George photos or graphs at least once a month.

Meanwhile, Tim introduced a new term after the first month. It was *Lean Council*. He explained this was another name for Jack's staff. The immediate purpose of this council was to discuss their progress against each of their KPI goals and then to develop plans to identify any obstacles and remove them.

Without going into detail, Tim told the Council that Lean had specific tools to deal with different problems. He went on to tell them that he would teach them about each tool and what indications to look for when deciding which tool to use.

Tim also said that they'd either have to find someone internal to the organization, or to hire someone from outside, who would become their full-time Lean expert. He promised to sit with Jack and Nadine to review the credentials for which they'd be looking.

The following week, Don asked to sit in on Jack's next Lean Council meeting. At the conclusion of business, Jack asked Don if he had any observations.

"Why did you enter the swamp?" Don asked.

There were quizzical looks around the table, but no one answered.

Don tried again. "Did you enter the swamp to kill alligators or to drain it?"

Long seconds passed, but Don waited. Then Sharon volunteered, "I think I get what you're after. We set out to change our culture, and you're asking if that's what we're still after?"

Don neither agreed nor disagreed with Sharon's response. He handed around sheets of paper illustrated with tables. He said, "Look, these are some of the questions that are asked on your monthly morale question-naire. I've dummied in some numbers to illustrate my point. Now, if these were real numbers, what is your biggest problem?"

Concern	# Responding	Total Responses	%
Work Hours	4	80	5%
No Growth	68	80	85%
Not Respected	72	80	90%
No Clear Direction	50	80	63%
Poor Pay	69	80	86%
Working Conditions	77	80	96%
Boss Doesn't Listen to Me	78	80	98%

The group studied the list and Jennifer quickly raised her hand. Don nod-ded to her, and she volunteered, "Boss doesn't listen to me."

"How did you find that?" Don asked.

Jennifer explained the process of looking down the list to find the largest percent of respondents indicating that had been a problem.

"Who here knows what a Pareto chart is?" Don asked.

Jerry and Sharon raised their hands.

"Okay," Don began, "what I'm about to show you is just a way of chart-ing the same data. It takes all the guesswork out of deciding what the order of importance is." He went to the whiteboard and drew the chart below.

"If you only had the capacity to improve one of these measures, which would it be?"

Nadine raised her hand, and when Don made eye contact, she said, "Boss doesn't listen to me."

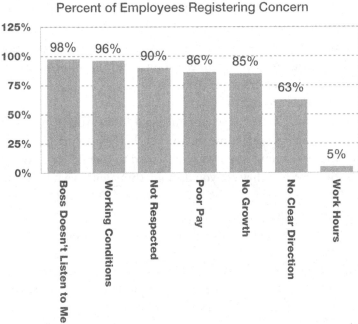

"I'm not disagreeing," Don replied, "but why choose that one?"

"Because it's their most common complaint," Nadine responded.

"POINT." Don stated. "Both the table and Pareto chart said the same thing, but the Pareto chart organized the data and made it visual. The more visual you can make things, the greater the number of people who will be able to understand it."

Don waited a beat for his message to sink in, then looked at Nadine and said, "Okay. Good. Then what?"

Nadine looked back blankly.

"What do you do once you know the biggest problem?" Jack asked.

"We talk about it," Nadine offered.

"Good start," Don replied. "Then what?"

There was silence before Nadine remarked, "Don, I know you want us to do something to reduce the number of employees who feel we don't listen, but honestly, I haven't got a clue. Does anyone else?" she asked, looking anxiously around the room.

Don waited. When no one else said anything, he said, "Remember me saying that changing a culture takes a long time, that you change the culture by changing one person at a time?"

There were nods around the room

"Well," he said, "THAT is what you've got to do. You've got to change the beliefs of each person. How do you do that? You start to listen. How does an employee know when you've listened to them?" He answered his own question. "When they see you do something with what they told you.

"Okay," Don began again. "Where do you start? How do you find out what's bothering your people?"

Someone half-jokingly responded, "We'd ask." The statement was accompanied by snickers.

Turning to them, Don asked, "And how would you do that?"

"We could ask them to complete a questionnaire," someone else volunteered.

There was a long pause before the same person said, "We'd place it on their desk at night with instructions to complete and return it."

"And how will you know that you got them all back, or whose was missing?" Don asked.

"We could have them turn it in to their supervisor …," the person started to say, then trailed off.

"Why did you stop?" Don asked, knowing the answer.

"Because it occurred to me that they already don't trust us. Why would they tell us the truth if they knew it could be tracked back to them?"

"Or," Don continued, "might they be so angry at you as to state their problems in angry or confrontational terms? Then you're left with open rebellion and no plan to restore order. How do you think that will end?"

They could see his point.

"First," Don lauded them, "you're right. You've got to ask, but *how* you ask is really important. Don't have them anonymously complete a questionnaire. Have them sit in front of a human who respectfully asks the questions and records their answers."

"Wait!" Nadine interrupted. "You've already done that."

"Right you are, Nadine." Turning to the larger group, Don asked, "What have you done with that data? Are you using what you learned to change anything, or are you just reporting it forward and hoping that your KPI dialogs will do it all?"

"Oh, dear," replied Nadine. "I know I'm not doing anything with it. What do you recommend?"

"This is the kind of thing that this group, this Lean Council, should deliberate," Don replied. "You should hold yourselves accountable to each other to make sure you're moving the cultural dial in the right direction."

The Council agreed and sent Nadine off to develop another, shorter survey that employees could complete themselves and turn in anonymously.

The following week, Nadine arrived with a six-question survey. She read the statements one by one. Each statement was to be answered using a scale of 1 to 5. A response of 5 said *strongly agree;* a score of 1 indicated that the respondent *strongly disagreed.*

1. "I believe I have adequate training to do my job."
2. "I know what *good* looks like in my job."
3. "I believe my boss cares about me and my success."
4. "I believe my opinion matters."
5. "I believe I have a future at Copper-Bottom."
6. "I believe I'm part of a winning team."

Nadine stopped there. "I should note that Don told us to expect very low scores. He said this will be like lancing a boil: you can't heal until you do it, but the experience will be painful.

"Don said that the whole point of a questionnaire like this is to find out where we are as we begin. These scores will form the baseline against which to measure progress. He also noted that the mere fact we are asking their opinion wouldn't be lost on them, but what really mattered would be how we follow up."

"I'd make one request," Jerry observed. "If you use the 1 through 5 scale on the first set of questions, it will give them an out. Answering with a 3 would allow them to avoid making a choice. It's an easy way to avoid controversy but would give us no sense of what to improve.

"I'd vote that we force their declaration by only giving them four possible responses: 1 through 4. That way, they have to state one way or the other whether they agree or disagree."

"I like that," said Jennifer, "but if that's our objective, let's just give them two choices: 1 for agree and 2 for disagree."

"Even better," concurred Jerry.

"I don't know," said Nadine. "I'm in favor of four choices. I think it's better to let them have the ability to flavor their vote. You know, give partial credit. By giving them the chance to say *Somewhat Agree* or *Somewhat Disagree*, we let them say, 'You've got room to grow, but you aren't all bad.' Does that make sense?"

They took a vote and Nadine's recommendation was adopted.

"There's one open-ended question," Nadine informed them. "It will have three blank lines below it." She read, "If you were in charge, name three things you'd change.

"What do you think?" Nadine asked, clearly proud of the questionnaire.

"I think we're walking headlong into a buzz saw," observed Jennifer Rosario, the Director of Sales.

"I agree," stated Sharon, "but I also think we've got to do this. Like Don said, all we've done so far is kill alligators. We need to start draining the swamp. They don't think we listen to them. If they tell us what's bugging them and we improve those things, then they'll see we listened."

Sharon added, "And by the way, nice job, Nadine."

Nadine's smile made it clear that she'd been hoping for affirmation of her work.

With the Lean Council's support, Nadine sent out the questionnaire and gave the participants two days to return them. By the following week, she had collated all the responses that were turned in. She'd used a locked box outside her offices for employees to submit the questionnaires anonymously. Now she presented the data to the Lean Council.

To no one's surprise, the scores on the first part of the survey were extremely low.

Earlier, when Friedman's survey team had conducted the morale questionnaire, they'd said that one of the hopeful things they'd found was the openness of Copper-Bottom's employees. Many of them answered the demographic questions about which department they were in and who their leader was. Some even named the person who gave them their day-to-day instructions.

The Friedman person also pointed out that their employees were no dummies. They knew that information could allow leaders to pinpoint them directly, so there didn't appear to be any fear of retribution from some leaders. "That," she said, "was a positive sign."

Presuming that morale could be improved the fastest by resolving the problems identified by the open-ended question, Nadine read down the list in order of the number of times it had been mentioned. The top three were

1. Inability to recall the most recent customer conversations on-screen
2. Constant mess everywhere, especially in Operations
3. Unsafe working conditions

"Can we deal with these?" she asked.

There was some discussion, but all pretty much agreed that the on-screen projection of real-time customer information was a corporate problem and outside their control.

"Wait," Jack said. "Do we just leave it there? This is a big deal to our employees and is clearly hurting morale. Can't we at least brief them on the progress being made?"

Skip raised his hand. "Jack," he began, "that's the thing. We don't know what progress is being made. We're totally blacked out of the process. Right now, we only find things out when we're informed of delays."

"Okay," Jack acknowledged. "Let's you and I take this offline, Skip. We need to see if there's anything we *can* do."

The second-greatest concern was that the office was a "constant mess." That was clearly within their ability to control. After some discussion about potential solutions, Jack appointed Sharon responsible for leading a team to develop some solutions and determine their costs.

Skip Fuller asked what constituted "unsafe working conditions." There were some examples Nadine had collected from the safety survey team. Some on the counsel thought that Nadine should send out another email questionnaire asking for specific examples, until Sharon observed that if they wanted to prove that they were listening to their employees, they should ask employees directly. They resolved that each manager would talk with their employees and compile a list to bring back the following week.

Before the session ended, Don, who had again asked to sit in on the Lean Council meeting, addressed Jack directly. "Jack," he said, "it will be extremely important that you publicly thank your employees for participating in this survey and for their candor.

"You'll want to say something to the effect that 'until we acknowledge what's wrong, we can't improve' and that you want them to know that you, and everyone who reports to you, want to improve the working conditions and relationships within the organization."

Jack called a short all-hands meeting that Friday. Nadine and her team presented the results of the first safety audit, after which Jack made the public declaration Don had recommended. There was neither cheering nor booing. It was as if the employees were reserving judgment until they saw how they would be treated.

At the following week's Lean Council meeting, Jack reviewed the top-level KPIs, all of which were either improving or holding their own. He then asked for Nadine and Sharon's reports. Sharon went first.

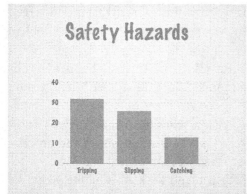

Following Jack's all-hands meeting, supervisors admitted to getting a good response to their Safety Hazards questions. The data was turned over to Nadine for collation. Following Don's guidance, she had arranged the data in a Pareto chart.

Sharon then projected the next slide, breaking down the sources of Tripping Hazards.

"Why are there drawers open?" asked Jack.

Sharon had to stop herself from rolling her eyes. The answer was so fundamental to the way her people had to work that Jack's question indicated how out of touch he was with the organization he led. That notwithstanding, she chose to deal with the sincerity of Jack's question.

"My people leave their drawers open to have ready access to their files. It's not necessary for first-time callers or for clients who haven't called in the last 24 hours, but when someone calls multiple times on the same day, the only way to access their file is to print the file and have it in their file drawer.

"Because they are in and out of their files all day, most of them just leave the drawer open."

Jack asked, "Why do they have to print it out?" Then answering his own question, he said, "That's right. They can't access the information on-screen for 24 hours."

"Agreed," Sharon stated patiently. "As we've said in the past, our computers never reflect real-time data. No data are stored locally. It's all retained on the corporate database back at headquarters. That database doesn't get backed up until after midnight Eastern time, so the minute they leave a customer's file, the most recent input disappears until the following day.

"That creates several problems:

- First, our employees can't access the notes from the customer's first call until the following day. They print their notes from the first call in the event that the customer calls back.
- Second, if the client calls more than once the same day, any new information has to be handwritten on the paper copy of the previous conversation, then input into the database the following day.
- Third, from a data analysis standpoint, entering the previous day's notes makes it look like any subsequent first-day calls were made on the following day, thus giving us bad information on how often customers make two or more calls on the same day.
- Fourth, because the person answering subsequent calls on the same day needs to have the paper notes, it pretty much means that repeat calls from that customer need to be routed to the original person who took their call. That necessitates whoever actually answers the subsequent call to find out who took the first call and park the new call on their phone line. Finding out who took the first call can be a process in itself and can take a lot of time," she concluded.

Jack was dumbfounded. He realized he didn't know as much as he thought he did about Sharon's operation. Looking at Skip, he asked, "So, is this why everyone is agitated about the delay of the new database upgrade?"

"It is, sir," replied the IT director.

Jack sat quietly for several seconds. Everyone else remained silent until he finally said, "Sharon, I am profoundly sorry. I had no idea of the *magnitude* of the problem. The fact that I didn't is my own fault and I'm embarrassed. Please accept my apology."

Jack's remark caught Sharon completely off-guard. She was used to bombast and bluster—the Henry Corn approach to bad news—turning it on the messenger and somehow making them feel responsible. In the back of her mind she thought, "There may actually be hope for us." She said nothing and hoped her face didn't betray her thoughts.

Turning back to Skip, Jack asked, "What can be done to hasten the upgrade?"

"Jack," Skip replied, "I don't think there is anything we can do. I mean, I know there's nothing I can do, and I don't think even you can hasten the upgrade. As I said earlier, this is all being controlled at Corporate."

Again, Jack paused. The fact that he had to ask Skip about the problem made it clear that he hadn't stayed on top of it. What an imbecile his people must think he was. No wonder morale was so low.

Coming out of his reverie, he stated emphatically, "Can't change the past, but let me pledge two things. First, I'm going to stay on top of this going forward and exercise as much influence as I can to get the new system upgrade rolled out.

"Second," he continued, "we're going to develop a local plan to resolve these temporary problems.

"I'm so sorry," he said again, looking at Sharon. "No wonder morale is so low."

Jack looked at Tim, who sat in on all his Council meetings. "Tim," he asked, "can you please help Sharon head up a project to develop a solution to the tripping hazards?"

"Absolutely!" was the younger man's response.

"I know this is only one safety concern," Jack admitted, "but let's walk before we run. Tim will help us solve this one, and maybe that will develop some credibility with our employees, showing that we really do care.

"Meanwhile, Sharon, will you present similar data on carpet snags next week? Oh, and before I forget"—he turned back to Tim—"how quickly can we get some results?"

Tim said, "We'll have remedial actions in place within three weeks, and a full solution within six. I could crash the first deadline, but applying your walk before running analogy, I don't want to overpromise at this stage. Is that acceptable?"

Jack nodded. "The sooner, the better," he replied.

Principle #29: Make data visible. Use charts so everyone can understand.

27

Walking

Tim met with Sharon later that afternoon. Together they created a list of people to include for their first Kaizen event. The list included people from Operations, IT, and Maintenance. It also included someone (an "impartial witness," as Tim called them) from Jerry's accounting group—not for their firsthand knowledge but for their unprejudiced observations of Sharon's group.

Since they already had background data on the problems they were setting out to resolve, they set the date of the event two Mondays hence.

Later that afternoon, Tim and Sharon met with Jack and reviewed what they hoped to discuss at the upcoming Lean Council meeting. Tim wanted Jack to know that it was customary to have the Council establish the goals and parameters for the event. This would be their first Kaizen, and he wanted the Council to understand their responsibilities to the team and to the Kaizen process.

Unsure of himself, Jack had little recourse but to agree.

At the Lean Council meeting, Tim and Sharon went over the list of people who would be engaged in the Kaizen event.

"Keep in mind," Tim reminded the Council, "a Kaizen event is a full-time job, and it will take a week. That means these people will be unavailable to do their normal jobs until the following week. You'll need to make appropriate accommodations."

"I only have two IT guys," Skip complained. "I can't be without one of them for a full week."

"What happens if one of them is sick?" Jack asked.

"I have to backfill," muttered Skip.

Jack only looked at the younger man.

"I guess I'll backfill," Skip said a bit sullenly.

DOI: 10.4324/9781003336051-28

"Okay," Tim said, "we need to figure out what we want the Kaizen event to achieve and any boundaries the team will have to work within."

"Since this is our first event," Sharon stated, "perhaps you can tell us what you mean?"

"Absolutely," Tim agreed.

"Well, to start, one of the goals needs to be that there will be no more open file drawers, agreed?" There was universal agreement. He wrote that on the whiteboard. "Anything else?" he asked.

No one else had any additional ideas. "How about clutter? Do you want them to reduce clutter by some percentage?" Tim asked.

There were nods. "How much?" he asked. After some dialog, the group agreed on 80% while acknowledging that it might be difficult to measure.

"Good point," Tim acknowledged. "One of the first things we'll do is to take photos of the *before* conditions. At the end, we'll take photos of the *after* conditions, and you can see for yourselves if they met the goal, even if only approximately.

"Next," Tim said, "are there any parameters they need to stay within?"

"Like what?" Nadine asked.

"Perhaps this is a good time to discuss the Kaizen methodology your team will be using," Tim stated. "Because Kaizen events are only a week long, the event leaders need to set some clear expectations. Here is a list of the bywords we'll expect the team to live by." He wrote them on the whiteboard.

- Focus on ACTION
- Tight focus on time
- Creativity before capital
- Quick & crude vs. slow & elegant
- Necessary resources immediately available
- Immediate results

"Can you explain?" Sharon asked.

"Absolutely," responded Tim. "First, the team isn't there to debate or to make recommendations. They are there to take guided *ACTION*. Because they only have a week to create actual change, their team leader will have a tight focus on time. He or she will have to limit discussion and move the team to action."

"Kaizen is more about using our brains than about purchasing solutions, so the team will be asked to use their creativity before they spend any money. The goal is to develop quick solutions, something they can use the following week. Events aren't about creating the *perfect solution*; they are about developing a workable plan. The team is able to do that because resources like maintenance or IT are immediately available. And finally, we're not looking for a *someday solution*. We're looking for an immediate solution."

"Does that make sense?" he asked Sharon.

"It does," she responded. "Thanks, Tim. That really puts our expectations in perspective."

Tim went on. "Although we aren't trying to *buy a solution*, teams often need money to purchase supplies and materials. Friedman gives its teams up to $500 to use in developing a temporary solution. The final solution may cost more, but the team has to work within a $500 limit. May we assume the same here?" he asked.

"Where does this money come from?" Jerry asked.

"Our first year, we had to pay for it out of the departmental budget of the department being helped. The following year, we created a Continuous Improvement Office and actually added a line item to their budget for Kaizen events.

"While I'm at it," Tim continued, "another thing we do is cater lunches for the team. We do that because we don't want them going out and coming back late. We also don't want them to lose focus by going back to their desk, or even to a lunchroom. Although nothing will impact the immediate results, we hope they'll bond with others on the team and start to form *relationships*. Oh," he said with a smile, "and because we pay for their lunch, we also reduce its length. That way they have more time on task.

"You good with that?" Tim asked Jack. There was quick debate within the Lean Council, and they agreed to at least do it for this event. It was further agreed that they'd monitor the results of this event and gauge whether they'd buy lunches for future events.

When that discussion was resolved, Tim continued, "We also give the team first priority when it comes to any IT and maintenance-related needs.

"Skip, for this event that priority would probably apply more to you than to maintenance, although it would still apply to maintenance should they need it." Turning to Jack, Tim asked, "To whom does your maintenance team report?"

"Sharon," Jack replied.

Turning to Sharon, Tim asked, "How many?"

"Two full-time," she responded. "They mostly work on preventive building maintenance and occasional rearrangement of office furniture and utilities."

"Okay, they're going to be in the same predicament as Skip. You'll want to give them as much forewarning as possible and let Jack know if they need overtime to make up for time spent on the event. If someone from the team comes asking for help, their request needs to be considered the same way you would an emergency.

"Finally," Tim concluded, "we'll need a place to meet where the team won't be disturbed and won't disturb others. Since we'll want to eat there, it would be best if it were a conference room, although we can create a space anywhere in the building, if we need to.

"That's something else we changed our second year," Tim said, addressing Jerry. "We created a new conference room. We called it the Kaizen room. Although others can use it, Kaizen events always have top priority on that space."

"That's a lot to ask," Jerry argued.

"Maybe so," Jack pronounced, "but we'll need to find a way. We need to put our best effort into this."

Jack cut off other complaints by stating, "Tim, plan on this room. See my assistant to book it. If you need anything else, come to me directly.

"Any other questions or concerns?" Jack asked.

No one had any.

Jack asked, "Okay, Tim, what's the next step?"

"Well, Jim, our Corporate VP of Operations, insists that all senior managers be present for the kickoff of each event. He says that events are that important. Don usually welcomes the teams personally, thanks them for participating, and establishes the reason for the event. We also typically invite the supervisor of the team's area since they will own the results of the event and be responsible for maintaining conditions.

"The other thing that Jim requires is that all senior managers attend the closing meeting, where the team gives their final briefing. I'd remind everyone that this event, and all future events, are chosen because they were deemed critical to the success of your organization. While it may not impact your discipline directly, a healthy organization improves everyone's life. Think about these teams as improving the health of your organization."

"Put it on your calendars," Jack said. "I'll expect each of you there for both kickoff and windup," he said to his team.

"The out-brief will be held at 11:30 on Friday and will last 30 minutes," Tim stated. "The team usually spends Thursday afternoon and Friday morning preparing. Most will be scared to death, given that public speaking is most people's number-one phobia, so they won't go any longer than they have to." He finished this last statement with a good-natured smile.

Principle #30: The Lean Council determines where all Kaizen events will take place and establishes the goals of each.

Principle #31: The Lean Council will establish any boundaries the team will have to work within.

Principle #32: The entire Lean Council kicks off every Kaizen event and attends the final report.

28

Finally, a Break

On Friday the 25th, Copper-Bottom's first Kaizen team gave their final presentation. True to Tim's word, the capstone presentation of the week's achievements took less than 30 minutes. The team seemed in a rush to get it over with, but they'd come up with two ingenious ways to eliminate having open file drawers.

The briefing had started with introductions, a recap of the event's goals, followed a series of *before* and *after* photos of the Operations area. Each pair of slides was explained by one of the team members. The changes were stunning. Areas awash in paper and folders were now neat and organized. Organizing systems had been hung on the wall in the media room. Each slot had the name of an employee on it, and printed items for that person were put in that slot. No more stacks of paper.

Then there were the individual cubicles. File drawers were open and papers spread all over the floor in the *before* photo, followed by a photo with drawers closed, floor clean, and files standing upright in file holders on desks.

Stationary cabinets with doors flung open and contents in total disarray in the *before* photo, followed by doors held open and contents neatly arranged in the *after*.

The differences were amazing.

Next came their ingenious ideas that had brought about the changes.

The first involved putting the small file stands—the kind easily purchased at any stationery store—on every desk. Each stand could hold up to 11 files at a time. The stand had a natural incline, so the desk owner could easily read the file tabs on all their files at once. The stands cost just over $20 each.

DOI: 10.4324/9781003336051-29

The second involved hanging the paper organizing systems on the cubicle wall next to the printer. Although it was a small cost, the change in the room was remarkable. There were no papers stacked on top of the printer or in its output tray. The adjacent table, which had papers strewn all over it in the *before* photo, was now bare except for a stapler, a staple puller, a three-hole punch, and a paper cutter. Each of those was neatly arranged on the surface, their locations outlined and labeled to indicate that they should be returned to the same place after use.

Then came the really ingenious idea. It involved assigning each employee their own phone number. That way, when the customer called back, they could reach the employee with whom they'd last spoken.

The team had done its research. Copper-Bottom already owned all the phone numbers, so there was no extra charge for that, but the switching gear in the company's phone room had always assigned the next available line to incoming calls. That made it nearly impossible to reach the same employee when calling back. By dedicating a number to a particular employee, if the customer called the same number as they had earlier, they would reach exactly who they intended every time.

Because some customers were better with names than with numbers, each employee would be given a laminated phone roster with names and associated numbers of their colleagues. If a customer called the wrong number and asked for someone, any person who answered could redirect the call.

Finally, employees would follow each initial customer interaction with an email to the customer's account on record. They would confirm that account as part of the first call. The after-call email would also contain the employee's name and direct phone number.

Although it was only an estimate, their phone carrier expected that dedicating the phone lines to individual phones would not exceed $250, and if they left the switching gear in place, the company could always switch it back for a nominal fee.

There was one final recommendation. The team observed that printing to a central printer meant having to leave one's desk to find the printout. If the employee's phone rang immediately after hanging up—which it almost always did during peak hours—the printed file of the previous conversation sat on the printer until the employee could retrieve it.

As often as not, printouts were pawed through, and pieces lost before the employee could ever get to the printer. This meant reprinting, which resulted in a massive amount of paper accumulating in the print area. The team recommended that each employee be given their own dedicated printer.

The IT member of the team had done research and found that reliable printers could be purchased for around $100. For ease of ordering ink and interchangeability, the team recommended that all printers be from the same manufacturer and of the same model. They'd also checked with procurement to find out how much the company spent each month on printer paper. They estimated that they could easily reduce that by 30%. The savings alone would pay for the printers. The team acknowledged that this was a temporary fix until the corporate IT organization was able to make their database in real time. The savings in the meantime would be well worth the investment.

After the team finished their out briefing, Jack and the directors applauded. One could see from the team's faces how much the praise meant.

Jack stood and thanked the team for a job well done. He concluded with, "It's Friday. I want each of you to take the remainder of the day off with pay. View this as our way of expressing our gratitude."

Tim had forewarned Jack that it was customary to give the team the remainder of the day off, but Jack hadn't committed to doing so. Now, having seen the results of the team's work and after learning about all they'd done behind the scenes, he felt it was a fair exchange.

The file stands were on all the desks by the following Tuesday. The phone changes took a few days longer, but it was the purchase of the printers that turned out to be the biggest problem.

Copper-Bottom's Corporate IT department screened all purchases of electronic hardware and software. When they saw the order for 34 printers, they immediately declined it.

Jack and his team had waited for the printers to arrive, but they never did. Instead, the rejected purchase order had arrived back a week later through the interoffice postal system. There was no reason given for the rejection.

Jack was incensed. He called his boss immediately, describing what his Kaizen team had done and why they'd made the recommendation. The purchase was well within Jack's signature authority and Jerry had identified budget for it.

Jack's boss agreed to "look into it" and called him back. When he called back later the same day, it was to explain that the IT department felt it was excessive to purchase that many printers. They had listed the fact that inexpensive printers had a poor maintenance history and that the cost of ink alone would be exorbitant.

Jack pushed back. "Boss," he said, "you've asked me to change the culture here. My employees have asked for these printers to improve their handling of our customers. It's well within my signature authority. Why can't I order them?"

"Jack," his boss said, "if we let every employee have a printer, we'd be spending tens of thousands of dollars a year."

Jack hadn't wanted to play this card but felt backed into a corner. He'd had Skip brief him on how long the database had been delayed and when it was currently set to be rolled out. He learned it had already been delayed six times over the last year, and the latest projection was that it would be delayed another five months.

"Mr. Franklin," Jack said, "The reason my people have to print out their screens in the first place is that they can't access their call notes until the next day. That's because the current database isn't real-time. It doesn't back up until overnight. If a customer calls back the same day, and our records indicate they do almost 68% of the time, there is no way to access the electronic record of what they talked about in the previous call. The only way to capture that information is to print out the file after the first call. Subsequent calls require handwritten notes on that printout, until the original notes become available electronically the following day, at which point the Customer Service Rep has to input the handwritten notes of all subsequent conversations.

"Meanwhile, we are already two years into IT's rollout of the new database. It has been delayed at least six times. Current projections are that it will be another five months before it goes live. While IT fumbles around getting the new database launched, my employee morale is in the toilet because of a host of problems related to having to print their client records to a single central printer.

"Now you're telling me that the very organization that can't perform its job on time is insisting that my people can't have the tools they need to do their job on time? Does that seem right to you? Is that the way Copper-Bottom treats its customers and employees?

"Sir, if you want me to change my organization's culture for the better, I'm asking you to bend on this one."

There was a long silence at the other end. Finally, George Franklin said, "Fax the PO directly to me. I'll have it back to you by morning."

There was another long silence, then the CEO said, "Jack, I'm betting on you. I want to hear good things from Charleston."

"Understood, boss. Thanks."

Needless to say, Jack had the PO faxed to Mr. Franklin's office within 10 minutes. It came back signed 10 minutes after that. There was a note on it instructing IT to purchase the printers for immediate delivery to the Charleston facility.

Finally, a break! They were off and running.

29

Our Best Selves

To Jack's great amazement, there was no need for him to exhort Sharon's organization to keep their file drawers closed. From the day the printers arrived, Sharon and the Kaizen team leader followed up on that task. Jack knew because he now walked the floor every day.

Within days, Skip had all the printers installed. With Tim's assistance, the Kaizen team had developed Standard Work on how to use the new filing system. After their installation, Sharon conducted refresher training on how the new system was going to work. The team had even created a standard for

- printing the customer's file;
- placing it in a folder;
- standing the folder in the holder alphabetically from front to back;
- how to annotate the folder, should the customer call back;
- how to destroy the folders and files the following morning, after verifying all the information from the previous day had been updated; and
- how to switch between the desktop printer and the main printer.

Within a week, one of her employees discovered that if they cut out a section of the left front corner of the file folder and oriented the file with the top on the folder's left, they could read the customer's name right off the printed document, without ever opening the folder. Sharon had the employee share this best practice with their colleagues, who agreed unanimously to update Standard Work to include this practice. This new practice allowed file folders to be reused and saved time writing the customer's name on the top tab.

DOI: 10.4324/9781003336051-30

Since the electronic files updated overnight, her employees acknowledged that the paper files would not be needed after making any updates the following day. They agreed to go through each file in the stand and enter any handwritten notes in the database. Then they purged the folder's contents according to Standard Work. That way, they emptied their file stands first thing every morning while reusing the file folders.

Clutter in the media center ended almost overnight, and Sharon made one of her employees responsible for maintaining the cleanliness and the supplies in the area. They immediately set about creating a minimum and maximum level for each item in the supply cabinet, including the new printer ink. That way, they never ran out but kept the number of supplies to a minimum.

Within the first quarter, the employee was able to place all the necessary supplies, including the ink cartridges for the new printers, in the much smaller bookcase they'd salvaged from another organization. One of Sharon's people had taken it home, cleaned and sanded it, and put a fresh coat of paint on it. All the supplies were now neatly arranged in the new cabinet and the shelves were labeled to indicate where each item belonged, as well as the minimum and maximum for the item. That freed up the large stationary cabinet for use by another group and prevented them from having to order a new one.

With floors now clutter-free of excess paper, the snagged strands of carpet fiber that had also been causing tripping hazards were now easily visible. Sharon and one of her employees went around the Operations bay, cutting all the loose strands back to the carpet's base.

Of course, the other thing that removing all the paper did was reveal how filthy the carpeting was. Sharon got three bids from local cleaning services and approached Jack with a purchase order. Jack readily signed it and personally walked it to Jerry. He asked Jerry to *find* the money.

The following weekend the carpets were cleaned. The effect on morale was amazing. Within days, both silk and live plants started to appear in Operations cubicles. It was like employees were *owning* the fact that they worked there and that they intended to stay. One could *feel* morale improving.

Someone found another set of used bookshelves and set them up in the media center. An entire set of policy manuals and work instructions were put on the shelves. That got them off the floor and out of individual cubicles, where they were rarely used. It also meant that there was now only one set to update when new policies were published.

At Tim's suggestion, the person Sharon had assigned to be responsible for the media center arranged all the manuals in alphanumeric order, then ran red tape down the spines in a vee pattern. This made it obvious if a binder was missing or out of order. The latter didn't happen after a photo of the correctly arranged binders was neatly pinned to the cubicle wall above the bookshelf. Tim referred to the photo as "visual Standard Work."

At the following Lean Council meeting, Sharon asked Jack if it might not be time to have a meeting with all the employees and explain what was happening. "It might also be a good time to review the results of our first morale questionnaire. The next one is just around the corner," she suggested.

Jack asked the other directors. All agreed that it would be good to "Own Their Story," as Don would say, and to let employees know what was up.

Jack committed to holding the meeting but didn't give a date, asking for time to think about what his message would be. "As I think about it," he announced, "I'd like to get input from each of you about what the message should be.

"Sharon," he continued. "I have a request for you. Will you have someone take new *after* photos of the area and update the team's final presentation? I want to send it to my boss."

Sharon readily agreed and had the updated presentation in Jack's email by the close of the day. Even to Sharon, the contrast between *before* and *after* was amazing.

To Jack's surprise, two of his directors suggested that he acknowledge what had happened to Patty Purcell and how it had been the impetus for the changes that were now taking place.

Jack weighted the pros and cons of such an action. In the end, he agreed that it was time to begin the healing of his organization, and the best way to do that was to confront the problem head-on. Before he did that, however, he wanted to speak with Nadine, his Director of HR, and then to Patty herself.

He had Nadine Sommers set the meeting up in the conference room, which was more neutral ground than Jack's office.

The day of the meeting, Nadine brought Patty in. Although she was tall and well groomed, Patty was ashen and visibly trembling. In an instant,

Jack's heart broke. "This," he thought, "is what an unhealthy organization can do to a human." He found himself fighting to keep tears from his eyes.

Jack hadn't known her name, but he recognized Patty instantly. He could tell from the loose fit of her clothes that she had lost weight. Now that he could put a face to the name, he could remember seeing dark circles around her eyes at their prior meetings. At the time, even her skin had been an unhealthy pallor. He was happy to see that she appeared in better health now.

After offering Patty coffee or water, both of which she declined, Jack got right to the point.

"Patty, I'm here to offer you my personal apology for what happened to you. I also want to thank you for calling me and my fellow leaders to become our better selves. Whether you realize it or not, you have started a change for the better in this organization."

He could see Patty visibly relax. She took a deep breath and her shoulders, which had been tightly locked, loosened.

"Patty," he continued, "I am ashamed of the way you and other employees have been treated. I will admit complicity in the act because I did not keep track of how my directors were behaving. I was interested in results, and that led to bad behavior going unchecked. I want you to know that I'm sorry for that, but especially for its impact on you. Can you forgive me?"

By now, Patty had tears sliding silently down her cheeks. These weren't tears of sorrow or self-pity. They were the result of finally having been heard. She nodded a "Yes."

Nadine gave Patty a gentle hug.

When she'd regained her composure, Jack began again. "Patty, because of your bravery in confronting the bullies of your life, you have been responsible for changing the entire organization. Because of you, your leaders are now trying to bring our best selves to work each day. Thank you.

"I also want to talk about your impact at a company-wide meeting. I'd like to discuss your critical role. I don't want to embarrass you, though, so I wanted to ask your permission first."

Patty remained silent. Jack continued on.

"As you and I both know, there are few secrets in an organization like ours. Everyone *thinks* they know what happened, and more often than not, it's wrong or only half the story. I'd like to tell your fellow employees the truth about what happened and what has come from it."

He waited again, then asked, "May I have your permission?"

Patty regained her composure and asked, "May I think about it?"

"That's only fair," Jack agreed. "Do you think you'll be able to let Nadine know by Thursday?"

Patty responded with a simple "Yes."

Jack stood and extended his hand across the table. "Thank you, Patty."

Patty and Nadine also stood. Patty shook Jack's hand. Her life coach would have been proud of her handshake. It was firm and far more self-confident than she felt. She'd even fought her instincts and looked Jack in the eye as she shook his hand.

Nadine gave her another much-needed hug, then led her out the door.

Two days later, there was a knock at his office door. Jack looked up to see Nadine in the open doorway. "Do you have a second?" she asked. As she spoke, Jack could see Patty step out from behind her.

"This can't be good," he thought to himself.

Standing, he motioned the two women to come in. Nadine closed the door.

When they were all seated at the table, Nadine said, "Patty would like a word."

"Mr. Simmons," Patty started. She had a 3×5 card in her hand. "I want you to know that you and Mr. Corn hurt me … a lot; not just emotionally but physically. You hurt my emotional and physical health," she said, repeating herself.

She stopped to compose herself before looking up from her card.

"Mr. Simmons, I can forgive you, but that won't undo all the hurt for which you are responsible. Since the day Mr. Corn belittled and berated me, I've been a nervous wreck. I'm a single mom and the sole source of income for my son and me. I've feared every day coming into work and being let go. I'm on prescription medications for anxiety and stress. I need sleeping pills to sleep. I've lost 30 pounds!"

Jack realized again how loosely Patty's clothing hung on her body.

"Mr. Simmons, no one wants things to change here more than me but not just for a week, a month, or a year. You employ great, smart people. You can't treat them the way you did me. I will support you if you'll commit to never treating an employee like that again.

"Can you commit to that?" she asked. By now she was no longer relying on her 3×5 card for her speech. She looked Jack directly in the eyes as she asked the last question.

Jack realized that this was no longer the timid, weak woman who appeared to have sat across from him earlier. This woman had backbone, resolve.

Jack thought for a second. He could readily commit to never *intentionally* hurt an employee, but he'd had no knowledge of Patty's problems until well after they had occurred. In fact, if it hadn't been for her lawsuit, it was highly likely that he still might not know.

"Patty, I could easily commit to never *knowingly* hurting an employee. I could commit to never *knowingly* allowing a member of my staff to hurt an employee, but we both know that things can take place about which I have no knowledge.

"I had no idea that Mr. Corn had treated you and others the way he did. In hindsight, should I have? There is a strong argument that I should, and in the future, I'll be on the lookout for it, but I can't promise to correct a problem of which I have no knowledge."

Patty was quiet for several seconds, seeming to weigh what Jack had said. As she did, her eyes never left Jack.

Jack used the time to think through what he was about to say next. "Let me go a step further. I think this will drive to the heart of what you are asking. I intend to work toward creating an environment here at Copper-Bottom Charleston where such behavior is intolerable. Is that acceptable?"

"Mr. Simmons, I understand what you've said, and I'll accept it, but I'd ask you to be more vigilant than you were in the past. Can you commit to that?"

Jack thought the last request was overkill, but in light of what Patty had suffered, maybe not so unreasonable. "I will, Patty."

"Then you have my permission to use my story," she said.

Patty gave a tight smile, thanked him, and left. There were no handshakes this time, but somehow Jack knew the air had been cleared.

On Friday afternoon of that week, Jack addressed a meeting for all employees in the cafeteria.

"Good afternoon," he opened.

There was a polite but disengaged response. By now, Jack was used to it.

"This meeting is long overdue," Jack stated, "but my staff and I felt it was time to clear the slate and tell you what is going on here at Copper-Bottom Charleston."

Without mentioning the lawsuit, Jack went on to discuss how Patty had been treated. "Based on what I've heard, Patty wasn't alone, so for all of you who have been mistreated, I want to offer my sincere apology."

Jack went on to talk about how the discovery of Patty's circumstances had led to major changes at their firm.

"The Chinese symbol for *danger* is the same symbol used to mean *opportunity*," he said. "What could have been our undoing is turning out to make us stronger. We have Patty to thank for that. Without her standing up to the schoolyard bully, we'd still be mired in our bad habits."

He reminded them about being challenged to change the culture and about involving Friedman Electronics to coach him and his staff. "Under different circumstances, Friedman went through similar growing pains several years ago," he said, "and emerged one of the strongest divisions in that corporation.

"Little by little, Friedman's Tim Stark"—he pointed to Tim, who was standing in the back of the room—"has not only helped us to see what we've been doing wrong but also ways to go beyond just making things right. He's showing us how to up our game and become our very best."

Jack acknowledged that along the way, he and his staff were learning new ways to lead and communicate.

"We're far enough into this transformation," he admitted, "that I am confident that we will stay the course and see it all the way through. My staff and I felt it was time to share that with you.

"Here's what you can expect going forward."

Jack outlined the purpose of the KPI boards and the metrics. He'd explained how these boards were intended to get leaders out of their offices and into the areas under their control, how the charts were intended to visually depict how each organization was performing and where help was needed.

"What they are not intended to do is to cause managers to revert to old behaviors and find fault with individuals. Their purpose is to highlight problems so we can work together as a unified team, supervisors *and* subordinates, to solve them.

"Okay, let me acknowledge right now that this is all new to us. We're human; we're bound to make mistakes and occasionally fall back into old habits. I'll ask your forgiveness in advance, but don't want it to end there.

I want us to have a code between us, and I want that code to be something Patty taught me.

"I want us all to hold each other accountable for bringing our *Best Selves* to each interaction. If any of us fall backs into old behaviors, I'm going to ask you to simply ask, 'Is that your *Best Self*?'"

He turned to his staff seated behind him. "That code should cause us to rethink what we just said or did. We should ask ourselves if what we'd just done or said was really representative of *Our Best Selves*. If it wasn't, then we need to take the appropriate action."

Looking again at the rest of the company, he said, "You've also learned a lot of ways to respond to the old behaviors. I'm going to ask you to hold yourselves accountable for changing those, knowing that we're doing the same.

"If your supervisor asks you if something you did or said was really a reflection of your *Best Self*, you'll know they're asking you to reflect on what you just did or said, and to make the appropriate response.

"This isn't a gimmick. This is just a code between us. You deserve our best selves, and we deserve the same from you. Let's hold each other accountable. After all, we're all one team: the Copper-Bottom team.

"Before we get all crazy and start using that question as our first response to every circumstance, let's agree that the more sparingly it's used, the more impact it will have. Make sense?" he asked. There were nods from the crowd.

"All right," he concluded, "this confession has been long overdue. I want you to know that I count it a privilege to work with each of you, and I look forward to what we can become as we all bring our *Best Selves* to each day and each situation.

"Thank you."

There was genuine applause this time, much more heartfelt than when he'd begun.

During the remainder of the afternoon, Jack made it a point to visit each of his subordinates in their offices. He didn't make a big deal of it, but he asked how they were doing and what challenges they were facing. He made a mental note to bring something to write on next time.

To no one's surprise, he was met with skepticism. It reminded him that his staff had also heard his words but were reserving judgment until they'd seen his actions. *That's fair*, he thought to himself.

30

The Map to Success

Over the next several weeks, life at Copper-Bottom Charleston fell into a new rhythm. The printers were still in use and papers were still off the floor, but there was now the slightest hint of what Jack would have called camaraderie between employees and their supervisors.

The second morale audit had been conducted, and scores had risen. Jack's boss called to acknowledge receipt of the latest numbers. "Keep up the good work, Jack," he encouraged him. "By the way," he went on, "that presentation you sent me about the event you conducted was amazing. I can't get over the difference between the before and after photos. I'd expect your employees are starting to feel more supported. Is that true?"

"I'm seeing glimmerings of it," Jack responded, "but we've got a long way to go. We've now rolled KPI boards down throughout the entire organization, and I expect to see morale improve as leaders start interacting with employees."

"Keep up the good work," George encouraged him. "Let me know if you need anything."

"By the way," he said as an afterthought, "good call on the printers. I can't get over the difference they've made."

Jack was grateful for his boss's praise; still, there was something *flat* about the behavior of the Charleston organization. There was no laughter. No expressions of joy. People came to work, did their job for eight hours and went home. Flat! Deflated!

Tim to the rescue!

At the next Lean Council meeting, Tim continued the Lean training he'd started weeks before. At this meeting, he presented what he called a Value Stream Map. It was a single page covered with boxes, arrows,

DOI: 10.4324/9781003336051-31

triangles, symbols, numbers, and words. It looked well ordered, but made no sense. As he began to explain it, the hieroglyphs slowly began to communicate to the Council.

"At its most fundamental level," Tim explained, "the Value Stream Map—VSM for short—shows the flow of work at Copper-Bottom Charleston from beginning to end.

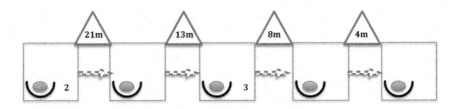

This isn't your VSM, but yours will look similar."

He pointed to the large rectangular boxes halfway down the page. "These," he continued, "represent the major steps in your process. They follow the process as it moves from left to right across the page.

"Each box has this symbol in it," he said, pointing to an oval within an arc. That symbol indicates that a human is involved in that operation. If the number of people at that step is greater than one, the number of operators is written next to the symbol. If there is no number, then it is presumed to be one.

"Below these *process* boxes are *data* boxes," Tim continued. "Data boxes contain information about the process. For instance, how long it takes to complete one full cycle of the process. We call that *Cycle Time* or *C/T*," he said, pointing to the C/T in the box.

C/T=186 sec
C/O 323 SEC
A/T =27,000
Defects=4/hrs
Uptime=95%

"Data boxes also portray how long it takes an operator to go from performing one type of operation to performing another. We call this *Changeover Time (C/O)*.

"The total amount of time operators are physically available to perform the process is referred to as *Available Time*, A/T. Available Time," Tim explained, "reflects the length of the operator's shift less any breaks, paid lunches, meetings, or other activities that take the operator away from the process.

"Defects speak for themselves," he continued. "These are the average defects created by the process in a given period of time, usually a shift.

"Uptime," Tim concluded, "is that amount of time the equipment at an operation is available to perform its task. In our company, we look primarily at our manufacturing equipment, but you may choose to look at your copiers, computers, printers, servers, or other equipment used in your processes. Even phones are equipment," he added as an afterthought. "If they are periodically unreliable, that affects your performance.

"Uptime is calculated by subtracting Downtime from Available Time. So, if your computer goes down for an average of 10 minutes a day and you've calculated your Available time to be 420 minutes a day, you'd use the following calculation:

$$(420 - 10) / 420 \times 100\%."$$

He quickly wrote the math problem on the board. "In this example, uptime would be 97.6% of available time."

"Connecting process boxes are dashed arrows." Tim explained that this symbol indicated that work was being *pushed* to the next process. He promised to explain what it meant to push work in a moment.

Above each arrow and between each process box was a triangle. The triangle contained a number and a unit of time. Tim explained that was the amount of Inventory ahead of each operation, and that inventory was expressed not in quantity, but in terms of the time it would take the receiving operation to process it at its current Cycle Time. "We use abbreviations like 's' for second, 'm' for minute, 'h' for hour, and 'd' for day," he concluded.

"Questions?" he asked.

Sharon raised her hand. Tim pointed to her. "Sharon?"

"You said you'd tell us what it meant to *push* work."

"Thank you, Sharon. You're right. I did.

"Okay," he began, "perhaps the best way to describe the difference between *push* and *pull* is to demonstrate it."

He went to the side of the conference room, where there was a printer. He took four sheets of paper and, using a straight edge, tore them roughly into eighths. He then asked, "Does everyone have a watch or a phone that measures seconds?" There were nods around the room.

"Okay," he said, setting the 32 scraps of paper down just above Skip's left hand. "Skip, I want you to pass one scrap of paper to your right every three seconds."

Nadine Sommers, the HR Director, was to his right. "Nadine, I want you to pass one piece of paper to your right every two seconds."

Jack sat to Nadine's right. "Jack," Tim instructed, "I want you to pass one scrap to your right every seven seconds."

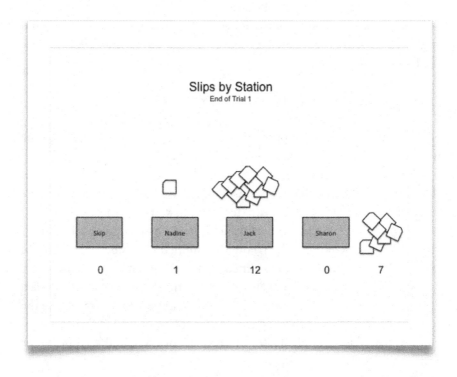

Finally, he addressed Sharon, who was on Jack's right. "Sharon, I want you to pass your slip of paper to the right every second.

"Does everyone understand their job?" Tim asked. The players all did. "One last thing," Tim offered, "if you don't have a slip in front of you at the time to pass it, wait until you have one; then start your countdown."

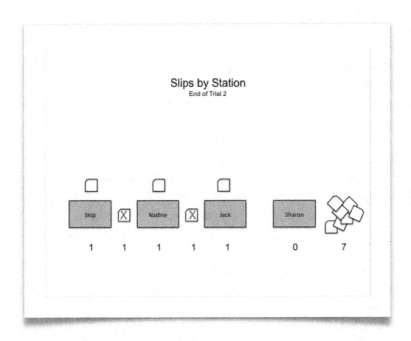

"Okay," Tim stated, consulting his watch. "Begin." Those not in the game watched with fascination.

Meanwhile, Tim went to the board and drew a chart he labeled "Seconds per Slip."

"STOP!" Tim shouted 60 seconds later.

"Jennifer," Tim called out, "tell me what you see."

Jennifer took a second to assess the players and offered, "Jack has almost all the slips."

"Why do you think that is?" Tim inquired.

Jennifer thought for a second before responding. "Jack is slower," she finally responded. Everyone laughed.

"Interesting way to state it," Tim observed. "You say *Jack* is slow as if the operator is the problem." He turned to the class. "That's a common practice: we find a problem and look for *who* is responsible. Fact is—and this is a really big deal—I could put anybody in that chair, and I'd get exactly the same result. What's really responsible is that Jack's *process* is slow.

"Okay," he continued, "what would happen if we dropped Nadine's wait time and she could pass every paper in just one second? How many more pieces would we get out?"

Jennifer thought for several seconds. "None," she finally stated.

"Why is that?" Tim asked.

"Because we wouldn't be changing the slowest operation."

"How about if we shortened Skip's wait time?"

Jennifer thought again. "Same thing. No more slips because the slowest operation never changed."

"Can we reduce Sharon's wait time?" Tim asked.

"Only if we eliminate her job," Jennifer responded without hesitation.

"What you've just seen is the result of a *Push* operation," Tim stated. "Push occurs when each operation *pushes* their completed work to the next operation, whether that operation is ready for it or not. If they're not ready, the Work in Process (WIP) just builds up in front of their operation until they're able to process it."

Tim pointed to the pile of slips in front of Jack's operation.

Then, pointing to the pile to the right of Sharon, Tim stated, "We only got seven pieces through this system. How much WIP did we have?"

The players all counted the slips in front of them. "Thirteen slips," Sharon offered.

"So," Tim summarized, "we have twice as much WIP in the system as Finished Goods.

"Jerry," Tim asked, "what costs are tied up in that WIP?"

"Well," Jerry began, "for sure, there is the cost of Raw Material and Labor. Presuming a factory or office, there's all the overhead and burden."

"So," Tim continued, "how many slips can I spread those costs across?"

"Twenty," Jerry responded.

"Explain," Tim pressed.

"Well, we released 20 pieces of material into production. We committed them to this product the minute Skip performed the first operation on them. They can no longer be used for anything else. So, there are 20 pieces either still in process or in Finished Goods. We'd allocate the costs over all 20."

"Don't take this the wrong way, Jerry, but you're thinking like an accountant, not a businessman."

Tim could see frustration play across Jerry's face. Was it a problem that he thought as an accountant? He *was* an accountant.

"Wouldn't you agree," Tim asked in a conciliatory tone, "that only *actual* revenue pays for everything? Revenue only comes after the customer pays. So let me ask you again, how many slips can I spread the cost across?"

Jerry got Tim's point. "Well, if the customer pays when we ship, then seven," he responded a bit sullenly.

Tim turned to the rest of the group. "So, what's the only way we can reduce our cost of WIP?"

Jerry responded immediately, "Ship more of what we start or build less." He thought for a second longer. "Or both."

"Great summary," Tim praised Jerry. "That's thinking like a businessman!" He could see Jerry visibly brighten.

"Okay, Jack, if we followed Jerry's advice, what would we do?"

"Start fewer slips," Jack responded.

"Okay, if we wanted to only start as many slips as we could finish, how would we do that?"

Sharon jumped in. "We'd slave our pace to Jack's. We'd only start as many as Jack and I could finish."

"How would we do that?" Tim asked.

"Well," Sharon began, "we'd only release new slips as fast as Jack could finish them."

"Great!" Tim approved. "Let me show you a trick for doing that." He grabbed a roll of painter's tape from his backpack and taped an 'X' on the table between Jack and Nadine. He then moved to the gap between Nadine and Skip and did the same thing.

"Now," Tim instructed, pointing to the blue Xs, "these are Kanbans or visual signals." As long as the Kanban is visible, meaning there's nothing on top of it, the preceding operation can pass a new slip to their right. When they do, they will place the slip on the Kanban. Once the Kanban is covered, the preceding operation can pull one slip into their work area but cannot pass it on until the Kanban to their right is empty, nor can they start any others."

"Is that clear?" he asked. There were nods from all the players.

"Okay, begin again."

"Wait!" Sharon called out. "Why isn't there an X between Jack and me?"

"Good question," Tim complimented her. "Ask yourself this: can you ship everything Jack sends you?" Sharon nodded. "Would we want to slow that process down then?" Tim asked.

"As a general rule," he explained, "once we get past our slowest operation, do we want to slow the process down?"

"Ah," Sharon stated. "I get your point. Okay, I'm good. We can begin."
Everyone chuckled.

"Yours was a good question, Sharon," Tim said. "I'm sure others were wondering the same thing. Any other questions?"

When no one spoke, Tim instructed Skip to begin. He started the stopwatch on his phone simultaneously.

Skip took a new slip off the pile of Raw Material, waited three seconds and put it on the 'X' between himself and Nadine. He then grabbed a new slip and pulled it into his operation.

As soon as Skip put the slip on the Kanban, Nadine took it, waited two seconds, and passed it to the blue 'X' between herself and Jack. She waited one more second until Skip's second slip was on the 'X' between them and drew that into her area.

Jack, meanwhile, took Nadine's slip off his Kanban, waited seven seconds, and passed it to his right. He then grabbed the next slip from the Kanban between himself and Nadine. Until he took it, both Skip and Nadine stood idle.

The moment Jack took the slip from the Kanban, Nadine pushed the one in front of her onto the 'X' to her right and grabbed another from the 'X' between her station and Skip's.

With the Kanban between his own station and Nadine's empty, Skip passed a slip to the Kanban on his right and grabbed a new one off the Raw Material pile. Then everyone waited for Jack to complete his seven-second wait. The moment he did, the chain of events happened all over again.

Tim let the sequence play out for 60 seconds, at the end of which he yelled, "STOP!"

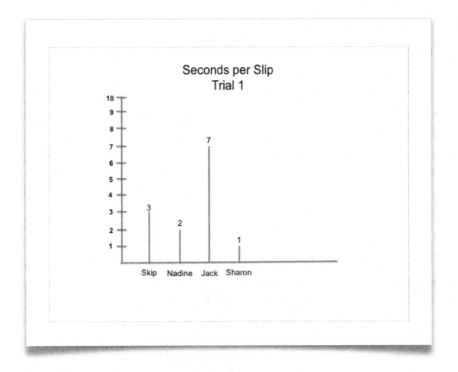

Again, Tim had the team count Finished Goods and WIP.

"How many more slips did we make?" he asked Sharon.

"Same number," she reported.

"How much did we shrink WIP?" he asked Jerry.

"Let's see," the Director of Accounting reasoned, "we originally had 13. We now have one at each of the first three stations and one on each of two Kanbans. That's five. So, we dropped WIP by eight slips or"—he did a quick mental calculation—"60-plus percent."

"Excellent!" Tim approved.

"And how much more revenue did we receive?" he asked Jerry.

"None," the other man responded.

"So, to summarize, we dropped cost but did not increase income. What would be the net result on the business?"

"We'd make more profit," Jerry stated.

"Good thing?" Tim asked the group.

He got a resounding "Yes."

Tim had the team pass the slips back to Skip, then began a new line of discussion.

"What we've just demonstrated is the difference between *push* and *pull*. In the first trial, we pushed the slips from one operation to the next. You saw the result. When we implemented the use of Kanbans, we didn't ship any more, but we reduced our cost of Work in Process by 60%.

"So tell me," Tim asked, "how could we complete more slips in the same 60 seconds?"

"We'd have to shave process time," Sharon stated. "For sure we'd need to shave Jack's."

"But what if all the things Jack has to do are important?" Tim asked.

Without thinking, Sharon said, "Then we'd have to redistribute the work somehow so that it was more evenly distributed and everyone ... er, every process, took roughly the same amount of time."

"Great analysis," Tim praised.

"Before we did that, wouldn't we want to see if we could reduce the time it takes to perform the operations?"

"Well, sure," responded Sharon.

"So how would we do that?" Tim asked.

The team seemed stumped. "You've heard me talk about Kaizen events," Tim offered. "Well, Jack's process is where we'd do a Kaizen event. We'd go in and analyze everything Jack does in his operation and eliminate any steps we can. What we can't eliminate, we'd reduce. If that didn't buy us enough, we'd look at creating a second station that performed the same operation as Jack's. We could also consider *redistributing* some of the operations from Jack's process to those before and after his.

"Is any of that making sense?" Tim asked.

"Sure does," replied Sharon.

"Absolutely," responded Jerry. Tim could tell this was starting to make a lot of sense to Jerry.

"Okay, without actual processes to reconfigure, let's assume we are somehow able to cut Jack's process to six seconds. That would get a couple more slips through the system, right?

"If that didn't buy us enough, we could redistribute some of Jack's process to others and hopefully some of Jack's time. What was the total number of seconds the old way?"

Jerry did the math out loud. "Three seconds, plus two seconds, plus seven seconds, plus one second equals 13 seconds."

"And if we divide 13 seconds by four operations?" Tim asked.

"Three and a fraction seconds per operation," Jerry responded.

"Very good," Tim agreed. "So, let's say we redistributed the work and now every operation takes three seconds except Jack's, and his will now take four seconds."

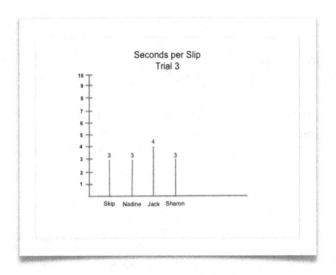

"Skip, you ready to start again?" Tim asked.

"I am."

"Okay, everybody. The process length for everyone but Jack is three seconds. Jack, yours is four seconds.

"Ready? Begin."

The line began again. Within 10 seconds, everyone had work in front of them. By second 13, the first slip entered Finished Goods. Then, every four seconds, another slip entered. At the end of 60 seconds, Tim called, "Stop!"

There were now 12 slips in Finished Goods.

"Jerry, remind us how many slips we got the very first time we ran this experiment."

"Seven," Jerry responded, "so we've almost doubled the process throughput."

"Would that mean more revenue?" Tim asked.

"Absolutely!" Jerry responded enthusiastically. "We've nearly doubled it, too."

"Did we do anything to increase cost?" Tim asked.

Jerry reviewed what they'd done before responding, "No."

"So," Tim summarized, "once we pay for the onetime cost of the Kaizen and for rearranging the processes to reallocate cycle time, we doubled our income. Good thing?"

"Great thing!" Jerry agreed.

Tim paused for long seconds. Everyone waited expectantly for what came next.

"Is this experiment germane to what you do?"

There was a short pause before Sharon spoke. "Heck, yes!" she said with a great deal of conviction. "It's absolutely germane. Especially the redistribution of process cycle times."

"Phew!" Tim said. "For a moment there I was beginning to worry."

That got a laugh.

"Here's what we haven't done," he said. "We have no idea how many slips," he pointed to the experiment, "the customer needs, or how long we have to deliver them. Let me illustrate my point," he said, going to the whiteboard. There he drew the following graph:

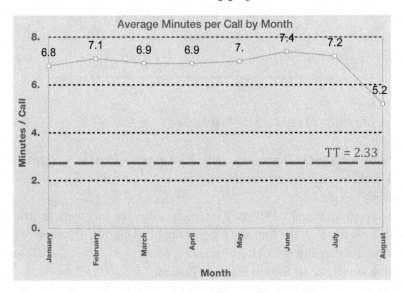

Tim drew a horizontal, red dashed line at about the 2.3 second point and labeled it *TT*. "What if," he began, "our customer actually needed our slips every two and a third seconds? Are we still doing okay?"

The group understood his point immediately.

"Okay," Tim said, breaking the silence. "Right now, you have no idea what you could do about it, but we'll come back to it later. As a professor of mine used to say, 'Little steps for little feet.' Let's start with a Value Stream Map of your operation and then take it step by step."

The team agreed to only measure Operations for now. For the next week, Tim, often accompanied by Sharon, timed the major processes in Operation's Value Stream. When they'd finished, they'd fleshed out many of the data boxes in the VSM: certainly enough to understand that Cycle Time (CT) and defects were the two major problems.

They also investigated how communication flowed between the various organizations within Copper-Bottom Charleston. Tim had expected it to be convoluted and wasn't disappointed. Organizations stockpiled information before communicating it, often doing a data dump within days of the end of the week or month.

Even more Byzantine was the manner in which customer information flowed.

At the end of the week, Tim sat down with Jack and Sharon. "Jack, I've got to say we're not ready for another Kaizen like the one just conducted, but we need to begin data-gathering. We need to take time to figure out how information flows between customers and your employees. I believe you have the ability to reduce the timeline by quite a bit. I'd guestimate 20%.

"Then we need to figure out what actions employees take in each situation, whether those actions are uniform, and what criteria they use to make their decisions.

"With your permission, I'd like to assemble a group of folks from Sales, Operations, IT, HR, and Accounting. I'd like to create a flowchart of how customer information enters the Operations team system and what transpires after it does."

"That's tying up a lot of our people," Jack observed. "Is it absolutely necessary?"

"Absolutely," was Tim's emphatic response. "I agree it's a lot, but I don't think we'll need a full week. I'm hoping to have it wrapped up in three days."

"Okay," Jack said. "Bring it up in the next Lean Council meeting and we'll decide when and where. You've got my support."

31

An Illogical Flow

The Lean Council understood why Tim's data-gathering event was so important and voted unanimously to support it.

Two weeks later, Tim was in front of a diverse team of employees. After Jack's kickoff, Tim outlined the plan for the event.

"I have a question for you," Tim began. "What is Copper-Bottom's *Value Add*? What do customers want from you? Why do they come to Copper-Bottom?"

The group looked stumped, so Tim prompted, "Do they come to you for moderately priced health insurance?"

There were universal head nods.

"Do you only have one type of customer?" Tim asked.

His question was met with silence and blank stares.

"Look," he began, "if we want to know why our customers come to us, don't we need to understand who our customer is? For instance, for some of you, the customer is an employer looking for benefits for their employees; for others, the customer is a broker shopping for insurance for a group of individuals or a small client organization. For others, the customer is the individual who already has your health insurance and has a question. Am I right?"

This crew's silence was starting to annoy Tim, but he could tell they were just bewildered by where this was all going. He knew he had to be patient, so he said, "For the next several days, we are only going to look at one type of customer: the individual already using your health insurance."

"Who here deals with those customers?" Tim asked.

Four hands went up. "Perfect." Tim responded. "What do you do?" Tim asked, pointing to one of the four.

"I'm a CSR," the woman responded. When Tim looked confused, she said, "Sorry, that's short for Customer Service Rep."

"Anyone else a Customer Service Rep?" he asked. A second woman raised her hand.

"Who else deals with that kind of customer?"

Two more hands went up. "What do you do?" Tim asked one.

"I work in Accounts Receivable," the young woman said. "A/R for short."

"And," Tim asked, pointing to the fourth woman, "what do you do?"

"I'm a supervisor of CSRs," she responded. "I talk with the *ugly* ones," she said, and the class erupted in laughter. Everyone knew that Janet got the angry customers who found something wrong with the CSR's service.

"Okay," Tim began again. "We are about to document the actual flow of information that occurs when a customer calls in. Note I used the word *actual*. I don't want you to repeat what you've been told or what the manual says. I want you to help this team to understand what really happens. Is that clear?"

There were a few nods, but mostly blank stares.

"Okay," Tim said. "We need ground rules.

- First off, silence doesn't speak. If I ask a question, I expect a response. If no one volunteers, I'll call on individuals. Clear?" Heads nodded. Hearing nothing, Tim asked again, "Clear?" "Yes," came a chorus of voices.
- "Second, you are on this team for the balance of the week. For that period of time, *this* is your job. We'll eat together and stay together. When we take breaks, it is to stretch, use the restroom, or make personal phone calls. When the break's over, I expect you back in your seat." Tim was hopeful that it wouldn't take the whole week, but he knew folks wouldn't argue if they were released early. Better to under-promise and overperform, he reminded himself.
- "Third, what you do here this week will set the tone for how Copper-Bottom Charleston processes information in the future.
- "And finally, we're all adults. If you need to stand up or go to the restroom, just do it. You don't need to raise your hand or ask permission."

"So, back to my first point: silence doesn't speak. If you don't give me a verbal answer to my questions, I will go around the room and ask each of you individually. You can't hide behind silence here. Your opinion matters a great deal. If you don't understand something, ask.

"We good?" he asked.

There was a raucous "Yes."

"Great!" he laughed. "Let's begin."

"When a customer calls," Tim began, "what's the very first thing that happens? Who do they speak with first?"

A woman whose name he'd later learn was Thelma said, "There is talk about us getting dedicated phone lines, but until that happens, the customer's call goes to an electronic switchboard. By answering a few questions, the customer tells the switchboard what they called about. The switchboard then routes the customer where they requested. Most go into a queue that gets answered by the next available CSR. However, if they have called before, they may have the phone number of the person who helped them last. If that's true, they can dial it directly. If they know the CSR's name but not their number, then the switchboard allows them to select that person's name from an electronic list. The system then dials that CSR's extension."

"So," Tim summarized, "if a customer calls in, they are put on hold until the next CSR becomes available. Correct?" The CSRs all said, "Yes."

"While on hold," Tim continued, "the customer hears some kind of pre-recorded message. Right?"

Several people, including Thelma, nodded in the affirmative. "And," Tim continued, "the recording invites them to dial an extension if they have one, or stay on the line and their call will be answered in the order received by the next available Customer Service Representative?"

"You've done this before," one of the team members said with a laugh.

"Yes, I have," Tim responded, "but I've only done it from the customer end of the call. This leads me to ask, what's your average wait time?"

To Tim's surprise, no one knew. He made himself a note on the whiteboard to find out from Skip.

Tim then went to a table and picked up a square packet of Post-it notes. Peeling one off the top, he put it near the top left of the whiteboard, orienting it with a corner up so that it resembled a diamond, rather than a square. Then he wrote on it: "Have extension?"

He then placed another sticky note to the right of the first. This one he oriented as a square. On it, he wrote, "Dial extension." Between the two he drew an arrow from the diamond to the square and labeled it "Yes."

He placed another sticky below the first, also oriented as a diamond. On it he wrote "Wait?" Then he drew an arrow down from the first diamond to the second, labeling it "No."

"Does anyone know what I'm doing?" Tim asked.

"You're creating a flow chart," one of the team members responded.

"Right you are," Tim said. "For those of you who aren't familiar with this style of flow chart, let me review what the symbols mean.

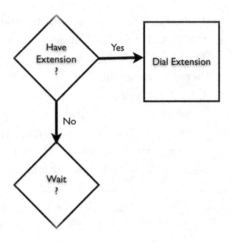

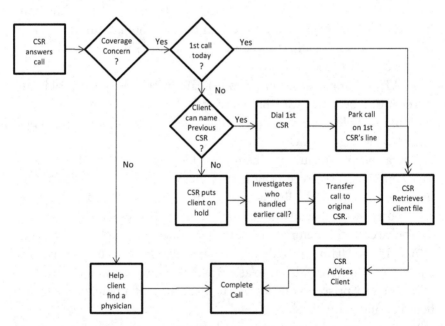

"Diamonds," he began, "represent decision points. Their contents are usually posed in the form of questions. Squares, on the other hand, are process steps. That means that some action is taking place at that step. Finally, the arrows indicate the direction of flow. Arrows leaving a decision diamond are labeled with the type of response that flow represents. In our case, the down-facing arrow is labeled with a 'No.'

"That means that it follows the logic of a 'No' response to the question 'Does the caller have the extension of a Copper-Bottom employee?'"

"Questions?" Tim asked the group before moving on.

For the rest of the morning, the team worked on the flow chart of a customer call. Calls fell into three main types:

- COVERAGE: calls related to customers wanting to know what their health insurance covered were handled on the first call 90+% of the time.
- BILLING: calls related to billing problems almost always entailed a call back.
- PHYSICIAN: calls seeking help with finding a primary care physician or specialist sometimes required the CSR to call the client back but most often were solved during the first call.

"What do you see?" Tim asked the assembly.

"Squares and diamonds," someone quipped.

"Fair enough," Tim responded. "How many?"

Someone quickly counted and said, "Thirteen."

"How many arrows?" Tim asked.

It took a second, but the answer came back, "Fourteen?"

"Here's what that's telling us," Tim instructed. "That's telling us that we have 14 opportunities to drop the ball. You see," he continued, "every gap between steps in a process represents a chance to fail in making a handoff, to drop things in the crack, so to speak, and to lose time."

"Remember that," he told them. "When we come back to work on this process, we will want to reduce the number of handoffs, and we are going to want to reduce the number of decisions we have to make. When we finish the first pass, we'll then want to make sure that any handoffs that remain have a positive *handshake*. That means we'll want both parties to do something that confirms the exchange took place."

"Okay," he concluded, "take a break. See you back here in 10. That's 9:12 by the clock in the back of the room," he said, pointing.

When everyone was back in the room, Tim dug into this mystery of why all billing questions were referred immediately to Accounting. He was informed that CSRs didn't have access to the accounting systems that contained the billing and payment data. "And," his informant continued, "Accounting has been instructed not to answer their phones until after all their postings have been completed. That's usually around 10 AM. By then, the customer has usually called us back one or more times. Those customers get referred to Janet," the informant told him, pointing to the supervisor who said that she spoke to the *ugly* customers.

That news baffled Tim, who elected to avoid confrontation with Jerry, opting instead to raise the problem vertically. First, however, he wanted to confirm what he'd heard with actual data and not folklore.

For the next two days, the team combed through the process of fielding customer calls. With his help, the team was able to reduce the concerns of the COVERAGE part of the flow chart from 13 to 7 steps.

Next, he asked how CSRs were able to give customer physician information. "Easy," shot back one of the CSRs, "we look the physicians up on our computers."

"Wait!" Tim stopped the person. "You mean to tell me that all that information is available digitally? Why don't you just post it on your website?"

"Are you kidding me?" someone responded. "Corporate IT can't even update our data in real time; you think they would spend time putting all that physician information on the website?"

"But it already exists in digital format," Tim countered in frustration. "It should be easy as pie."

"There are a lot of things that *should be*," Janet responded with equal frustration. "Trust me, we've tried … and more than once."

When Tim left Copper-Bottom that night, he was really frustrated. He called Don after supper. "Got a second?" Tim asked. When Don said yes, Tim asked if he could review a problem with him, then proceeded to tell him about the issues he'd uncovered.

"Any recommendations?" he asked Don after he'd finished.

"See if you can set up a meeting with Jack tomorrow and text me the time. Let's tackle this together. Meanwhile, what are you thinking?"

Tim knew what he thought would solve the problem but hadn't put much stock in being able to sell it. To be honest, part of the institutional gloom of Copper-Bottom had begun to affect him. No one seemed capable of doing anything other than what they'd been directed and, even then, only with difficulty. Employees seemed to have to work around extremely dysfunctional systems.

"Well," Tim responded to Don, "if this were Friedman, I'd ask you to talk to Jim and get IT to kick into overdrive. They are a huge impediment to this site. I have to believe they are adversely affecting all the sites. I also have to believe that someone back at Copper-Bottom's headquarters has a lot of juice to be able to keep the sites from pushing the upgrade forward."

"Which upgrade?" Don asked. "Both!" Tim said in frustration. "They need the new database that refreshes in real time, and they need the web-site upgrades I was just talking about."

Don was quiet for several seconds, then cautioned Tim, "Keep in mind, their corporate headquarters doesn't think the same way as ours. They might agree to do all the things you ask but then expect reciprocal reductions in force. Before we get involved, I need to lay some groundwork. Can you give me a couple of weeks?" Tim agreed to do so. "In that case," Don said, "let's not have that discussion with Jack just yet."

The following day Tim asked the group how they might gather some data that they could use to convey the magnitude of their problems.

"Transfers?" Tim asked. "Is there anywhere we can gather data about how many calls you get a day and how many of those get transferred?"

Silence. Then one of Skip's people timidly raised her hand. "Yvette?" Tim acknowledged her. "Do you have an idea?"

Yvette cleared her throat and said, "We have call logs."

"You mean you have logs of all incoming calls?" Tim asked.

"And outgoing and transfers," Yvette admitted. "We could export the data for, say, the last three months into Excel and then sort it by direction of call, incoming or outgoing, length of the call, and destination, for example, Accounting or Operations. If you'd like, I could get you a sample."

"Please," Tim said.

While Yvette was gone, the rest of the team helped Tim fill out a table on the whiteboard. The table contained a list of the information he felt they'd need to describe the magnitude of their problem. The list contained the

- number of problems resolved in one call,
- number of Billing calls,
- number of calls looking for a network physician, and
- number of CSR to CSR or CSR to A/R call transfers.

When Yvette returned, she had several sheets of paper printed with all the call information. She passed these around. The logs had date and time information, the phone number where the call originated, and the number of the extension that answered. If the call was later transferred, the log showed the number to which it was transferred. It also showed the total length of each call.

Yvette explained again that she could export all that information to an Excel spreadsheet where it could be further sorted and analyzed.

"Analyzed?" asked one of the CSRs.

"For instance," Yvette continued, "we could look up everyone's numbers and add a column in Excel that has the name of the employee assigned the phone. Or we could sort between incoming versus outgoing calls. We could also identify transfers and so on."

Tim pointed to the board. "Can we get the information to fill this in?" he asked.

"Absolutely!" Yvette responded.

So for the remainder of the day, the team analyzed three months' worth of calls, breaking them down to answer the questions on the board. At the end, they'd filled in the table.

14,421 = Total Calls Received in three months
3,894 = Calls resolved in a single call (27%)[1]
5,913 = Billing calls (Transferred to Accounting 41%)
4,615 = Other CSR (Transferred to 2nd CSR or A/R 32%)

The data amazed the team. Most had never kept their own data, nor was this kind of data kept by anyone at Copper-Bottom.

"What have we learned?" Tim asked.

"That we take a boatload of calls in a month," Janet offered.

"Ok. Good observation," Tim agreed with a chuckle. "What else?"

"That almost three-quarters of the calls we field need to be transferred, either to Accounting or to another CSR. That's amazing!"

"That CSRs resolve the customer's problems in a single call more than a quarter of the time," Cindy observed.

"Do you begin to understand the meaning of the quotation *Knowledge is power?*" Tim asked. "Can you see how what we've learned has framed our future discussions?"

There were nods around the room.

"Okay, next step," proclaimed Tim. "We now need to collect some more data, but this time in the field, at individual CSRs' desks. Here's what we're going to do."

Tim outlined the next steps.

Each team member was given a clipboard and a stopwatch. On the clipboard was a table. In the first column were the numbers 1 through 20 in sequential order. Tim explained that the team would split up and start to measure

CSRs as the CSRs took calls. They'd record the time the call came in, the time it concluded, the action the CSR took, and, if transferred, to which group.

They took a quick break while Tim created the form in Excel. Afterward, he sent the team out with clipboards and pens. They were instructed to meet back in the conference room for lunch and to bring their data.

When the team met at lunch, Tim input the data they'd gathered into an Excel spreadsheet.

"Here's what you found," he told them as they ate. Consulting a strip of paper, he began writing numbers on the board. "Calls ranged from a low of 3.5 minutes to a high of 12. The average call was about 9 minutes, which matches up with the three-month data we collected earlier. The average call length during the three-month period had been 8.6 minutes.

"The average time it took to answer client questions on first-time calls was 2 minutes and 57 seconds. Let's call that 3 minutes."

Date:		CSR:		
Time:		Observer:		
	Time Call Answered	Time Call Concluded	Action Taken	Transferred To
1				
2				
3				
4				
5				
6				
7				
8				
9				
10				
~				
20				

"The data you collected today indicated that the answering CSR transferred the call almost 56% of the time. That's higher than what we observed in the three-month study.

"Today's data also show that more than half of the calls were subsequently transferred to Accounting. That implies a billing concern. The other transfers were internal: CSR to CSR. Now," Tim continued, "this is where it gets interesting. Most of you used your heads and actually measured how long it took to find the CSR who had last spoken to that client. Anyone want to guess?" he asked.

"Three minutes," someone guessed.

"Way too low," someone else said. "I'll bet it's closer to five."

"Anyone else?" Tim asked.

There were head shakes.

"Nine and a quarter minutes," he stated. There were low whistles around the room. "That would imply that CSRs are able to answer questions pretty quickly if it's an original call. CSRs spend the rest of their time hunting for the CSR who last spoke to the customer."

"That's crazy," someone stated, "but only to see the actual numbers. I think that those of us who are CSRs had a pretty good idea that it was something like that."

"After lunch," Tim explained, "you'll be gathering more of the same information. Now that we know it's an issue, please make sure to time how long it takes to find the CSR who had taken the call the day before."

By the end of the day, the master spreadsheet was far more populated, and there were definite patterns forming.

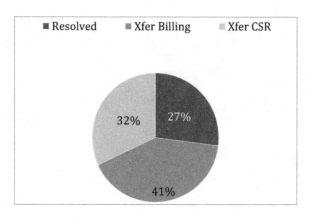

Although it occurred more frequently, transferring callers to Accounting was the quickest activity. When it came to transferring calls within the CSR community, it took three times longer to find the original CSR and transfer, than to just answer questions. That was because finding the original CSR took a lot of leg work.

Clearly, the best future alternative would be to give CSRs the ability to answer any customer questions, but that necessitated a new or updated database—one that was instantly accurate.

"Was there anything they could do now?" Tim asked himself.

He decided to go over that with the team in the morning. They needed to resolve some of their issues, even if only temporarily.

NOTE

1 No new calls from the same number within three days.

32

Unkinking the Hose

The following morning, everyone was fresh. It was their last full day, and they all felt the need to show progress, something more than just data collected. Tim tapped into this emotion and asked two questions: (1) Is there any way to know who a customer spoke to yesterday without physically tracking them down? (2) Is there any way that CSRs could gain access to the client billing information so they didn't have to transfer those calls?

Tim went to meet with Jerry to get the answer to the second. Meanwhile, he left the team leader, Cindy, in charge of finding an answer to the first question.

Tim had formulated an answer to the first but wanted to see if the team could come up with a more creative one. He was glad he did. The team came up with a far simpler solution.

Jerry, on the other hand, was a disappointment; predictably so. He refused to give CSRs access to the accounting data. He assured Tim his people would respond within the 24-hour window but maintained that CSRs would have to continue to forward customer calls to his people.

On his way out of Accounting, Tim passed Patty Purcell's cubicle. "Tim?" she asked timidly from inside her cube. "Do you have a second?" Tim stepped in and sat in the chair.

"I take it," Patty began, "that you've been in speaking with Jerry. Did you get what you needed?" Knowing Jerry as she did, Patty already knew the answer. Tim admitted that he had not.

"What were you looking for?" Patty asked.

"Permission for CSRs to access the accounting database so they can answer customer questions in one call."

DOI: 10.4324/9781003336051-33

"I could have told you the answer before you asked," Patty stated with a knowing smile. "Although it's not the same thing, can I give you something that will help a little?"

"Sure," Tim said.

Patty reached into her center desk drawer and handed him a sheet. "This is our department's phone roster. It not only has the name and phone extension of our accountants but which clients they service. It should help the CSRs direct the calls to the right person in the first call, at least."

"Thanks," Tim acknowledged. Slipping the page into his binder, he said, "You're acting like you'll get in trouble for sharing this with me. Is sharing this a problem?"

Patty didn't answer his question. "Jerry means well," she began, "but he sometimes doesn't see the bigger picture. He's very worried about protecting the data he's been entrusted with. Understandably, he's ultra-sensitive with the clients' personal information. He sometimes acts as if the rest of the company isn't."

Patty paused as if she had more to say, but then seemed to think better of it. She gave Tim a sweet smile and wished him good luck.

When he got back to the team, Tim explained that he'd struck out with Jerry, then, without revealing its source, offered the list Patty had given him. Cindy examined the document then looked at the other CSRs.

"It's the Rosetta Stone," she exclaimed in awe, handing it to another woman.

"What exactly is the Rosetta Stone?" Tim asked Cindy.

"Well," Cindy began, "it always made sense to us that Jerry had assigned certain accountants to handle specific groups of clients, but whenever we've asked for a document that gave us those assignments, Jerry refused, saying there was no such list. By inference, he must have forbidden his people from sharing this document outside of Accounting. How you got your hands on this I'll never know. I'm sure it wasn't from him. He's a very secretive person," Cindy concluded.

Knowing what he now knew, Tim suspected that if it became known that the CSRs now had the Rosetta Stone, Jerry would instigate a witch hunt to find out who gave it to them. He knew that would lead right back to Patty. He decided it was time to go to Jack.

He collected the document, but before heading off in Jack's direction, Tim asked Cindy if her team had made any inroads in knowing which CSR a customer had spoken to the previous day.

"I think so," Cindy responded. "Arlene, do you want to tell Tim what you discovered?"

Arlene cleared her throat and said, "We noticed that the telephone logs contain the 'from' and 'to' phone numbers. Once we export the log into Excel, we can sort the list for the customer's number. That, of course, is also part of the CSR's record. Once we find the customer's number, we can see who they reached here. We tried it over 30 times and every time, we came up with the CSR's number in less than 40 seconds. Once we got the hang of things, we got it down to about 25 seconds."

"Impressive," complimented Tim. "How would you gain access to that information each day?" he asked after thinking about it for a second.

"That's the next step," Cindy agreed. "We need to go to Skip and see if he'll give us access to the previous day's data. We don't need it further back than that. After 24 hours, our database is accurate; it's just those first 24 hours."

Tim left the team to seek Skip's assistance, then he went in search of Jack. When he found him, Jack was just concluding a phone call with a third-party sales company. Tim knocked on the door frame.

"Hey, come on in," Jack greeted him. "How's the team doing?"

Tim gave him a quick rundown before explaining the reason for his visit. "Jack," he began, "the team's mission was to reduce the length of time the client waits for Copper-Bottom to get back to them regarding their concern. As you know, the database is not up to date, so when a call comes in for a billing problem, the CSR can only forward the call to a general accounting number. From there, the Customer Service Rep loses track of the call and has no idea if the client's question has been answered at all, much less in a timely manner. When I questioned Jerry, he would only commit to his people answering the call within the 24-hour window.

"Since the CSR is already responding to other client queries, it just seems logical to allow them to answer accounting questions, too. So I went to Jerry and ..."

Jack stopped him. "Let me guess. Jerry refused to give the CSRs access to billing information."

"Correct," Tim responded. "As I was leaving, one of Jerry's people gave me a closely held document that at least has the name of his accountants and an alphabetical list, by last name and first initial, of which clients each serves. That would allow the CSRs to direct the caller to the correct accountant and get them one step closer to resolving the client's problem."

Jack's face brightened.

"But," Tim continued, "I've been told that if Jerry found out who leaked the document, that accountant's job might be in jeopardy. I'm now reluctant to disseminate the document."

"Can you tell me who gave you the document?" Jack asked.

"Patty Purcell."

"Oh, brother!" Jack put his head in his hands. "As you know, Patty was the one who filed the original lawsuit when Henry Corn berated her and Jerry refused to come to her defense. I'm afraid you called it correctly. If Jerry gets wind of this, he'll likely use it as an excuse for retribution against Patty."

Tim remained quiet for several seconds. When he finally spoke it was to say, "Is there any Copper-Bottom document that states that Jerry is not allowed to give other employees access to client billing information?"

Jack thought for a second then said, "No."

"Have you, or possibly a predecessor, told Jerry not to share that data?"

Again, Jack said, "No." After a pause, he continued, "But think about it. If anyone else gives the client the information and the client finds an irregularity, a CSR isn't going to be able to adjust the account. I think that Jerry's right that it's proper for the CSRs to forward the call to his people." Then, before being asked, Jack answered what he knew was going to be the next question. "However, I can see no harm in giving CSRs this 'Rosetta Stone,' as you call it."

Pausing, he asked, "Do I need to do something?"

"Jack, it sounds like the smartest thing we can do is to keep Patty's name out of all this. Can you contact Jerry and ask him to give us a copy of whatever breakdown he has indicating which of his people handles which clients?"

"I sure will," replied Jack, reaching for his phone.

It took serious arm bending, but Jerry finally brought a copy of the document to Jack's office.

"Thanks, Jerry," Jack said. "This is the most up-to-date, right?"

Jerry hesitated. "Let me check."

"Tell you what," Jack said. "Have someone bring a copy to Tim in the conference room as quickly as possible. Thanks again."

As Jerry left and Tim stood to leave, both men hoped they'd just avoided another train wreck. "Thanks for acting so quickly on this, Tim. I hate to think what might have happened had Jerry discovered this."

"It's none of my business …", Tim began, then stopped abruptly.

"What?" Jack inquired.

"Well, don't you think that would be a really silly reason to let a person go? I mean honestly, when I think of the potential consequences, I shudder to think that Jerry can act that unilaterally."

"Good point," Jack agreed. "Let me get HR to make sure Jerry understands that he cannot take any disciplinary actions, especially regarding Patty, without first clearing it with HR and then with me." Jack recalled that the board had given him those instructions but that he hadn't passed them on to Jerry.

By the time Tim got back, the team had developed two solutions and were making plans to implement them.

1. Regarding CSR to CSR transfers, the team proposed to use Skip's call logs to ID with whom the customer had last spoken.

    Skip had volunteered that there was a 29-character field in the call log that was no longer used. He suggested that the field could be repurposed to input the last CSR's first initial and last name.

    Another part of the team attempted to use the call log to ID the CSR *without* the benefit of the 29-character field. Once the log had been exported into Excel, the task proved extremely easy.

    After the team had practiced the technique, someone observed that it made more sense that the CSR put their name in the 29-character cell as soon as they hung up the call. That meant that the call log could be used directly and cut out the whole download and export to Excel. It could be used live in a background window of the CSR's screen.

    The team was about to make that recommendation when someone observed that they might as well just make CSRs responsible for their own list of customers. That led to a quick sift of the total number of clients and the computation of how many each CSR would have to cover.

    Someone asked if there was a way to figure out which clients were most likely to call. There were several opinions offered, but when each was tried, none proved reliable.

    Finally, the group agreed that while it made great sense to assign each customer to a CSR, they weren't ready for that. "Walk before we run," someone said. Once again, they decided to stick with the call log.

2. By now the team had an official copy of the Rosetta Stone and an assurance that they'd receive an updated copy every time it changed. Using the Rosetta Stone, they could quickly ID the name of the accountant assigned to their clients.

That led to a new discussion: could the CSRs be reorganized to match up with specific accountants, thereby forming a CSR-Accountant team? The idea gained immediate favor until someone pointed out that there were one and a half CSRs to every accountant.

Back to the drawing board. The team agreed to stick with the Rosetta Stone to identify the appropriate accountant.

Additionally, the team agreed to start collecting new data on call length in general and also by type of call (Physician, Billing, CSR Transfer).

Just before lunch, the team gave their final briefing to Jack and his staff. Tim had choreographed the PowerPoint presentation so that each team member had a part. Aside from Cindy, who was the team leader, everyone else only had to speak on two slides. Cindy introduced the team, stated the team's mission, and reviewed the goals the team had been given. She also did the wrap-up and asked for questions.

By the end of the briefing, Jack and his staff were impressed. The team had gathered data, isolated their problems, and set actions in place to resolve their two most flagrant time hogs. The team promised to continue to capture call length by type and update the chart in the CSR area.

When they finished, they received an ovation from the Lean Council. It was clear from their demeanor how much the praise meant.

33

Confrontation

Tim was straightening the conference room after the team's final out-brief. With his back to the door, he sensed rather than saw someone behind him. Turning, he saw Patty Purcell standing in the doorway.

"Patty," he said. "You're a sight for sore eyes."

Patty blushed and said, "Good to see you, too, Tim. Am I interrupting?"

Tim let out a laugh. "Hardly," he said. "You're a welcome distraction. What's up? By the way," he cut off her response, "Jack got Jerry to give us an official copy of the Rosetta Stone and a promise to keep the CSRs updated on any changes."

"That's great," Patty responded. "I presume that by Rosetta Stone you mean the document I gave you, right?"

"Correct," Tim responded. "We wanted to decouple the team's possession of the document from you. This way, Jerry gave us the document personally. He has no idea you were involved."

"Thanks," Patty responded. "That was a smart move." She stopped. "Well," she began a bit hesitantly, "I was wondering if you were free for supper?"

Tim was taken aback. It had been weeks since they'd spent the day at the beach. Since then, they'd seen each other in passing, but had only spoken the one time, about the Rosetta Stone. It wasn't that Tim wasn't interested in Patty, but it was shortly after they'd met at the beach that things at Copper-Bottom had become far more intense. He'd found himself living and breathing the efforts to get them back on the right course. Even as the thoughts tumbled through his mind, he knew that was an excuse.

If he was honest, there was another problem. Patty had been at the epicenter of the events that led to Tim being here. He still felt a tension between pursuing a relationship with her versus the possibility that doing

DOI: 10.4324/9781003336051-34

so would taint his ability to change the leaders of this company. He'd put his job obligation ahead of his personal interests. Again, in all honesty, he'd hoped that he'd be able to pursue his interest in Patty when his obligation to Copper-Bottom was over. Unfortunately, he'd never discussed any of that with her.

He took a mental step back and thought about how it looked from Patty's perspective. She'd made it clear at the beach that she was interested in seeing him again. They'd even tentatively talked about plans. By not following through, he'd left Patty to think that she wasn't appealing or that he wasn't interested in a woman with a child. He hadn't intended any of that, but he could see that it would be easy to form that conclusion from her point of view.

Coming to ask him to supper had really taken a lot of fortitude. He had to give her credit: whatever work she'd done with her life coach had given a lot more self-confidence than most women. Most would have just moved on and been angry with him. Patty had not.

He leaped back from his mental journey and stammered, "Patty. I'm stunned. I just realized that I owe you a huge apology for not reaching out to you after our meeting at the beach. I am embarrassed and really sorry."

He thought for a second and then said, "I'd really like nothing more than to have supper with you, but I need to talk with you first. Can I meet you in half an hour at the Starbucks on the corner?"

When Patty didn't respond immediately, Tim said, "That sounded dumb even to me. You're here now.

"I'm sorry," he said. "Let's try this again. Will you have a seat?" he asked, gesturing to a chair.

Patty sat down a bit reluctantly, then said, "Tim, I feel like I'm creating a problem. I didn't mean to. Maybe I should just go." With that, she slid her chair away from the table and started to stand.

"Patty, stop! Please," Tim pleaded.

Eyes cast down, she sat again but looked ready to bolt at any second.

"Thank you for staying," Tim began. He took a seat across from her. "I left the beach definitely wanting to see you again. Then something happened here, and I let myself get buried with work. But that's not all. I've also worried about how spending time with you might impair my ability to do my job here."

Patty looked up and straight into his eyes. "Look, Tim, the last thing I want is to be a problem to someone. I just thought we'd had a good time at the beach and wanted to see if there might be more." She stood again.

Tim also stood. "Patty," he pleaded, "will you give me one more second? Please?"

Patty didn't leave but remained standing.

"Patty, I really want to see you again, and I'd love to have supper with you and Scott tonight. I just don't want you to think if I don't later acknowledge you here that it's because I don't care about you. Getting Copper-Bottom healthy is important to my company and, by extension, to me. Can you and I do both?"

Tim couldn't read Patty's face. It was as if she had a mask on, but she was still looking directly into his eyes.

At length she said, "Let's do this. The dinner offer is still out there, but not for tonight. You think about it. I'll think about it. If you'd like, you can call me tonight." She stopped but then went on. "I want it to be clear. The ball is in your court. I will not reach out again. I'll be cordial, but I'll understand if that is all you want out of our relationship. If you want more, you'll have to make an effort."

The last words stung, but Tim knew he deserved it.

Patty didn't wait for his response. She turned gracefully and walked out of the room. As she did, Tim acknowledged once again how attractive she was and felt pain at her leaving. He admired the pluck it had taken to ask him to supper and to stay for the difficult conversation that had ensued. He realized, once again, that he really liked Patty as a woman. He definitely admired how strong she was.

He finished preparing the room for the next day, then, on impulse, pulled his phone out of his pocket. Typing the first three letters of her last name, Tim found Patty's number and dialed it. He had no idea what he was going to say, but he wanted Patty to know he was interested.

The phone rang twice before she answered with, "I haven't even gotten out of the parking lot." Her voice sounded a bit peeved.

"I try to learn from my mistakes," Tim responded, "especially the big ones. I just wanted to know when a good time would be to call you tonight."

"There may be hope for you yet." She chortled. He could hear the mirth in her voice. "Scott's usually in bed by 8. I try to have my clothes laid out and everything ready for the next day by 9:30. Somewhere in that hour and a half would be the best time on a weeknight." Then she added with mock offense, "Now may I drive home?" They both laughed.

"I'll call around 8," Tim concluded. He paused, then said, "And thanks, Patty."

He was punctual, and the call had been a very good one. He doubted that Patty had made it to bed by 9:30, but they'd made plans to have dinner that coming weekend. Tim had offered to take her out, but they agreed that they should keep things low-key for the time being. "Let's eat at my place," Patty had offered, adding with a touch of humor, "Heaven knows what your place looks like." They both laughed.

When he hung up, Tim found himself grinning from ear to ear.

34

The Turning Point

On Monday, Tim returned to Friedman to meet with his own team. Since he'd missed their normal Friday meeting, each team member gave a brief update on the progress they'd made the previous week.

Their work was on track. Those who had conducted Kaizen events the previous week gave a brief synopsis of their accomplishments. They'd updated the value stream map to reflect the new stats. Each had met or exceeded their event's goals. As was the practice, after each event, they transitioned ownership of the process back to the supervisor. Although not on the team, the supervisor had been part of the daily briefings. Each was familiar with the gains achieved during the event. At the post-event transition, the supervisor became responsible for maintaining them.

This transfer was a formality, but it was symbolically important. Tim's team had briefed the leadership team, including supervisors, each evening of the event, so supervisors were fully abreast of what the team had been doing. This private transition briefing, however, gave supervisors a chance to ask questions and seek any additional information. Tim's Continuous Improvement team remained responsible for assisting the supervisors for up to six months. During that time, they were on call to the supervisor any time they needed help.

After the event, the supervisor was expected to keep up any new charts on their KPI board. History showed most of those charts would continue to show improvement as the supervisor and their team further refined the gains made during the event.

His other two subordinates were preparing for events still on the horizon. There were data to gather, team members to choose, a value stream map to create or update, and a team leader to recommend to the Lean Council. Plus, there were all the other event preparations: restaurants to

DOI: 10.4324/9781003336051-35

deliver their meals, event kits to restock, training materials to assemble and photocopy. Even without collecting data, it could easily take two weeks to prepare for an event. Tim's people were all seasoned and could manage 98% of it on their own, but they liked knowing that he had their backs and would support them if they ran into an obstacle.

By 10 AM, Tim was back at Copper-Bottom. He met with Cindy, who reported that she'd met with Skip. She'd gotten digital call logs from the past six months and gotten one of her people to export the data into Excel. Once in Excel, the employee had created a tab for Average Call Length. They copied and pasted the call length data into the new tab, separated it by month, then calculated the average call length for each month. With this data, they created a chart showing call length by month.

"Look at this!" Cindy said excitedly.

She showed Tim a chart that revealed that the average call length since the Kaizen event had dropped almost two minutes.

"That's even though we still have to refer billing questions to Accounting," she said with excitement.

Tim did some quick calculating. "Your call length has dropped by over 20%," he said. "That means you will start having people who aren't fully occupied. What do you intend to do to use this newfound time?"

Cindy had been so excited by her own news she hadn't considered the consequences of what that news meant.

"Uh," she said. "Does this mean I'm going to have to let people go?"

"Absolutely not!" Tim stated. "This is a good problem to have. How can you make something great out of this new capacity? Ask yourself, *what projects have I always wanted to tackle, but have never had enough time to get it done*? THIS is the time."

"But what happens when that project is over?" she asked, still not seeing the silver lining in the cloud.

"Let me ask you," Tim began, "can you afford their labor?"

"I think so," she said, then asked, "Can't I?"

"Or course you can." Tim was emphatic. "You've been able to pay for them all along because of the way Copper-Bottom has structured its prices, so the money's there to continue to pay them. The question is, What productive activities will you have them do?

"Think of this," Tim continued. "If you don't do anything, everyone will have an hour or more of free time each day, but you'll have nothing to show for that time. If you select one or two people and put them on special assignment, everyone else will close ranks to get the job done. Life will be normal. Meanwhile, you'll be tackling major projects that will make EVERYONE'S job easier, perhaps even saving more labor."

"This gives you a chance to spend more time training your people, or you could conduct another event, or you could totally 5S the CSR area, organizing, labeling ..." He stopped, feeling as if the options were endless.

"What's your employee attrition like?" he asked.

"It used to be pretty high," Cindy said, "but of late, it's down to about one or two people a year."

"Okay," Tim said, "think of your problem this way. If you don't replace them, in a year or less, you'll be down to your correct size. Until then, you have an extra person or two who can help you make your group super strong. What if you could assign your best person—the one you're grooming to replace you when you get promoted—to begin rethinking the CSR process? Could they come up with better training? A better process? A stronger team?

"When the time comes that one of your people resigns or gets promoted," he continued, "you may need to put that person back into their old CSR job, but what can you do with them in the meantime?"

"Wow," Cindy said, "you're right. I don't *have* to let them go. They are fully paid for. I need to change my mindset and start thinking of where we need the most help.

"Do I have to continue to use the same person, or can I use different people on different projects?"

Tim could see Cindy was starting to see the possibilities. These were good questions.

"You'll assign the person with the right skills to each project," he said. "But you knew that. And think of this, Cindy, you'll be growing your people and your organization. You'll be giving them chances to demonstrate their skills and stretch their knowledge. Don't those seem like good things?"

"Oh, Tim," she said, spontaneously hugging him. "This is *great* news. I'm excited. I need to spend some time thinking about what we need to tackle first."

"Consider this," Tim warned her, "your people are no dummies. They're going to start to see they have time on their hands. What's happened in the past when that was true?"

"We let someone go," Cindy replied in a dispirited voice.

"What do you think they're going to worry about when they begin to notice that, day after day, they have time on their hands?"

"I see where you're going," Cindy said.

"So," Tim asked, "how do you turn their thoughts from the negative to the positive?"

Cindy thought for almost a minute. "Well, if I understand what you just said, they'll quickly see the extra time and expect a layoff. I may as well admit it and tell them my plans to redirect their extra time."

As she thought, she brightened considerably. "As long as they already know what I know, I can tell them straight out and also let them know how we intend to use the new time productively.

"Oh, my goodness!" she squealed. "This feels *so* good. I can be HONEST!"

"We call that being *transparent*," Tim said. "You can confide in your people now and acknowledge both the hard and exciting truths."

"Okay," Cindy responded distractedly, writing the word *transparent* on a pad. "I need to spend some time thinking about what I want to do first." Then she asked, "If I can tell my people about this, can I ask for their input?"

"Absolutely!" replied Tim, "but I'd wait until you have more data, and you can confirm the new trend."

From Cindy's office, Tim went to Jack's.

Sticking his head in, Tim asked, "Got a sec?"

"Just" came Jack's response.

"I wanted to give you a heads-up," Tim began. He went on to explain one of the advantages of Lean: increased capacity. "That comes in many forms: floor space, machine time, people whose jobs become easier and who have more time on their hands as a result. In the past, there may have been a sense that you'd need to cut your staff back, but that actually works against you. You see, you have trained people who already fit your culture and understand the Copper-Bottom ground rules. That's no small thing. If you got rid of the people made excess by Lean, you'll have two problems: one short-term, one long.

"The short-term problem is that the moment your people realize that by being more efficient someone will be let go, your Lean program is over. Your people will stop volunteering improvements and will only do what's required.

"The long-term problem is that, by letting those people go, you lose the opportunity to take on new business or make your work even more efficient. From what I can tell, your momentary excess labor conditions solve themselves through attrition in a year or less, but you have the good fortune to have a momentary opportunity to use their knowledge and skill to improve things."

Jack said nothing, his face blank.

"I'm telling you this because the event we just conducted appears to have reduced per call CSR time by almost 30%. If that proves to be true, you will have excess time on your CSRs' hands, but what I've proposed to Cindy is that she take one or more CSRs offline and use them to 5S or further improve the CSR process. For example, they might create Standard Work of some of the more complicated CSR processes, actually documenting the single best way to do things that they sometimes get wrong. Or they could rethink some of their processes, shortening them or making them less error-prone."

Again, Jack listened silently. When Tim finished, he spoke.

"That's great news, Tim, but why wouldn't I want to drop our cost by reducing staff? Wouldn't that make us more competitive? It seems to me that I have a chance to reduce the Charleston campus's costs. Why wouldn't I jump on that?"

Tim's excitement from a minute before sank. He suddenly understood why Copper-Bottom had such culture problems. He thought for several seconds before saying in a steely, quiet voice, "Jack, that is certainly your prerogative, but if that is how you treat your employees, it's no wonder that you have a sick culture. This is the other shoe that your people have been waiting to drop. If you lay people off because they found a way to save time, you show them that nothing's really changed in the way you manage, and that means that nothing will change in your culture.

"I'll be honest," Tim continued in a voice barely above a whisper. "If that is how you intend to respond, today will be my last day. I'll notify Don." He stood and left Jack's office.

The euphoric feeling he'd gotten while talking to Cindy was gone. Tim was now crestfallen and, truth be told, angry.

With morale numbers continuing to rise, Jack had been ready to show corporate that he was back on his game, improving morale *and* reducing headcount. Tim's words caught him up short and, quite frankly, stung. As he replayed the situation, he realized that if Tim had worked for him, he'd have fired him on the spot for being so insubordinate. Jack was hurt and angry. A bad combination.

That was when his phone rang and changed the course of events at Copper-Bottom of Charleston.

"Mr. Simmons?" a female voice asked.

"Yes," he responded.

"Please hold for Mr. Franklin."

This couldn't be good, Jack thought. *Why is the CEO calling me?*

The line crackled momentarily. "Go ahead, Mr. Franklin," the female voice said.

"Jack," a male voice boomed. "George Franklin here. I hope I've caught you at a good time."

In all his years with Copper-Bottom, this was only Jack's third interaction with the CEO. The first one was when he was summoned to Corporate Headquarters to be given 90 days to improve the culture. He knew that deadline had been extended, but he'd lost count. *How many days has it been?* he asked himself. After his conversation with Tim, this call had the portent of being a really, really bad one. He waited what seemed like forever until George Franklin's voice continued.

"Jack," Mr. Franklin resumed, "I'm hearing good things out of Charleston. Your financials look strong, and your customer service ratings are the best in the corporation. Whatever you're doing there, keep it up!"

The knot that had formed in Jack's stomach slowly released.

"Thank you, Mr. Franklin," he found himself responding rather mechanically.

"I suppose you weren't expecting good news from me," Mr. Franklin stated. "I hadn't thought of that. Forgive me. I just wanted to compliment your team on their hard work. I'm sending you a little something through inner office mail," The excitement in his voice was unmistakable. "Keep up the good work. I hope to visit you next month when I meet the COO of Friedman Electronics to tour their factory there."

With more excitement in his voice than he felt, Jack said, "Great! I'll look forward to having you."

35

A Second Start

Jack hung up the phone and let out a long cleansing breath. He'd been caught completely off-guard by the CEO's phone call. The call had started with dread, but ended on a high note. Thinking back to the first time he'd been called to Mr. Franklin's office, he realized that by the grace of God, he'd been spared.

Jack had barely put the receiver in its cradle when the phone rang again. This call was from Don.

Upset and not wanting to waste a word on pleasantries, Don jumped right in. "Jack, what were you thinking? Why would you ever consider reducing headcount after a Kaizen event?"

While Jack had been on the phone with the Copper-Bottom CEO, Tim had called Don. Still in the Copper-Bottom parking lot, Tim had told Don of his conversation with Jack. Tim had been nearly apoplectic as he explained Jack's plan to reduce headcount. What he heard infuriated Don as well. Hadn't they warned Jack against this very thing? Now he was blatantly ignoring their advice. Don found it hard to repress his own anger. After everything he and Tim had done for Copper-Bottom, Don took Jack's behavior as a personal affront.

Don pressed on. "Jack, it's abundantly clear why the culture at Copper-Bottom is so poor."

Don waited two beats before saying, "Jim, my boss, just called me to inform me that your CEO is about to visit your facility. Jim has invited him to visit our plant and show him another example of what's possible when you employ Lean. In light of your recent decision, I'm about to ask Jim to cancel and to inform your boss that we'll be ceasing our support of your cultural improvement. What do you think George's response will be?"

DOI: 10.4324/9781003336051-36

Jack felt sick to his stomach again. "Don," Jack began.

Don was silent on the other end of the phone.

"I made a mistake. I figured it out before your call. We can still make this work."

"What makes you think *we* want to help you now?" Don asked.

Jack had no idea where the next words came from. "Look," he began, true contrition in his voice, "I admit I made a mistake. I thought about my personal gain over that of my organization. It was *old* thinking, but I caught myself. I haven't taken any action, nor do I plan to. Isn't that worth something?"

Long seconds passed. Finally, Don said in a quiet voice, "It is, Jack. I just need some time to settle down. Can I call you back?"

"Sure," Jack responded. Don hung up.

At least Don hadn't slammed the phone down, Jack thought. Still, he felt terrible unrest until Don called back an hour later.

Heaven knew Don had made his own mistakes. He wanted to give Jack the benefit of the doubt, but before he did, he needed to calm down. Then he needed to hear Tim's full story. As he usually did in such circumstances, Don walked out to his shop floor. He gained great respect for his people when he was there. Afterward, he'd frequently be in a state of awe at how much his people did for Friedman.

No matter where he went, to Engineering, or Maintenance, or Accounting, or Marketing, he came away with the same sense of awe and respect. He could no longer understand leaders who didn't listen to their people, who had no idea what problems their employees encountered, who hadn't discovered how important it was for them to use the full power of their office to help their people overcome the obstacles in their work.

Returning to his office in a better frame of mind, Don acknowledged that there was no doubt that Jack had screwed up. Even Jack admitted it. But truthfully, there was no question that the situation could be salvaged. So far, the entire incident was between Jack, Tim, and himself.

With new perspective, Don called Tim and invited him to his office.

When Tim arrived, he was still wound up. He hadn't had the benefit of overhearing Don's recent phone call with Jack. It was going take some time for Tim to come to peace with all that had transpired. Don knew the best way to begin that process was to just listen to Tim's thoughts on what had transpired. Then he'd tell Tim what had transpired since he'd left Copper-Bottom and then have Tim walk him through *next steps*. He wanted to get Tim thinking constructively and to move past this momentary hiccup.

After Tim finished recounting what had gone on at Copper-Bottom, Don explained what had occurred since. "Here's the thing, Tim," Don assured him. "We can still make this work, but I wonder if this isn't as much my fault as Jack's."

Tim looked at Don, puzzled.

"Think about it," Don pursued. "Jack's response was totally in keeping with how he's been taught to think: business school and decades of previous leaders all emphasized that his primary, if not only, job was to protect and improve the company's bottom line; not grow his people. His response implies that I haven't done a good enough job of explaining to the Copper-Bottom leaders what changes Lean thinking requires.

"You and I know that the two pillars of the Toyota Way are continuous *improvement* and *respect for people,* but they don't. I think it's time I had that discussion with them. We made coaching performance about developing dialog with their people. That was a good thing, but did I explain why it was important? They need to understand that coaching is as much about respecting their people as improving performance. It's about developing rapport with their subordinates. As their people feel respected, morale and *the culture* will improve. As employees feel respected, they become more open to offering their insights that can help the organization improve. In short, respect for people leads to continuous improvement."

Tim now understood what Don was driving at.

He was quiet for several seconds. When he finally spoke, he said, "It wasn't just you, Don. I let myself get enticed into confusing bold improvements with achieving our mission. You're exactly right. I need to refocus on developing respect for people. *That's* what will change their culture for the better.

"If you think about it," Tim continued, "Copper-Bottom has actually made significant strides. It's just that they're so new to this that their leaders don't think of what they're learning as a lifelong behavior. As so often happens, they see what we've been doing as a project with a finite duration. They are expecting that when we leave, what we've taught them will be over and they can go back to the way things were. I think we need to restate that there's no going back, that what they're learning is the way things will be for the rest of their lives."

Pausing a second, Tim went on. "Realizing that's how they see things makes Jack's behavior a lot more understandable. Hopefully, your conversation has helped him to see why his initial instinct was not in keeping with his new course of pursuit."

Pausing even longer, Tim said, "I owe him an apology, don't I?"

Don asked, "Had a consultant talked to you that way, how do you think you'd feel?"

"Put that way, I'm sure I owe him an apology," Tim stated.

"I think so, too," Don said. "I'm not condoning his initial response, but I am confident that your apology will go a long way toward restoring relations with him, so yeah, apologizing is the right thing to do, and the sooner the better."

Shifting gears, Don asked, "You good?"

"I am, sir," Tim replied.

"Okay then," Don said, returning to his earlier discussion of respect for people. "How do we get Copper-Bottom to think in those terms?"

Tim thought for a moment. "We've got to go back to teaching senior managers Lean leadership behaviors."

Although he knew the answer, Don asked, "How do we do that?"

Tim responded, "We've got to train them to spend more time with their people. They need to get firsthand knowledge of what their people are doing so they can see the obstacles their people face and help remove them."

"And how do we do that?" Don asked.

"I think we should begin Gemba walking with the leaders," Tim replied, "and using the walks as coachable moments."

"And what do we want them to learn?" Don asked.

"That their wealth lies in their employees and that a significant part of their job is to grow and mature their employees; yes, grow the business, but to do so in a way that grows their employees at the same time."

"Okay," Don said, "and how do they do that?"

"Let me think," Tim said, growing quiet.

"Well …," he began after several beats. What followed was stream of conscious discussion, but on target all the same.

"… when we started, we said that we'd teach them to create Key Performance Indicators and then to use those to *coach* their people. As with most new initiatives, Copper-Bottom's leaders took to creating KPIs readily enough, but looking back, I realize they've been treating KPIs as an end in itself. They don't see how critical they can be to growing their people and managing their business.

"Plus, KPIs are being used by some to continue the old blame game. So, if we're going to get the train back on its tracks, we'll have to begin there: Coaching.

"I see your point, Don," the younger man said. "This is going to take you. Clearly Jack doesn't fully understand, so he can't lead this. I think he's going to require someone he considers a peer to guide him and his leaders through this. Besides," Tim admitted sheepishly, "I may have burned a bridge there."

Until the last sentence, Don had nodded his agreement. It always pleased him when Tim saw the bigger picture as well as the small one.

"I think you wounded Jack's pride," Don admitted, "but I think he also saw the passion you have for Lean and his people. I suspect he's a bit ashamed that you had more passion for his people than he did. He'll come around. But you're right, for the time being I need to lead the next phase."

"One other thing?" Tim asked.

Don nodded.

"We know leadership—as versus management—is about setting an example for subordinates to follow. Anyone can *talk* change, but leadership is about *being* that change, *modeling* that change. Neither Jack nor his direct reports are modeling that change yet. We had said from the outset that we were going to teach them to use KPIs to change their relationship with their people. I think we need to do more work there.

"Your boss," Tim continued, "has taught us that leaders need to start generating time to actually see what's going on. That means they have to eliminate or delegate more of what currently occupies their time on a day-to-day basis.

"When they're not in meetings, Jack and his executives stay in their offices. What does Stephen Covey call it? 'Majoring in minors'? The result is that they rarely get out to their actual work areas to observe what's going on and listen to their people. Think about what a surprise it was to Jack when he learned that the software his people depended on didn't refresh for 24 hours and that they were printing all that paper to work around a busted system.

"Not only do Copper-Bottom leaders not coach; they don't make humble inquiry and certainly don't use the Socratic method of coaching their people.

"I know these are *behaviors* and not activities, but isn't that what we're trying to change: Behavior?

"I mean," Tim continued, "we came here to help them change a culture."

Then, in a moment of candor, Tim confessed, "I'm starting to see that I've behaved as if I've been working in our own organization. I keep forgetting that the folks on the ground floor, where I've been working, always adapt quickly. It's senior and middle managers who fight the change. I know that, yet I took my focus off them. That's my error."

Don realized that Tim's profession was a close cousin to Hansei: the Japanese act of self-reflection, expressing contrition, and developing a plan to improve. Don chose that moment to pick up the thread. "Tim," he admitted, "you're not alone. It's too easy to fall into old habits. I haven't visited as much as I should have, and, to your point of a minute ago, I need to be the one to work with Jack and his staff.

"I guess," Don concluded, "we need to start again.

"How about this," Don asked. "Let's start with Jack and his direct reports. I'll invite them here today at"—he consulted his watch—"3:00 this afternoon? We'll give them a factory tour and pair them up with their counterparts in our organization. We'll ask them to spend no less than half an hour a day for the next couple of weeks with their counterpart from Friedman, preferably when the latter is Gemba walking. We can even get our people to go there and coach them as they Gemba walk."

"I like that!" Tim agreed. "That is exactly what they've needed. They've had no example to follow and no one with whom to commiserate."

"How about I meet them in the lobby and guide them to the large conference room? You can meet us there," Don suggested.

Plans made, the pair agreed to meet in a little over an hour.

36

Truly Leading

Don's plan totally disrupted Jack's day, but he wanted to show Don he was willing to do what it took to get his organization back on track. He asked his subordinates to drop everything and meet him at Friedman Electronics at 2:50.

As they entered the conference room, Tim could see from the faces of Jack's people that they weren't happy to be here. They saw this impromptu meeting as a big waste of time and wondered how Friedman felt they had the authority to take them away from their business. Nonetheless, what followed changed the tide and truly impressed Tim.

At 3:01, each of Don's direct reports filed into the conference room. Don introduced each by name and title, and asked if Jack would have his people pair off with their counterpart.

When that process was over, Jack began what might be considered the Lean altar call.

"No doubt those of you from Copper-Bottom are wondering where this is all coming from. Let me put this meeting in context."

Don could see Jack squirm, as if the mistake he'd made earlier in the day was about to be revealed, but that wasn't the way Don worked.

"We agreed to help Copper-Bottom *change their culture*, whatever that means." There were smiles and rib jabs among the Copper-Bottom people. "Well, let me give you a look into Copper-Bottom as we arrived," Don continued.

"You'd just settled a lawsuit from an employee for creating a hostile workplace. You had a senior staff member refuse to participate in anything that would cause him to change his behavior, and he ultimately had to be terminated. You had a workplace that could best be described with the terms 'squalor' and 'chaos.' And you had a workforce that operated in an atmosphere of fear.

"Jack," Don paused, "is anything I said incorrect?"

Jack was a trooper, but then he and Don had discussed this during the call that set this meeting up. "No, Don," he acknowledged. "Sadly, that is an accurate assessment."

"Okay," Don continued, "the purpose of this visit isn't to beat you down or humiliate you. Actually, I want to acknowledge that I've let you down. There were things I should have done, but haven't. Forgive me. We've asked you here to acknowledge my failure and to give you a picture of what a workplace *can* look like.

"What I'm going to ask each of you to do is to take a walk alongside your counterpart. We're going to start at what we call our Division's *Wall*," Don said.

The Friedman personnel led their counterparts to the wall of the plant where Don's KPIs were posted.

Don turned to his procurement manager and asked, "Andre, will you identify yourself and explain what we're seeing?"

"Hi, everyone. I'm Andre. I am the procurement manager for this division of Friedman Electronics. And this," he said, sweeping his arm across the wall like a TV spokesperson, "is our division's *Wall*." Andre added emphasis to the last word. "We post our division's monthly performance metrics here. These graphs reflect how we're performing as a division of Friedman Electronics."

Andre paused to let what he'd just said sink in, then said, "Of course, the top row displays our performance against the critical measures of our business, as set forth by our Corporate Headquarters." Without looking at the board, Andre used his fingers to count off their key metrics: "Employee Safety, Product Quality, On-Time Delivery, and Product Cost, which we break into labor cost and material cost.

"So, looking at the Safety KPI, this run chart shows that we're currently at 99.85% injury-free against a goal of 100%. In the note," Andre said, pointing to the *NOTES* box on the chart, "I can see that we had a slipping injury three months ago. It was not a lost-time injury, but the mere fact that the incident occurred suggests we lost our focus on Employee Safety."

Don stopped his procurement manager and asked, "Andre, why is Safety first?"

Without hesitation, Andre responded, "Because we believe that our employees are truly our most important asset. They rely on us, their leaders, to keep their workplace hazard-free. We believe that when one of them is injured, it means their leaders failed them. An injury could mean that they lost an hour or more being examined by a physician before returning to work. It could also mean months of convalescing after a serious injury.

"To our business, it means lost productivity, but to our employee, it means lost income. Short-term disability only pays 60% of the employee's wage. That can really hurt them financially and make them resentful of the company that let them get hurt in the first place. That also creates an atmosphere in which employees don't trust their employer to take care of them, and that invites everything from gossip to resignations.

"As managers," Andre continued, "each of us feels we let our employees down if they're injured."

Switching gears, Andre said, "Of course, injuries are a lagging indicator, meaning something's already gone wrong by the time we can measure it. We prefer to look at *leading* indicators: measures that predict that something *may* go wrong. We conduct a weekly safety audit as well as daily workstation audits to try to catch things that have the *potential* to create an injury.

"Should I keep going?" Andre asked Don.

"Please." Don smiled.

"The next KPI is Quality. We know that no matter how quickly we deliver or how low our price is, the moment our products go into a customer's products, they affect our customer's reputation in the market. If our product fails, it gives our customer a black eye. That's not good, so our first measure of Quality is a leading indicator: Quality at the source, or the location where the product is actually built.

"Every handoff, from one operation to the next, involves a quality check by the operation receiving the product. In essence, each operation *buys* the product from the previous operation. To do that, they inspect the product for the value-added improvements made at the previous operations. If they find any defects, they do not accept the product and return it immediately to the previous operation for correction. They also record that incident on a document they turn in at the end of the shift. We add up all those defects and examine them by product, operation, department, and division.

"It's worth pointing out," Andre said, interrupting his own monolog, "that we do the same thing with paper processes in our offices. As we process documents from one operation to the next, the first act is to scan the document for flaws and errors. If there is a flaw, or something missing, it is returned for correction.

"The second, and far worse, measure of Quality is from field returns. A field return means that the product got to our customer, and they found the problem. Any time that happens, it makes the quality of *ALL* our products suspect. So far this year, we have not had a single field return. We also went all last year without one.

"As I said, we take quality extremely seriously. Any questions?" Andre asked. There were none.

Continuing, he said, "When we accept an order, we make a commitment to our customer. We promise to meet not only their specifications but their delivery requirement. Some companies disregard the customer's delivery needs, replacing them with their own standard lead times. Our belief is that our customers come to us for their most dire needs. If humanly possible, we will agree to their delivery date. If not, we will tell them what we *can* achieve. If they agree, that becomes the delivery date.

"Since you don't come from our industry, I can only tell you that our approach is novel. We used to charge an expediting fee when we agreed to the customer's delivery date, but we no longer do. Do we leave money on the table? Sure, but we try to cultivate long-term *relationships* with our customers. We believe that if we meet their needs this time, they'll be back with future orders. We're right more often than not."

Looking up at the chart, Andre said, "By the way, our on-time delivery is currently sitting at 98.7% for the year, with over 15,000 orders and 225,000 line items shipped.

"The next measure is of our product's cost. As I said, we look at our Cost of Goods Sold, or COGS, as a way of understanding how we're performing." Andre pointed to a graph which had what looked like a straight line. On closer inspection, the line dipped down slightly the further to the right it got.

"It takes a lot of work to keep our GOGS low," Andre continued. "For instance, we work with our designers to design with the least expensive and highest-quality materials available. We aren't looking for *cheapest*. We want the lowest price among those materials already identified as meeting our rigorous specifications.

"We work with our suppliers to ensure that they are constantly on the lookout for better, more efficient ways to make the things we buy from them.

"We don't beat up our suppliers, as some suspect, but we do constantly challenge them. We work with them, too. We have ways of making it worth their while to keep their Quality and On-Time Delivery high while dropping their price. They can't always meet our expectations, but they take our business seriously and do their best to meet our needs. We consider them more than suppliers. We think of them as *partners*, as they truly partner with us in the development of the best product of which we are jointly capable of producing.

"Like most organizations, we also monitor labor costs, both direct and indirect. We have yet to cut an employee to make our product less expensive, but we constantly try to find ways to reduce the labor content in our products. The result is that we can make more products than before with the same number of employees."

"What about morale?" someone asked.

"Great question," Andre said. "We used to conduct a semiannual anonymous survey to find out what our people felt about working here. Two things changed that. The first was that we reached a point at which our scores leveled out for six consecutive semesters. They were all in the high 90s. Then, we started being measured by a well-known financial magazine and we found that our employees consistently rated us among the top 10 employers in our field.

"Not to be smart"—Andre smiled—"but we decided to let the magazine do the legwork while we concentrated on what we do best." There were nods from the Copper-Bottom leaders.

"Anything else?" Andre asked Don.

"No, Andre, nicely done," Don complimented him.

Changing topics, Don said to the group, "Let's move to a board a level below mine. Any of my directors want to volunteer?" he asked. Three hands shot up. Don pointed to his Engineering Director. "You sure you're up to this, Amy?" he asked with a wink and a smile. Amy's immediate response was to put her fists on her hips and give Don the evil eye. That drew a laugh from the crowd.

"Okay," Don agreed with a laugh. "Engineering it is."

Amy led the tour to the Engineering bay, where they found her KPI board right on the aisle as they walked in. Its location guaranteed that all her people saw it coming and going.

"Like Don's board," she began, "we measure the same four metrics: Safety, Quality, On-Time Delivery, and Cost." She pointed to her safety chart. "Our department conducts a weekly safety audit. We use a standard checklist and look for things like exposed wires, extension cords, trip hazards, slip hazards, etc. There are 20 questions on the checklist. Each week's score is recorded on the department's run chart, and we discuss it at our weekly briefing."

Engineering's safety chart showed a line that vacillated between 97% and 100%. Amy pointed to the previous week's audit, which also hung on the KPI board. It listed all of the things they inspected and the score they'd received for each.

For each item measured, the form outlined conditions that met the requirements for that score. Each item could receive a score from 0 to 5, with 5 being the highest. All but a few of Engineering's scores were 5s.

"Next up is Quality," Amy said, pointing to that chart. "My team and I agreed that Engineering Change Orders (ECOs) would be an apt measure of our quality. We figured that, unless the customer paid us to change a drawing, a change order as much as implied that there had been something wrong with the original document, or at least that the drawing had been ambiguous and needed clarification. Further, my engineers and I agreed that not all ECOs resulted from defects; some were actually a proactive attempt to improve our design, so we set the goal for ECOs at two or fewer per month."

Amy pointed to the trend line. It was averaging 4 per month for the last three months but had been as high as 28 in the previous year. The line had steadily trended down.

"Admittedly, we seem to have hit a plateau," Amy acknowledged, "but we agree as a team that we'll break through the barrier in the next couple of months. We're already brainstorming ideas on how to reach that goal."

She pointed to the On-Time chart. "Like Don, we look at On-Time Delivery from our customer's eyes. Our primary customer is manufacturing. If we're late, they need to make up the time. That often leads to bad outcomes of either quality or schedule, so," Amy pressed forward, "we set the project manager's desired date as our delivery date. We had a terrible time meeting it at first, in part because our engineers were used to designing everything from scratch and using components that were often just entering the market: what some call *bleeding-edge technology*. That created a host of problems in manufacturing, but we had our own set of problems with designing products with the latest technology."

"Like what?" asked a Copper-Bottom manager.

"New electrical components often have bugs that need to be worked out and frequently suffer from infant mortality. If the supplier makes modifications to eliminate a problem, and up-revs their drawing," she continued, "that causes us to up-rev our own drawing, and that results in an unanticipated ECO."

"What does that mean: up-rev?" someone asked.

"Good point," Amy agreed. "'Rev' is an abbreviation for a *revision*. When we first produce a drawing, it doesn't have a revision number. Each time we modify it, we increase the drawing's revision level. For example, the first revision becomes *Rev A*. The next *Rev B*, and so on. Did that answer your question?"

"Yes, thank you."

"Where was I?" Amy asked herself out loud. "Ah, yes, how we reduced the bulk of our design changes. So, as a team, the Engineering department decided we wouldn't use a component in our designs until it had been in the market for at least six months, or unless the supplier could offer us data that showed the part's quality was stable. In those cases, we left the option open to use it earlier.

"The other problem we discovered that drove our design changes was the fact that we designed everything from scratch. Every design started *tabula rasa:* as a blank slate. That meant that we had to suffer through our own drawing mistakes until the design became stable.

"One of our engineers suggested that we start with a design that was already stable and simply modify it to meet the new purpose. The rest of the engineers agreed that made sense. After beta testing the concept, the team agreed to adopt that as our standard. The number of design errors that decision prevented was staggering.

"Keep in mind," Amy instructed her audience, "every one of our design changes had to be paid for by the project manager, and sometimes drove our product cost to be uncompetitive.

"Then there was the problem that design changes often delayed our on-time delivery to our internal customer: manufacturing. In the end, both project managers and manufacturing got on our case and aggressively challenged us to improve. We have a way to go, but we're a lot better than we used to be," she concluded.

"I'll say," someone said sarcastically from the audience.

"Thanks, Cheryl," Amy replied equally sarcastically, singling out the employee who had commented.

"For those of you who don't know, Cheryl is our Director of Manufacturing," Amy informed the group.

The crowd laughed.

"Amy," Don asked, "how did your engineers feel about being measured?"

If she'd been prepared for the question, it wasn't obvious. "Of course you know the answer, Don, but for everyone's benefit, I'll simply say they hated it. There were all kinds of conspiracy theories about what was about to happen once the numbers came out: There'd be terminations, reorganizations, alien abductions, you name it; however, when we got them involved in defining how we'd measure, those concerns melted away."

Amy paused a second, then added, "Although I'm not sure anyone would volunteer it, I think the team is proud of their accomplishments. They know they've made a lot of progress and that they are making Friedman more competitive."

One of the Copper-Bottom people raised their hand. "So, if you have fewer design changes, have you let people go? I mean, it seems to me that you wouldn't need as many engineers if you weren't having to repair your drawings." By the time she finished asking the question, the woman was blushing. She knew that to answer, Amy was going to have to divulge business-critical information.

"Very insightful question," Amy complimented the woman. "Let me answer you with equal bluntness. Before we started on our Lean journey, Jim, our corporate Vice President of Operations, made it clear that no one would lose their job because of Lean. He was emphatic and gave us his rationale.

"He said, 'The moment you start using Lean as a tool to identify people to let go, becomes the moment the implementation of Lean stops, and things stop improving.'

"That statement made a lot of sense to me, but Jim went on. He said, 'Layoffs are the sign of weak management. Weak managers see excess people as a problem. Strong managers see them as an opportunity. Freed up employees represent new capacity to do even more work. Strong managers,' Jim said, 'look for ways to use that new capacity fruitfully.'"

Amy was getting worked up. "Most organizations have statements in their marketing material that says something to the effect that 'our employees are our most important asset.' Right?"

There were nods and murmured assents.

"Makes for great PR," Amy continued, "but then you get to their accounting organizations and find that they carry people as liabilities on their books. Machines are book assets, but people are liabilities. That means that the moment the stuff hits the fan, the controller is advising that we need a layoff.

"Anyone see the duplicity in that?"

This time, there was a more vocal agreement.

"Well, I found out that, here at Friedman Electronics, we practice something called Lean Accounting. The upshot is that we count people as assets."

Amy paused before going on.

"In the years since Jim told us we were never to lay anyone off because they found a way to eliminate themselves or a colleague from a process, I've thought about his statement a lot. Here are some of the conclusions I've come to.

"Do you mind?" Amy shot Don a glance. He gave her a thumbs-up.

Amy used her fingers to count off the list.

- "The cost of the now-excess employee is already fully accounted for in the price of our product, so even though they are not needed to do their old job, their cost is already accounted for and fully funded.
- If you're creative, you can always find ways to redeploy people to *make* their work more impactful. We realized that we had design projects we'd never been able to tackle because we were always too busy. So we took a senior engineer and put him in charge of those projects. One of the tasks we charged him with was finding ways to develop drawings faster and with fewer errors. That is what resulted in our decision to modify previously successful designs when making new products. In addition, he developed a new protocol for designing products. We also asked him to evaluate the possibility of redeploying engineers to the factory floor. After study, he suggested that engineers be made an integral part of each manufacturing cell, and that they be held accountable for designs that impact those cells.

That decision has led to a reduction in assembly time, manufacturing cost, and an increase in overall product quality.

- In addition to what Jim had said, I slowly came to recognize that continuous improvement depends on employees being willing to take a risk, being open to trying something new. People who don't trust their leaders to protect their jobs are fearful of change and will not take risks. They will not suggest labor-saving techniques if it means that they, or another employee, will be let go as a result. In short, continuous improvement *only* occurs in a climate of trust and transparency.

"Did I answer your question?" Amy asked.

"You did," the woman answered, a bit awed.

Amy waited as the silence grew. "No doubt some of you are saying to yourselves, *This is a manufacturing company, we don't make anything. How could any of this apply to us at Copper-Bottom?* Am I right?" she asked.

No one responded, but she could tell she'd hit a nerve.

Amy pointed to the woman who'd asked the last question. "What do you do? What processes do you use?"

Again, the woman blushed crimson but responded, "I speak to customers and advise them about their medical plans."

"What starts your process?" Amy asked.

"Usually, a phone call from a customer," responded the other woman.

"What ends your process?" asked Amy.

"The customer hanging up after their questions have been answered."

"Are there steps in between?" Amy asked.

"Yes. Of course," came the response.

"So," Amy summarized, "your job involves performing a process. Is that about right?"

The woman nodded.

"Guess what? My job starts when I get an engineering design request from a customer, usually a program manager. And it ends when my team delivers a design. So, you and I both use processes to do our jobs, and it's processes that we have in common. That's what links all of this," Amy stated, sweeping her hand around the building.

"There's another thing we have in common," she pointed out. "We both accomplish our jobs for people and through people. So, we share People and Processes in common.

"Here's my point," summarized Amy. "Lean isn't about an industry or whether you have a product or service. It works anywhere there are people and processes. Don't get hung up on the whole product-versus-service thing. Think about it. My team and I provide a service inside a company that manufactures a product. Lean works for us both. And our lives—those of my team and I, as well as those of the manufacturing team—are better for it."

If Amy had gotten through, it wasn't clear. The woman who'd asked the question had her head down the whole time, as if listening intently. Now she quietly nodded, eyes still downcast. When the crowd moved on, the woman hung behind and asked Amy if she might call her later. Amy gave her a business card and said she'd look forward to it. The woman quickly rejoined the tour.

37

Standard Work and Water Spiders

The last KPI board they visited was for someone who worked much closer to the product. The speaker, although neat and presentable, wore cotton clothing and had signs of light dirt on his pants. They learned that he was Scott Bennet, supervisor of the final assembly crew.

After Don introduced him, Scott walked to his KPI board and began explaining his KPIs. It was clear that he'd have rather had a root canal, but his discomfort with public speaking was not the result of a lack of knowledge.

"My first KPI is Safety," he began in a bit of a monotone. He quickly explained that his crew conducted a daily safety audit, looking for things like frayed wires, broken machine guards, leaks, sharp objects, basically anything that could cause an injury. "Each operator has a safety audit form specific to his or her area. I compile those scores and that number gets posted here," he said, pointing to his Safety chart.

Scott was about to move to his next KPI when Don asked, "Scott, can you explain the sheet below your Safety chart?" The Copper-Bottom crew realized these sheets had been below every chart they'd seen thus far.

Action Item List

Item#	Date	Problem	Description	Responsible (Name)	Due Date	Status	Comments
1							
2							
3							
4							
5							
6							
7							
8							
9							
10							
11							
12							

"Yes, sir," Scott said, a bit flustered. It was clear that Don had thrown his rhythm off.

"That's an Action Item List. If we discover something during our audit, it's my job to log it here. The team identifies who the owner will be, and it's usually the person who is closest to the problem. The owner then identifies and takes the appropriate action. In a safety example, that usually means writing a maintenance work request. I log the REQ# here, too.

"Every line item on the Action Item List has a requirement to identify the problem, the owner, the action taken, and a due date. We do that so that there is always someone whose job it is to accomplish the action by the due date. It's my job to follow up on all open actions and make sure progress is being made.

"As you can see," Scott said, pointing to his KPI board, "every chart has an Action Item List below it, and we review those every morning during our daily huddle to make sure all open actions are being completed on time."

Scott looked at Don, as if seeking permission to move on. Don nodded.

Pointing to the second chart on his board, Scott said, "Our second KPI is Quality. Here we post the sum of the defects we discover during the day." The chart revealed that Scott's team was averaging about six defects a day against a target of five.

"How come you're above your target?" someone asked.

"Ah, yeah," Scott began. "Well, we recently added a new operator and they're still learning the ropes," he explained. "Plus, we dropped the goal from 10 to 5 defects per day a little over two months ago. I suppose it might help to understand that this number used to be over 100 every day and we're now faithfully below 10."

"Scott," Don suggested, "maybe it would help the Copper-Bottom folks to understand what you count as a defect."

"Yes, sir," Scott replied. Thinking for a second, he said, "We have a cell here." He motioned to the work benches arranged in a U-shape behind him. "My people assemble metal cabinets in a pass-along line. The first operation takes painted parts and begins snapping or bolting them together. As you can see, the assembly is pushed along rollers to the next operation, and the next and the next; each operation adds their value to the assembly.

"At each station, the operator's first job is to examine the raw material, or work in process, for defects. At the first operation, that might be a flaw in the paint or a burr on the part. Once the operator discovers a flaw, they cannot use that part. They mark the flaw on the part with a grease pencil and set it on their *defects* table." Scott pointed to a table near the paint area.

"Of course," he continued, "if a subsequent operation finds a flaw in the way the previous operation assembled the part, that too is counted as a defect. But instead of putting it on the defect table, the assembler stops the process and reviews the problem with the previous assembler. The previous assembler then has to repair the problem and pass it back. After correction, the product gets reviewed again and is only accepted when it's correct. Using this methodology, we ensure that defects become opportunities for immediate feedback and, if necessary, retraining. Although we corrected the defect, we still add it to the list of defects discovered."

There was a stack of Action Item Lists below the defect chart. Scott explained that *every* defect got recorded, along with what action was taken and by whom. "Assemblers keep blank copies of defect sheets at their bench." He walked over and took one from a stack on an assembler's bench, passing it to the crowd.

They could see a mechanical drawing of a part on the sheet, along with a column of words. Scott explained that the assembler marked an 'X' in the area on the sketch where the defect was found and then circled one or more of the words. "For example," he explained, "if the assembler finds a dent on the part, he'll 'X' the area where the dent was found and circle the word *dent*."

Scott flipped through the sheaf of Action Item pages and said, "We used to require the assembler to stop and log each defect on the Action Item sheet, but realized that was taking away from valuable assembly time. Now we ask each operator to submit a single-page defect log for their station each day. That shows me how many defects we had at each station. I post the composite here, but keep separate charts in my office to track defects by station. I use those charts during my weekly review with each assembler, and we talk about their plans to improve. We also review the previous week's charts to make sure that operators aren't backsliding. Having charts by station also helps me understand if I need to retrain my people or elevate problems to my boss. I'd do that if we were consistently getting defective work passed to us from other groups, like paint or metal fab."

Scott realized this had been a long explanation and sheepishly asked Don, "Is that what you meant, sir?"

"That's super, Scott," Don encouraged him.

Scott continued, talking about his Schedule and Cost charts. On his schedule chart, he said, "We need to produce a certain number of parts each day in order to meet customer demand. To do that, we need to produce a certain number an hour. Every hour, the lead assembler tracks the line's performance against that target.

"So," Scott said, pointing to a small board at the end of the assembly line, "you can see we need to make 13 of these assemblies every hour to meet demand. In the first, second, and third hours they hit that number. In hour four, there was a problem and they only made 11. You can see to the far right of that board that, Pete, our lead assembler, took action to catch up. I can't read it from here, but I know he called maintenance to repair an air hose for a pneumatic wrench and contacted me to get another assembler to help them catch up.

"You can see that in hour 5 they assembled 15, which put them back on track. So, on this chart," Scott summarized as he pointed to his Schedule KPI, "I show the total number of parts assembled each day against the target of 104, or 13/hr × 8 hours. As you can see, we're very consistent about making that goal. My folks know that to miss that goal means missing our commitment to our external customer and … well, neither Cheryl nor Don look favorably on that." The crowd chuckled in response.

Scott explained that his Cost KPI was a function of labor and material. Labor was calculated by the number of people on his line times the number of hours they worked. "I don't need to worry about what we paid each worker. My job is to keep hours in control. So, for instance, I went an hour over today when we added an assembler to catch back up after the air hose problem. We made our daily commitment, but we paid for an extra hour of labor to do it."

"When it comes to material, we use Standard Work, so we know the exact number of screws, nuts, bolts, washers, and panels we need to assemble this product. We also know the cost of each component. With those two things, material costs are easy to calculate. Labor costs are equally simple, and their sum becomes the product's cost.

"For example, it's pretty safe to say that we'll make 104 assemblies today. We know the cost of all the components, but we added two more hours of labor, or two people at an hour each, to meet the demand. That will increase today's costs."

Someone raised their hand. "Can you explain this *Standard Work?*" they asked.

"I can," began Scott. "Let me see if I can make my explanation short." He paused as he formulated his response.

"Standard Work is the single best way to perform a job as of today. For instance, we use Standard Work to assemble this cabinet." He walked over to a bench and grabbed a thin binder. He handed it to the Copper-Bottom employee who had asked the question. The binder was soon making its way through the crowd.

On the first page were photos of the components and tools used to assemble the cabinet at station #1. Each component was neatly laid out and grouped with like components, so it was easy to see and count what was needed to complete this assembly. One didn't need to count, though, as every part was labeled with the names and quantities of the components, as were the tool and cabinet parts.

Page two contained step-by-step photos of station #1's assembly process. Each photo showed what took place at that station in sequential order. There was also a photo of what the finished assembly looked like when the work at that station was complete. There were text boxes and arrows indicating common problems to look for before counting the process as complete.

In every case, the photos were labeled and, where appropriate, arrows pointed to the exact spot where the action was happening. While elegantly simple, it was equally informative. There were very few words, and most were verbs explaining what action was taking place in the photo.

"I should point out," Scott broke the silence that had ensued as the Copper-Bottom people examined the book, "that this is the best known way to perform this assembly *today*. As we learn new techniques or use different tools, we update the Standard. Until we do, every step must be performed the same way every time, and that is the way documented in the Standard.

"It's my job," he explained, "to make sure that the standard is being followed. Every day, I observe my people performing their tasks and make sure that they are adhering to the standard. If not, I point out the error and work with them until they are able to perform the task correctly. I've been doing that a lot with our new assembler," he noted, "but he's about 85% of the way there."

There was a pause while Scott waited for the binder to circulate through the crowd, then he began again.

"Creating Standard Work is a bit more involved so I won't get into that, but every step is timed, and the number of stations and operators are calculated. Because they're timed, we can calculate exactly how long each subassembly takes, and how long it takes to make an entire assembly. We balance those times so that every station is within seconds of the others. That's how we know that we can make 13 assemblies per hour.

"Now," Scott stated, "since we know exactly what hardware and panels are used in this assembly, and since we also know how long it takes to build a cabinet, it's easy to calculate the cost per assembly."

"Wait!" It was Jack this time. "You're calculating cost at your level?"

Scott looked at Don as if he'd said something wrong. Don gave Scott a smile of encouragement but answered this question himself.

"Good catch, Jack. One of the things my team and I realized was that, by the time we calculated the numbers in Accounting, any ability to control them was long past. We decided to let the people with the ability to control our spending keep track of it.

"Scott," Don asked, "Can you explain what you do each day to track your cost and how you do it?"

"Yes, sir," Scott responded. "Cost is one of the ways I get assessed. Even though Accounting will calculate the cost for our books, I review my costs daily. At the end of the month, we're generally within pennies of what Accounting calculates.

"I share an employee, Avery, with another supervisor. Avery keeps track of our inventory for us. From Standard Work, we know exactly how many panels, nuts, screws, bolts, and washers go into every product. Every day, Avery makes sure that our consumption for that day matches what we produced.

"In addition, Avery matches our consumption with our receipts. All our panels come directly from paint. Avery monitors panel receipts and consumption. Our hardware suppliers deliver our hardware right to our supply bins. They do so in whole boxes. When Avery opens a new box, he always counts what's already in the bin, adds the quantity in the new box, and ensures the new count matches his records. That way, we know exactly what the hardware cost of our product is at this operation."

Scott looked at Don. "Is it all right to talk about our plans?" he asked.

Don nodded with a smile.

"Right now, operators spend about half an hour *picking* their materials for the day. They then arrange it for ready use at their stations. When it comes to hardware: nuts, bolts, screws, and washers, they never want to run out. They often *pick* more than what's needed, for example, they'll just fill a bin with bolts or nuts, never counting. That means that, at the end of the day, Avery has to account for everything left in their bins in addition to what's left in the stock bins. So, we are looking at implementing a new position called a *Water Spider*.

"The role of the water spider is to stock each station with exactly what they'll need to build ONE product. Once per assembly, the water spider replenishes the line while the assemblers continue to work. Data say that with an extra half an hour of assembler time, we should be able to build one additional product per day. That turns out to be worth well more than the cost of the additional labor.

"To implement the water spider role, we'll be bringing on a new assembler who was made excess on another line. That will allow us to replace our best cabinet assembler, who will become the water spider.

"In addition to being a material handler, the water spider is also a utility player. They are typically the most experienced assembler on the line. In our case, that assembler is Gabe. Because Gabe can already perform any job on the line, his knowledge and skill make it possible for him to step into any job to spell an assembler while the latter takes a restroom break or gets a drink of water.

"Moreover, if the line falls a little behind—like today—the water spider can step in and help catch it up. And"—Scott smiled—"his labor is already part of my cost, so I won't be charged more when he helps us catch up."

Scott looked at Don, who said, "Great job, Scott. Thank you." Scott nodded at Don, and the tour moved away.

38

Putting It All Together

The group returned to the conference room. Once they were all seated, Don asked, "What did you see?" It was an open-ended question that resulted in a variety of insights. Don nodded at each, not seeming to be looking for any particular answer.

When the observations stopped, he asked, "Were there any similarities between the measures on my board and those of my subordinates?" After a moment of silence, someone said, "Their KPIs all measured the same things as yours."

Don said, "Good observation. The fact that we all measure the same things creates *alignment*. Alignment ensures we're all pursuing the same goal. Further, every last person knows how their contributions lead to the company's success. KPI boards, from top to bottom, create that link."

Next, Don asked, "If an operation begins to slip, how long do you think it takes before the leadership team knows?"

Silence. Then another Copper-Bottom employee said, "It varied. In Scott and Amy's areas, their boards got updated daily, so you'd know the next day, but Scott's lead person's board got updated hourly. For that one process, you'd know every hour."

"Great observational analysis," Don complimented the woman. "So, if I can fill in the blanks, would I be correct in saying that here at Friedman, the closer we get to the actual work, the quicker we know if there was a problem?"

The woman thought for a second and said, "Yes."

"Do you think that's important?" asked Don.

"Are you asking me?" the woman stammered.

"I am," Don said. "What's your opinion?"

"If I were to guess," she responded, "I'd say that it was important."

Pointing to another Copper-Bottom leader, Don asked, "Would you say that the sooner we know there's the problem, the sooner we can take action to resolve it?"

The employee nodded.

"Now, here's a tough question," Don began. "Tell me, who was in charge of our assembly process? Who ran each operation?"

There were several seconds of silence as the Copper-Bottom leaders thought back, then someone volunteered, "It seems like the person closest to the work was actually in charge, that they had the authority to solve their own problems. I mean, the lead assembler kept track of performance and had authority to resolve problems quickly. And Avery was in control of inventory. They both reported their findings to Scott, but I didn't get the sense that they went to Scott to ask how to handle every problem."

"So," Don picked up, "would it be correct to say that Scott's job was to create the framework in which his subordinates had authority to act, and to account for their overall performance?"

"Yeah, I guess it would," came the response.

"Did you get a sense," Don queried, "that Amy made all the decisions in the Engineering department?"

Again, the Copper-Bottom leaders reflected before someone answered. "No. She talked about the team agreeing on how to measure defects. And she said she appointed her most qualified engineer to propose solutions to the way they created new designs."

"So," Don summarized, still looking at the last respondent, "would you say that Amy's job, like Scott's, was to set the ground rules within which everybody worked, then to monitor their performance?"

The Copper-Bottom employees reflected on what they'd seen, and slowly heads started to nod.

"Last question." Don grinned. "How do you think Scott and Amy's people feel about performing their jobs?"

Some of the Copper-Bottom leaders discussed their thoughts among themselves before one of them raised her hand. "We'd guess they enjoy what they're doing. It seems they have authority to *act* when they see a problem; that they are able to give input and that it gets listened to."

"Very good," praised Don. "Did you see anything of value to your own jobs in how these manufacturing leaders worked?"

Silence. Don waited.

Finally, a male Copper-Bottom leader volunteered, "I think we all see applicability," he started, "but the problem is that we have no authority to do any of that ourselves."

"Fair answer," Don thanked the man, but he nudged Jack inconspicuously. There was no need. Jack had gotten the message.

"One last point before moving on to the next topic," Don said. "The process we just used—walking around the workplace and engaging with our employees—is called *Gemba walking*. Gemba is Japanese and means *the real place*, as in the place where something you're interested in is occurring. For example, if you want to see a design being created, Gemba, the real place, is Engineering. If you want to understand a problem with your paint system, Gemba is your painting operation. Toyota leaders believe that the best way to understand a problem is not to read about it on your monitor or to have someone tell you, but to go and see it for yourself. We strongly encourage those of you in the room, the leaders of Copper-Bottom, to adapt that behavior.

"Gemba walking," Don advised, "is the perfect time to connect with your people, understand their problems, and to coach performance."

Don paused. "Anyone wonder where our leaders find the time to Gemba walk?"

39

Winning Back Time

Don began a new discussion. "Why are *you* in the room? What is the point of bringing all the Copper-Bottom leaders here to see this?"

There was long silence that no one moved to break.

When no one responded, Don stated, "The reason is to share what I had to learn the hard way: culture is all about leadership. In short, where you lead, the culture will follow. Perhaps more to the point, *how* you lead is how the culture will behave."

"You're going to find," Don stated, "that I use the Socratic method. That means I ask questions to provoke the listener to think. I have found that, if I just tell people things, they have no investment in the information. If I ask them to come up with a response, they are required to think, and that deepens the knowledge within them.

"So, let's start with some questions. How many Copper-Bottom directors do I have in the room?"

Five people raised their hands.

"Can someone tell me what a typical day is like?" Don queried.

No one spoke at first. Finally, Sharon Ferrari, the Operations Director, raised her hand.

"My workday starts around 7:00 to 7:15. I head directly to my desk and check my phone for voice mail and employee callouts. If there were callouts, I send a quick email to the appropriate supervisor and annotate the individual's time sheet.

"Let's see. … Next, I begin to respond to emails. That usually gets me to around 8:00 or even 9:00. After that, I go over the CSR call logs from the day before to see how many calls there were, what types they were, and so on. I add that data to a spreadsheet I keep. Then I take a quick tour through the building to get the pulse of the organization. I can usually

DOI: 10.4324/9781003336051-40

sense what kind of calls we're getting early in the day. Often, the folks who call in early have pent-up frustration over something they discovered the night before. If not, it's just the run-of-the-mill queries.

"The rest of the day is spent in meetings and filing reports." She stopped. "That's pretty much it."

"Thanks," acknowledged Don.

"Sharon, as is my wont, let me ask a few more questions.

"Question 1: What is the purpose of Copper-Bottom? What is its mission?"

Sharon thought for a second and responded, "To provide the best service allowable by the customer's package and to provide a return to our shareholders."

"Thank you," Don replied. "Can you tell me which of your daily activities connect to either of those expectations?"

Sharon thought, began to open her mouth, then closed it. She thought longer. Again, she started to comment but again chose to remain silent. After a full 10 seconds, she finally said, "None, directly. I can see that many of them provide tangential support, but nothing I do directly touches the client or shareholder."

"Thank you, Sharon. That was a very honest assessment."

Turning to the rest of the audience, Don asked, "Who here works for Sharon?"

Five people raised their hands.

"Question 2: How many of you *touch* customers or shareholders?"

There was a moment's pause, and then all five hands went up. Turning back to Sharon, Don asked, "If you wanted to have more impact on your customers or shareholders, how could you do it?"

The answer was obvious to everyone in the room, but Sharon wanted to make sure she wasn't stepping on a landmine before responding. After a second, she said, "I'd have more direct contact with the people actually dealing with the clients?"

"Sharon, I know I'm putting you on the spot, but bear with me. Do you think your employees could give you insights into your customers, what they want and don't want? Do you think your employees could, through you, help Copper-Bottom become a better service provider?"

Sharon didn't hesitate this time. "Now I can see where you're going and won't disagree with you, but who will do all the other things that I do to keep the organization running?"

"I'm not the one to answer that for you, Sharon, but the people in this room are. I'd suggest that you ask them when you get back."

Addressing the crowd, Don said, "Sharon is not unique. Most of us have been trained that our people *report* to us and have an obligation to execute as we instruct them. I'll be the first to admit that leaders have to set the expectation and hold subordinates accountable, but that's a tiny part of what we need to do. A large part is to—and this will seem upside down at first—support those who are serving our customers, whether they are internal customers or external."

"At the end of the day, the role of leaders, in an organization with a healthy culture, is to support those who report to them and to blaze the trail for their organization: *go ahead* of the team to discover the best path forward. Strangely enough, that usually comes by humbly listening to your employees' and customers' problems and finding a solution, often with the help of one or both.

"Now," Don continued, "those two things occur only when there has been a clear path established for good performance and when there is an expectation of accountability. Not that there needs to be a harsh disciplinary process, but everyone needs to know the rules and that straying outside of them has consequences.

"So, let's come back to Sharon's question: 'Who will do all the things I now do?'

"To that, I'd respond with a question: *what value does what you currently do provide to Copper-Bottom's customers, to your shareholders, or even to you?*"

As Sharon pondered the question, Don waited. In the silence, he turned on a projector that cast two words on the screen: STOP DOING.

STOP DOING

"Jim Collins advocates that leaders need to have a STOP DOING list. It is, he asserts, just as important as a TO DO list. Collins's claim impacted me as if it were a stone wall that I'd hit at 80 miles an hour. The act of stopping something implied that it had been wrong or, at least, that it had outlived its need. I couldn't believe that was true.

"Yet I was so shaken by Collins's statement that I took it into a period of self-reflection. Only after pondering his statement for days did I see the profound wisdom of it.

"Here's a personal example," Don continued. "I used to hold a weekly staff meeting. I argued that I needed that meeting to know what was going on. Those meetings frequently rambled on for over 90 minutes. During that time, my staff and I were tied up and away from those we supported. When I was finally honest with myself, I admitted that the information we gained was already old and that we'd already missed the critical window to use it in timely decision-making. What, I asked, would happen if I discontinued it? I put the question to my staff and together we came up with a much better solution.

"We now host a daily stand-up meeting at which all discipline leaders update fellow leaders on changes that have taken place in the last 24 hours. The new meeting is fast-paced and factual. Decisions are made on the spot, the results of which will be assessed in less than 24 hours.

"Now, in 10 minutes or less, my staff learns exactly what has transpired in the previous 24 hours and how it will affect their discipline. In summation, we save 40 minutes a week and get much more timely information.

"Let me admit, I'd never have gotten there on my own. It was only at the prompting of a business leader I truly respected that I was willing to challenge my own long-held beliefs."

Don let silence settle again, then put up a second slide. This slide had one word: Delegate.

DELEGATE

"A lot of the burden leaders face is self-imposed. By that, I mean we force ourselves to sit through meetings and read reports, believing that *our* decision-making prowess is needed to solve the problems our organization faces. Like Solomon, we listen to the details and issue our proclamations, as if we know just what to do by virtue of our position.

"Don't get me wrong," he continued, "there is some truth to the belief that all I experienced getting where I am has helped me know what to do, but might I be drawing the same imperfect conclusions as those leaders I learned from? Why not appoint subordinates to gather and analyze data for you? If nothing else, you'd be training your future leaders to make decisions based on data rather than on their *gut*.

"Most of your employees will see it as an honor to be asked to do work for you. More importantly, you are starting to deepen your bench. Do you know what I mean by that?" he asked.

Someone raised his hand. "Do you mean develop a greater number of skilled employees?"

"That's exactly what I mean," Don replied. "Think about it. If your employees felt that you were passing down to them sound decision-making practices, wouldn't most feel that was a sign of respect for their talent?"

Heads nodded in the crowd.

"Remember," he reminded them, "the first thing you do is to eliminate anything that doesn't add value. Only then do you delegate."

Don projected the last slide.

GO AND SEE FOR YOURSELF

"Here's something to think about," Don continued. "At Toyota's Georgetown, Kentucky plant, more than half of the 10 hours executives spend in the plant are spent out of their office. That means they are walking around, seeing what their people are doing, and what problems their people are running into. Much of the work that fills the days of other executives, the Toyota executives have eliminated or delegated.

"Because they spend so much time seeing the business firsthand, they are much more in tune with what is going on and what problems their people are experiencing. That allows executives to bring the full weight of their position to bear in helping to eliminate problems.

"What do you think?" Don queried. "Could that work at Copper-Bottom?"

No one spoke, but they could sense a new energy in the room.

"Tim," Don asked, "could you come up here?"

Tim walked to the front of the conference room.

"In the weeks ahead," Don explained, "Tim is going to be meeting with Copper-Bottom executives. He'll be doing the following:

1. Working with each of you to review your hour-by-hour activities
2. Helping you to eliminate around 25% of those activities

3. Helping you to delegate another 15% of the remaining activities
4. Helping you to create something called Leader Standard Work: a new list of activities that each executive sets for themselves to complete each day
5. Accompanying executives on daily Gemba walks
6. And finally, Tim is going to sit down with your HR personnel and key employees asking: "What are the core VALUES of Copper-Bottom?"

When those things are completed, we'll all meet back together, if that's okay with Jack." Don turned his head to Jack, who nodded.

"Thank you, Jack," Don stated.

After Jack's "Okay," Don began again. "Here's what I'd like you to do." He handed out forms on which to keep track of how individual leaders spent their time. The form was divided into 15-minute increments and ran from 7 AM until 6 PM.

Day: _____		
Date: _____		
Activity	**Time**	**Code**
	0700	
	0715	
	0730	
	0745	
	0800	
	0815	
	0830	
	0845	
	0900	
	0915	
	0930	
	0945	
	1000	
	1015	
	1030	
	1045	
	1100	
	1115	

Activity	Time	Code
	1130	
	1145	
	1200	
Activity	**Time**	**Code**
	1215	
	1230	
	1245	
	1300	
	1315	
	1330	
	1345	
	1400	
	1415	
	1430	
	1445	
	1500	
	1515	
	1530	
	1545	
	1600	
	1615	
	1630	
	1645	
	1700	
	1715	
	1730	
	1745	
	1800	
Legend		
C = Correspondence/Reports		
E = Email		
G = Gemba Walk		
L = Lunch (Meal)		
M = Meeting		
P = Phone Call		
V = Vacation		

"What you'll want to do with this," Don instructed, "is to track how you spend your day. I'd encourage you to use the key at the bottom of the page as much as possible," he said, pointing to the key. "You'll see we've covered the usual ways most of us spend our time, for example, P for phone calls, M for meetings, C for correspondence, and so on.

"After two weeks we'll total up the time spent on the various codes, then calculate the percent of time spent doing each.

"Pretty easy assignment. The only way you can fail is if you don't truthfully record what you do. Record exactly what you do, no matter how you think it will be seen. Don't change your schedule to match what you think will look good. Do what you usually do; just record it. You will see how informative this can be.

"Any questions?" Don asked the group.

Later, Don sat with Jack and reviewed the same ground rules, asking again if he had any questions. "Nope," Jack responded. "I think I can do this." He smiled at Don, but the latter could see Jack felt this activity was beneath him. Don, who had risen to leave, sat back down.

In a quiet voice, Don said, "Jack, we can stop this now if you'd prefer. I'm not here to waste your time. You want to change your culture, right? We're trying to help. Sadly, some things have to be done the hard way, and leading is one of those things.

"So say the word and we're gone, but if you want to change this organization's culture, it will only happen if *you* lead the change. So pick your poison."

Don stood again. "Let me know your plan."

The following day, Don got a call on his mobile phone. It was Jack.

"Got a sec?" Jack inquired.

"Sure," Don said, pushing their last conversation out of his head.

"Don," Jack began, "this is really hard for me, and I'm afraid I'm botching it all up."

"The time form?" Don asked.

Jack barked out a laugh despite himself. "No, changing," he responded. "I haven't seen what the end product of a "'changed me'" looks like, so I can't wrap my head around the things you're asking of me and my organization." There was a pause. "Don't get me wrong," he continued, "I'm not stopping anything, nor am I talking about this with anyone but you, but I'm just having a problem. I mean, if this stuff was so important, why don't they teach us about it in undergrad or business schools?"

"Excellent question," responded Don, "but all I can give you is my opinion. Here's what I can *tell* you. Do you have kids?"

"A couple," responded Jack.

"Ages?" asked Don.

"Ten and 12."

"Then no doubt you've learned the hard way that you can't ask a kid to eat a food that you're unwilling to eat or to perform a chore that you're unwilling to do. Am I right?"

There was silence at the other end of the phone, and Don sensed he'd struck a nerve.

"Employees are the same way. They watch our behavior and pattern their own after ours. If you ask them to do something that you're unwilling to do, they will read your behavior as stating that the task isn't really necessary or worse, that it's beneath you ... but not them. They'll do it as long as someone oversees them, but the moment they can get away without doing it, they will abandon it.

"If you want subordinates to change, it must be evident that the new behavior is important enough that you'll do it. That requires that you lead by example.

"In this case, if you want employees to free up their time and refocus their energy on more important things, you've got to do it yourself.

"This isn't just about setting the example. Freeing up your time is going to be even more important to you than to your subordinates. For you to do the job that will change your culture, you're going to need to shed a lot of the things you now do."

"Okay," Jack responded resolutely. "Let's see where this goes."

He meant it. It wasn't that he doubted what Don and Tim were doing. It was just that he was used to leading, not following. He felt a little bit resentful of being given direction by somebody other than his boss. Nonetheless, Jack was curious to see where this was going. Besides, his boss was coming, and he wanted Don to have a favorable report about his support of this process.

Principle #33: Culture is all about leadership. How you lead is how your culture will behave.

40

Acknowledging Values

On Tim's next visit, he met with Nadine Sommers, the Director of Human Resources. They were joined by a small group composed of Nadine's staff and a few key employees. Nadine informed them that they were there to develop a list of values held in common by Charleston employees.

Tim gave each attendee a pad of sticky notes and asked them to *silently* write one value on each. He instructed them that the values they wrote needed to be ones they believed Copper-Bottom employees already held or should hold. "Please do it in silence," he instructed them. With those simple instructions, they went to work.

When everyone was finished, Tim asked them to *silently* put all their Post-its on the room's whiteboard, then be seated.

When everyone was seated, Tim asked participants to go back to the board and silently read every note. "When you finish, sit back down."

Again, Tim instructed them to go back to the board and this time talk amongst themselves. "Eliminate any duplicates, or, if two are written the same way but were intended to mean different things, modify one of the two to say what was meant. When you're finished, be seated."

When the last of the team was seated, Tim asked if they'd found any values missing. There was some lively discussion, at the end of which Tim gave them a few minutes for members to silently add new Post-its.

When they finished, Nadine took a photo of the board with her cell phone. Attaching the photo to a text message, she tapped out a few short instructions and sent it to her administrative assistant. She asked the latter type it into a single-page list and deliver it to the conference room as soon as possible. Tim, meanwhile, sent the group out on a break.

When the administrative assistant delivered the list, Tim and Nadine read it then made copies for each participant. Participants were invited

DOI: 10.4324/9781003336051-41

back in and were asked to distribute copies of the list to every member of their department, and have employees turn them back in to HR within three days. Instructions at the top of the list asked employees to circle no more than five words that most exemplified what they believed were the values of Copper-Bottom Charleston.

The following week, the group reassembled. When the returns were tallied, the following values had been chosen:

- Honest
- Caring
- Customer-focused
- Hardworking
- Going the Extra Mile

Nadine reviewed them at the following Lean Council meeting and, at Jack's direction, posted them on the HR bulletin boards, in addition to sending emails with the list attached to everyone who had an account.

Within a week, the division's web page listed these values. Several managers posted them in their departments.

41

Leader Standard Work

A week later, Tim started meeting with individual executives to review their daily time usage. Tim had arrived with a summary form and, with the help of the manager, totaled and ranked each activity by the amount of time spent performing it. Almost without exception, executives said things like, "I had no idea I spent so much time doing that."

Legend	Sum of Minutes	% of Day
C = Correspondence/Reports		
E = Email		
G = Gemba Walk		
L = Lunch (Meal)		
M = Meeting		
P = Phone Call		
V = Vacation		

The next step was to get each manager to identify those things that didn't need to happen at all. Meeting with them individually, Tim asked them to be specific by naming the report or meeting or email that they intended to eliminate and to record it on the form he provided.

Then Tim asked them to identify any activities that still needed to be done but didn't need to be done by them. Directors were told to record these on the same form and to document the name of the person to whom they would delegate the task.

DOI: 10.4324/9781003336051-42

Activity	Eliminated	Delegated to

When they'd finished, Tim found that most executives had been able to eliminate or delegate the activities that had occupied between 25% and 40% of their time.

Activity	Duration	Times/Week

Next, the executives were instructed to list the remaining activities and next to each, write the number of times a week each needed to be performed and the approximate time each should take: for example, staff meeting, 1/wk, 40 min.

When that task was complete, Tim suggested they begin the process of delegating. Executives met with their subordinates, explaining what they were being asked to do and why. Without exception, subordinates willingly accepted the additional duty.

Tim had encouraged executives to keep a list of what they delegated and to whom. He suggested they hold on to this record for a couple of months, at least until they were able to ensure that the people were following through.

At the end of the week, Tim held a brief meeting with all the executives. He said, "The point of the exercise you've just gone through was not to give you more time to fill up with non-value-adding tasks, but to get you out of your offices and onto the floor, where your business is really taking place. The goal is for you to see what's really happening in your business. The time you've won is precious. *Fight* to keep it unencumbered!"

The following week, Tim met collectively with the executives. In that short meeting, he talked about the fact that leaders also needed to have a standardized process they followed. "That process," Tim explained, "is called Leader Standard Work."

Tim paused. "I suspect you've all heard the story about the professor who began class one day by placing a large-mouthed glass jar on his desk. As the students watched, he proceeded to carefully place several large stones in the jar, many of which barely fit through the mouth. When he had fit as many as he could without going above the mouth, he asked the class, 'Is the jar full?'

"Most students responded that it was, but then the professor brought out a bin of smaller rocks from below his desk and began putting these in the jar. He'd shake the jar at intervals until the gravel filled in around the large stones. When the gravel was at the top of the jar, he asked again, 'Is it full?'

"The students, now wary, said nothing.

"Again, the professor reached below his desk and, this time, withdrew a bin of sand. He promptly began troweling sand into the jar, again shaking the jar until the sand filled in the crevices.

"Again, when he finished, he asked, 'Is it full?'

"He got no response.

"The professor paused for effect and then pulled out a pitcher of water from below his desk. This he slowly poured in the jar. He continued to pour as the contents settled. When the water finally reached the top, he declared, 'There! Now the jar is full.'

"'What was the point of that exercise?' the professor asked his audience. The students were stumped. When no one answered, he said, 'The point is to demonstrate that, if you don't put the largest stones in first, you can never get them all in.'"

Following the story, Tim handed out sheets on which were printed a partially complete table. "These," he said, "are a typical Leader Standard Work checklist. They contain a list of activities most executives engage in, but I'd encourage you to personalize the list.

"You'll note that the table has a space for each day of the workweek. This is where you'll indicate whether or not you were able to complete the task. We typically use a green '0' to indicate we completed it and a red 'X' to indicate that we did not."

Leader Standard Work

Name: _____

Month and Year: _____   Week: _____

From & To Dates

Daily Activity:	M	T	W	Th	F	Notes
Write Out Daily Activities						
Conduct Gemba Walks						
Coach Subordinate KPI Boards						
Conduct Subordinate Performance Reviews						
Conduct Staff Meeting						
Attend Lean Council Meeting						
Attend Division Staff Meeting						

Complete	0
Incomplete	X

"So, what happens if you find yourself with a lot of red Xs?" he asked.

"The fact these activities are on your sheet reminds you that you deemed them important. If you're not getting to them, you'll want to ask yourself why and develop a corrective action plan.

"Are you not making time for tasks you identified as critical? Are you slipping back into old habits? Do you need to redouble your efforts to break old habits in favor of new ones? Did you miss writing some things on your checklist that you now realize need to be added? In short, the Leader Standard Work form is *your* tool to give *you* feedback. Are you changing to meet the new requirements of your organization, or are you responding using the same old approaches? Constantly ask yourself what you intend to do in response to your discoveries?

"One thing I am *not* advocating is that you account for every minute of your day. You want to intentionally leave blanks in your schedule to think and to plan. Remember, one of the attributes of leaders is that they seek to understand where their discipline or their industry are going. That means you're going to need to make time to read books, periodicals, and blogs. You'll want to attend discipline and industry lectures, conferences, and workshops.

"As you begin to understand where your discipline and your industry are going, start asking yourself what you need to do to get yourself, your organization, your company there first. Make sure you're talking with your co-workers and learning where their disciplines are going. Learn how you can facilitate each other's efforts and develop a mutual plan.

"Later, I'll teach you a tool that will help you crystalize a company-wide plan for your future, but for now, focus on improving your personal skills and knowledge within the context of the company mission."

Tim gave the participants time to examine the LSW form before beginning again.

"Let's talk for a second," Tim stated. "What's the significance of that story about the professor in the context of this discussion?" His audience looked stumped. Tim waited them out. "What are we talking about?" he asked. Again, he waited. Finally, someone volunteered, "We've been talking about how we spend our time."

"Okay. And what significance could that story have on how you spend your time?" Tim asked.

When no one volunteered, Tim said, "The answer is that you've got to treat your day like it's a large-mouthed jar. This Leader Standard Work checklist is your large-mouthed jar. As you ponder which activities you're going to put on the list, your first priority has got to be your *big rocks*, those 'Must Do' things that only you can do. Continue to ask yourself, *'What actions do I need to undertake to provide sound leadership in my field of expertise?'*

"If you don't know the answer to that question, ask yourself, *'What do I need to do to discover what those actions are?'* Again, you need to make time to discover what actions are critical to the future of your discipline and organization. The time to ask those questions belongs on your calendar. I'd argue it also belongs on your Leader Standard Work."

Tim paused. When all the executives' eyes were on him, he said, "Your organization needs you to provide leadership. To do that, you need to carve out time to think about where your organization must go and the path it needs to take to get there. Those *things* take time, but because they're not life-and-death activities, most managers put them off. DON'T!" Tim raised his voice as he spoke the last word. He then repeated it more softly. "Don't."

"One caveat: Don't do it alone. Make sure you're talking with Jack about your plans. Let Jack and your peers *steer* you so that your future plans best serve the entire organization and not just your personal organization.

"Management is about making sure the right things get done, and that's important, but leadership is about deciding what those right things are. You are all in leadership roles. You need to be able to lead *and* manage, but keep in mind that right now, nobody below you is devoting time to leading. That's why leading has got to be so critical to you, why it's a big rock.

"Okay, let's assume you've got the big rocks on your Leader Standard Work. What's next? You'll need to make sure that you fit in the gravel, for example, those meetings that YOU must hold. Before you add meetings, you may want to restructure their length and agendas." Tim paused.

"I'm probably preaching to the choir, but never hold a meeting without an agenda. And make sure your agendas estimate the amount of time that will be devoted to each topic. Try hard to stay within that time. I'm not suggesting you squelch dialog. I'm encouraging you to schedule those conversations on another calendar but that you do not tie up the rest of the participants unless the topic impacts them all."

Agenda

1. Review today's agenda (5 Minutes)
2. Review last plan and prior assignment updates (15 Minutes)
3. Discuss topic A (10 Minutes)
4. Discuss topic B (10 Minutes)
5. Discuss topic C (10 Minutes)
6. Develop plan & make assignments (10 Minutes)

"Just a reminder: when you attend KPI huddles, your role is to be a silent observer but to also reinforce the importance of the huddle with your presence. If coaching is needed, that takes place in a one-on-one, preferably immediately *after* the huddle.

"This form doesn't contain them, but are there activities you need to be sure to accomplish monthly or quarterly or semiannually? Consider creating boxes on your Leader Standard Work (LSW) form for those activities and group them by their frequency.

"As you already learned, it's easy to commit all your time to activities. Don't be afraid of blanks on your calendar. That's when you'll deal with unforeseen opportunities.

"*IMPORTANT, NOT URGENT:* There is a condition referred to as the *tyranny of the urgent*. It occurs when others feel something is *important* because it's on fire. As you've already learned, you can fill your days fighting fires, but from here on, you need to focus on what's critical. You need to have a list of things that you know to be important; things that will move all the right dials. That's where leaders focus their efforts. If fires need to be fought, develop a fire brigade to handle them, but keep your efforts focused on the important and critical.

"The LSW form I've shown you is how you will keep your daily focus where it needs to be. Review your Leader Standard Work list first thing in the morning or at the end of the previous day. The things on your LSW checklist are the things you need to make every effort to accomplish. You can fit smaller activities (gravel and sand) around these, but you fight like hell to avoid missing even one big rock.

"*MAKE TIME TO THINK STRATEGICALLY:* Where do you get the items to put on this list? You create them during a time of strategic thinking, often with your boss or your colleagues. Some organizations have retreats where this is the focus. Others use the annual goal-setting part of the employee performance review cycle for this purpose. At the end of the day, no matter how you accomplish the establishment of the items on your list, it's important that you do it.

"Not only should you create major goals, but you should break them down into smaller goals. The completion of these smaller goals should lead to the completion of the major goal. You'll need to set a date by which each of these smaller goals needs to be accomplished and use your daily calendar as the tool for scheduling these actions.

"What if you miss a date? You'll do the same thing you'll ask your subordinates to do: create a recovery plan. A recovery plan includes a new plan to complete the task, whether that's a single event or a series of activities.

You'll then need to set a new completion date and hold yourself account-able to meet that new date."

Tim stopped and assessed the room. He was pleased to see that his audi-ence was paying rapt attention. Most had been taking notes. "Anyone have any questions?" he asked. There were lots. He addressed them all.

Principle #34: "The time you've won is precious. *Fight* to keep it unencumbered!"

Principle #35: *"SET ASIDE TIME FOR REFLECTION"*: It's not for me to tell you, but I would strongly suggest you begin to set aside time at the beginning or end of the day to reflect on what this LSW checklist is telling you.

Principle #36: *"SEEK ADVICE"*: You're going to want to reach out to people you think of as current industry leaders. Don't be afraid to admit that you don't understand something. Admit to it up front, but make it clear you don't want to remain ignorant. Ask for their instruction. Ask for their advice. Ask for their reading lists; ask who influences them. In short, begin the climb up the hill of knowledge that leads to industry leadership.

Principle #37: *"JOURNAL"*: I'd also like to encourage you to keep a journal of your thoughts. That journal will have the most value if you periodi-cally review what you've written and how those thoughts impact you today. Write about how those thoughts have matured or atrophied and why.

Principle #38: Leaders have got to *make* time to think deeply about the future and about how their organization will affect it.

Principle #39: *"MAKE TIME TO THINK ABOUT THE FUTURE"*: Leaders can't afford to put off thinking about the future. Leaders have got to *make* time to think deeply about the future and about how their organi-zation should affect it. From there, you need to plan the activities that strengthen your organization and the services it provides.

Principle #40: Senior leaders ensure that changes and improvements are good for the entire organization, and not just their own discipline.

Principle #41: *"MAKE TIME TO GROW YOUR PEOPLE"*: What else? Well, aside from planning the path forward, growing their people is one of the most critical tasks of a leader. You need to *make time* to do that. That means making time for one-on-ones with each member of your staff at least quarterly, preferably monthly, and for visiting their KPI boards, preferably with the owner, as often as they get updated. That allows you to stay informed about problems and trends, as well as to understand what they are doing to improve and grow their organization. After all, strong, well-trained employees provide the services your customers crave. You'll also be looking for what is hindering them and to find ways to remove those hindrances, either personally or by taking it to your boss or even the Lean Council.

42

Objective Performance Evaluation

"What does good performance look like?" Sharon asked a group of managers.

Silence.

"Come on!" coaxed Sharon. "How can you evaluate subordinates, even yearly, if you don't agree on what good performance looks like?"

The class looked at her blankly.

"Let me explain what your silence is saying. It says you evaluate your subordinates based on how you *feel* about them. Would you agree that's not very scientific? We could also argue that such a system is open to judging employee performance more on your relationship than on their skill. Would you agree?"

Although no one responded, Sharon could tell by their averted eyes that she'd hit a nerve.

"Of course, saying that puts the blame on you, doesn't it? It's YOUR fault that you evaluate your employees using feelings rather than empirical data. However, blame is not where this discussion is heading, because if we're honest, what are your alternatives? Is there a tool that allows you to evaluate your employees using an honest assessment of their skills? Is there even a tool that lists what skills your subordinates are supposed to possess?

"I want you to look at this," Sharon said, passing around a printed page. "I'll make an Excel version of a similar document available to you, but for now, let's get familiar with the form.

DOI: 10.4324/9781003336051-43

		Employee Title		
	Employee Name			
Name: **Charles Stewart**		Title:	Journeyman, Sidewalk Repair	

Tasks / Skills	Expected	Actual	Gap
Can break concrete with sledge hammer	3	4	1
Can make concrete with concrete mixer	3	3	0
Can trowel concrete	3	2	-1
Can use concrete float	3	1	-2
Can form sidewalks	3	3	0
Can form steps	3	2	-1
Can operate vibrator / compactor	3	4	1
Can shovel gravel	3	4	1
Can break forms	3	2	-1
	27	25	-2

Expected Skill Level

Actual Skill Level

Skill Gap

0 = No experience, knowledge or skill
1 = Very little experience, knowledge or skill
2 = Can perform with oversight or assistance
3 = Can perform without oversight or assistance
4 = Can perform at mastery level; can train others

"At the top of the form, we find the employee's name; next to it, the employee's job title. This employee is named Charles Stewart. He is a Journeyman Sidewalk Repair Technician. Just so you know, there are three levels of this skill: *Apprentice, Journeyman,* and *Master.* Each has different *levels* of the same skills.

"Below the title block, we find a list of all the skills a Sidewalk Repair Technician should be able to perform. Just a reminder: these same skills are expected of the Apprentice, Journeyman, and Master. The only difference is the level of proficiency at which each should be able to perform the skill. For instance, an Apprentice might be expected to perform the skill at a 2, while a Journeyman is expected to perform it at a 3, and a Master needs to perform it at a 4.

"In the column titled *Expected*, you'll post numeric values indicating the level of proficiency at which this employee is expected to perform. That level needs to be consistent with all other employees holding this job title. So, for example, a Journeyman may be expected to perform most skills without assistance (level 3), while one or two they need only be able to perform with oversight (level 2).

"Any questions so far?" Sharon asked.

There were none.

"Well, if you have questions later," she said in a singsong voice, "you know where to come."

Returning to her previous dialog, she continued. "You'll observe each employee that reports to you as they perform every skill. You'll rate their performance according to the table. Once you've rated their performance, you'll compare their performance to the expectation for their skill level, and note any gaps.

"To calculate the gap, subtract the EXPECTED value from the ACTUAL value. In most cases, this value will be zero or positive. That says the employee is qualified to perform that task. If the value is negative, I want you to circle it. That is a skill in which this person needs to improve.

"Skill gaps mean that the individual can't perform their current job. In the beginning, that may not be uncommon, but you'll want to work with those people until they at least can perform at the expected level."

Sharon shifted back to the form. "Let's look at our example. Charlie here is a Journeyman Sidewalk Repair Technician. The numbers in the *Expected* column are reflective of a journeyman's skill level. You'll note in the actual column that our man Charlie exceeds some expectations but is also deficient in several as well.

"What do you think?" Sharon asked. "Based on your assessment, should Charlie have been deemed a journeyman?" There were headshakes around the room.

"Nonetheless, that's how he's been ranked and he's getting a Journeyman's pay. How do you think other Journeymen feel about the fact that Charlie can't perform the same skills they do but earns the same pay as them?" Sharon didn't wait for an answer. Instead, she asked, "Who do you think they blame for that?"

"Charlie's leaders," someone volunteered.

"So, what's got to happen?" Sharon asked.

"It's pretty obvious," another person said. "Charlie has to be put on some kind of recovery plan."

"Any recommendations for how we could do that?" Sharon asked. She was avoiding giving them answers and was asking questions to make them think through the solution, just as she'd been taught.

"I'd pair Charlie with either a Master or with individual employees who scored 4s in the skills in which he was weak. I'd have them tutor Charlie in the performance of the skills he is weak in; then I'd retest him."

Someone else volunteered, "I'd also give him a clear deadline by which he needs to be proficient."

Sharon pointed to the second woman and gave her a wink and a thumbs-up.

Addressing the first woman, Sharon complimented her and said, "Good plan. Anything else? How would you deal with the fact that Charlie can't perform the job now?"

The woman thought for a second and then offered, "I'd place him on probation. That's when I'd give him the deadline by which he needs to be proficient."

"Okay," Sharon summarized, "what you've said is that we're going to give Charles *Guidance, Direction, & Suspense*. You're going to tell him exactly what he has to do, to what level of proficiency, and by when. Excellent!"

"I know I can count on you to be fair," Sharon encouraged them. "Even your best people have some flaws and weaknesses. Likewise, except in rare cases, even your worst have some skill.

"Okay, for each skill group reporting directly to you, you'll want to type in the expected skill levels on the first spreadsheet. Don't put a name on it yet. You should create a similar form for everyone that works for you that has that same title.

"Here's how I do it," she went on.

"I create the master that includes the skills and expected skill level for a particular skill group, for example, all Journeymen. Then I label the spreadsheet tab with the name of one of my Journeymen. Excel has a 'Move or Copy' feature that you can access by putting the cursor on the tab, then right-clicking; a dialog box will pop up. In the dialog box, check the box labeled 'Create a Copy' at the very bottom of the pop up. Excel creates an identical sheet in a new tab." She demonstrated on-screen as she spoke.

"We good?" she asked, looking around the room before going on.

"Once I have created tabs for each of my subordinates, I can enter the names of each subordinate who holds the same job title on their own tab. Within each tab I add the employee's name. You can also enter an employee number if you want.

"Now I make appointments with each person in that skill group and begin to observe each of them performing the skills. As they do, I rate their performance. Of course, I can also just observe them as they just do their jobs. Sometimes that's less intimidating," she said with a smile.

"While I rated them on a paper copy of the Excel sheet, I now return to my office and input the data in the actual spreadsheet. The EXPECTED values won't change from sheet to sheet, but the employee's ACTUAL rating will. As you enter the ACTUAL values, the spreadsheet has been set up to automatically calculate the GAP.

"You'll do that for every employee in that *skill group*. I find it easiest to set up formulas in the forms that do the math.

"Now, this is critical," she said, "if multiple supervisors have people with the same title working directly for them, make sure you all agree on what the EXPECTED skill level should be and what good performance should look like. It might take someone from HR to broker a consensus if supervisors can't agree. Oh, and don't hesitate to video the best person you have performing the task. It's hard to argue with an actual performance. Plus, it will make it easier for others to pattern the same behaviors."

Sharon paused before asking, "What do you think? Does this form belong in a person's performance review folder?" It took a fraction of a second before the chorus replied, "Yes."

"Think about this," Sharon continued. "Could this skills matrix, as it's called, form the basis of your performance discussion each month? For example, 'Charlie, you are currently scoring a 2 against an expectation of 3 in this task. What are your plans to increase your skill level? How can I help? Where do you intend to be when we sit down next month?' Make sure you record Charlie's answers.

"That will give you something to talk about next month. Did Charlie achieve what he said he would? If not, why not? Make a note. What are his plans to recover? If he never seems to *get around* to improving his score, what does that tell you?" She let the question hang.

"Never, except under the most unusual of circumstances, should you let an employee stay below expectation for longer than 90 days. After 90 days, if their skill doesn't increase, then you either need to downgrade their title or part ways. Does that seem fair to everyone?" she asked. The group agreed it did.

"Remember: you set the bar for the value the employee needed to have in order to perform the job. If they're below that value, what does it tell you about their ability to perform the job? Are they qualified to hold the title?" she asked. "And receive the pay?" she added after a pregnant pause.

"Think about it," she continued. "You're talking with data. This isn't a statement like '*I think*' or '*I feel.*' This is 'Here's where you are and here's where you need to be. What do YOU intend to do about it?'

"The ball is in their court. Plus, you're applying a standard fairly.

"Or 'Jill, you are scoring a 4 against an expectation of 3 in this task. Would you be willing to work with a few of your peers to help them improve their performance?' Make sure you document her response. If she agrees, you now have a potential new trainer in that skill."

Sharon paused to let her participants catch up mentally. "Step back for a second," she said at last. "How consistent does this tool make you as a boss? How does it streamline the conversation? Every month your employees know you're going to discuss their skill level. Can you also talk about behaviors? Absolutely! Can you talk about special assignments? For sure. But think back to where Charlie was being paid for skills he didn't have. Can that happen anymore? Will his peers appreciate the fact that Charlie's being held to task and that their skills are being recognized?

"Now," Sharon allowed, "they may still not like you, but they have to admit that you're treating everyone fairly." She delivered the last statement with a broad smile.

"How about other performance measures? Can you talk about things like how many calls they took this month against a target number? Can you discuss customer feedback, good and bad, and what your employee plans to do about it?

"Stay on task during these meetings. You can hobnob later. Right now, your goal is to make sure that the employee in front of you knows how they rank in your eyes.

"What do you think?" Sharon asked. There was a lot of positive energy in the room. She could tell she'd gotten through.

"Two last thoughts, then we'll take a break," she informed them.

"First thought: you're going to want to create a master list that has the individual scores of everyone in the same skill group, so, for instance, all apprentices on one list and all master craftsmen on another. What you'll be doing on this list is to look at any organizational skill gaps. That will point to weaknesses in training and in your ability to execute as a department. That's next to impossible to tell from an individual sheet, but when you line the scores up, you can see how many or your subordinates have a gap greater than zero. I even conditionally format the composite sheet so that cells with negative numbers turn red. At the end of each row of skills,

I sum all negative scores. If they are above a certain threshold, that should lead to action, like group training rather than individual training.

"Second thought: as we start out, we're just going to use this tool to assess current job skills, but in the future, we could meet with subordinates, determine what career paths they want to pursue, and start evaluating them against the skills needed to perform that job (their 'promotional' skills). That way, we are growing them toward where they want to be next, which can also be part of your monthly discussion.

"Okay," she said. "Take a break."

43

Coaching the Middle

When everyone returned from the break, Sharon began again.

"Next, I want to talk to you about *coaching* your subordinates. The goal of everything your leaders are trying to do is to live the behaviors we want you to mimic. Easier said than done, right?" She was joined by the laughter of the participants. "Nonetheless, as Tim constantly tells the execs, 'People follow your feet, not your words. If we want to change behaviors, we have to exhibit them first.'

"So, what behaviors do we want our subordinates to follow?" she asked. She didn't wait for a response.

"First, we want them to conduct their own huddles, but rather than *tell* their subordinates about everything on the board, we want them to *ask* their subordinates what they're seeing. Most will get it, but it's okay if some of their subordinates get it wrong. That allows your subordinate to do the next thing, which is to *ask* their subordinates questions that steer them on course. If they just can't get there, it's okay to tell the subordinate what they're seeing, but continue the process of asking first. Eventually, everyone will get it and that means that you're making them stronger.

"After your subordinates have people who understand their KPI boards, let those people lead daily huddles. Have your subordinates rotate who they use, so their people don't think they have favorites. They don't want to develop a 'Mini Me,'" she said with another smile. That statement was also met with laughter.

"Why do you think we want you to lead this way?" she asked when the laughter died down.

"Because it gets our people addressing their accomplishments?" someone volunteered.

"Yes," Sharon agreed. "Anything else?"

"Because it gets them to understand charts and talk to their peers?" someone else contributed.

"Also true, but do you think it gives them a sense of pride that YOU asked them?" There were nods. "Here's the point of it all," Sharon explained. "We want our people to feel that their leaders respect them." She stopped. "What do we want them to feel?" she asked.

"That we respect them," came a chorus of responses.

"Excellent!" affirmed Sharon.

"Anybody want to guess why that's important?" She pointed at Justine.

"Oh boy," Justine began. "Well, it sure can't hurt morale." That brought snickers.

Justine continued. "Because they feel they have an important role in what we do for our customers?"

"Doing great, Justine," Sharon complimented her. "How do you think people who feel respected treat our customers?"

"I'd have to believe they'd treat them with respect, as well," Justine responded.

"And how do you think that makes our customers feel about Copper-Bottom?" Sharon asked. She could see the lights of understanding come on in the group.

"One more thing," Sharon went on. "We learned from Friedman that people who feel respected, and *listened to*, are far more likely to offer suggestions that will improve our products and performance. Think about the implications of that on our business.

"Who are the Subject Matter Experts in our employees' disciplines?" she asked.

"They are," someone volunteered.

"So who do you think has the best ideas for improving our products and services?" she asked.

Sharon could see she'd made her point. "The difficulty is," she continued, "that if people don't feel respected, they won't offer their ideas. If they feel they're only here as a warm body or as a voice on our phones, they see no point in improving *our* business. And," she emphasized, "that's just how they see it, isn't it? People who don't feel respected see Copper-Bottom as *OUR* business, not *theirs*. After all, they just work here; they're just hired guns; they have no stake in the action, so why help improve it?

"Unfortunately, that's the way our previous director made people feel, isn't it?" She asked, referring to Henry Corn.

There were nods around the room.

"So, we've got our work cut out for us," Sharon concluded. "And remember, we're humans. We're bound to mess up along the way. Ask your folks to be patient with us as we work to get better.

"If your folks feel they've not been treated respectfully," she added, "what should they ask us?"

"Is that your best self?" the chorus responded.

"Superb," Sharon agreed.

"Let me ask you," she said, starting in a new direction. "Are the KPI boards the only place we want our employees to feel respected?" There was a chorus of "Nos."

"Well then, how do we make them feel respected everywhere?"

Participants made suggestions: talking to them, listening to them, and asking for their opinion.

"All great answers," Sharon agreed. "How about *growing* them?" Sharon asked. "Do you think it would matter to them if, when you have your one-on-one meetings with them, you ask what they'd like to do next within the company?"

"It sure would," someone responded.

"Don't you think you're smart enough to plug them into the right resources and to get them the right training?" she asked.

"Let me rephrase that," she said, "*I* think you're smart enough to plug them into the right resources and to get them the right training.

"I know that a position will need to open first, but don't you think they will stand a better chance if they can already perform the skills of that job?

"My point? When you meet with your subordinates, show interest in them beyond their current jobs. Show interest in *them*. Take notes, and during subsequent one-on-ones, talk about their professional interests.

"Later, as your subordinates get their own KPI boards, you'll want to attend as many of their daily huddles as possible, but as they get better, you can dial back to one or two times a week. If you can't get to huddles, keep visiting KPI boards to *see* what's going on.

"It's appropriate after the huddle has dispersed to hold your immediate subordinate back and to ask questions. If you sat through their daily update, you don't need to ask them questions about their KPIs or their intended Action Items. Those should have already been covered in the huddle. You'll want to know how they think they're doing and if there is anything you can do to help them.

"Remember," Sharon reminded them, "You're there to build your subordinates up, to improve their skills, to make them better, not to show your superior knowledge. This is about them, not you.

"If their KPIs are flagging, have them walk you through their Action Item Lists. That should tell you their plans to improve. If appropriate, make suggestions. Beside your one-on-one sessions, these exchanges are where you drive change: personal, professional, organizational change. When subordinates realize that you're staying abreast of their performance, keeping track of how they are overcoming problems and meeting deadlines, they will be more faithful about staying on top of things themselves.

"Now think about this," she took a momentary diversion. "Are conducting huddles, recording data, documenting Action Items, and following up on those actions, skills your subordinates used to perform? Can you see how you're growing them? Can you see how you're preparing them for greater roles?

"Make sure they connect the same dots. You want your subordinates to realize that this process is making them stronger and more valuable as leaders."

There were smiles and approving nods around the room as the class began to see the deeper implications of what they were being asked to do.

"It's also appropriate to ask your subordinates if there is anything you can do to help them. At first they'll be leery, but when someone takes you up on your offer and you come through, you'll start to get more requests. When that happens, you'll start to see subordinates come to you for guidance and assistance in other professional matters as well. Your subordinates coming to you for advice and guidance is a great sign. Admittedly, you're not looking for friends, but you *are* looking to create a real relationship that can serve you both.

"So, let me ask you," Sharon inquired, "is anything I've shown you hard?"
There was a chorus of "Nos."
"Is anything I've shown you going to take a lot of time?"
Again, a chorus of "Nos."
"Is there anyone here who couldn't coach daily?"
This time there were no responses.
"Okay," Sharon suggested, "let's go to Jack's Wall and his KPI board."
When the group got there, Sharon pointed to the Safety KPI chart. "As I suggested you do, I'll lead you through the first one. Let's review what this chart tells us.

"First thing, what are we measuring?"

"Safety," came the answer.

"Great. What's our target?"

"One hundred percent Safe Workplace."

"Where are we performing?

"Ninety-nine percent," someone offered.

"Can you tell how we're measuring it? Are we using a leading or a lagging indicator?" Sharon asked.

"Leading" came the reply. Then, as if anticipating the next question, the responder stated, "The chart states that it's the cumulative score from a weekly safety audits."

"Any idea why it's not 100%?" Sharon asked.

"The Action Item List indicates that there was a file drawer left open in Accounting, and the action was to add file drawer hazards to the daily staff meeting."

"Whose action was it?" Sharon asked.

"Marianne F.'s" came the response.

"When was she supposed to do that?" Sharon asked.

"Yesterday," came the response.

"Okay," Sharon began, "what did we learn? Note: I'm not asking what you learned about Jack's safety metric, but what you learned about the Socratic method of drawing people out and getting them to address their metrics."

"That it's all about asking non-confrontational questions to draw them out," one of the group stated.

"That you kept drilling down until they got around to answering the question about what *action* they have taken and what was the outcome. I presume," continued another, "that you'd ask them what their next *action* would be if they hadn't already solved the problem. Is that correct?"

"You're absolutely correct," Sharon affirmed. "You're growing a leader here, so you want to teach them the behaviors that leaders use to get to the root cause of a problem. And what if they've tried several things and the problem persists? Then what?"

The respondent seemed stumped. Everyone else was quiet and looking at Sharon for the answer. "Then," Sharon answered her own question, "YOU get them help. Call someone like me or Tim to take them to the next step. You observe what that helper does or says, and next time, both you and your subordinate will know how to handle that problem."

"But isn't that admitting defeat in front of our subordinates?" someone asked.

"Think about it this way," Sharon responded, "if Jack, who knows a lot about our business, said he didn't know the answer but would get someone who did, wouldn't you respect that? Especially if, when the expert showed up, Jack came with them to learn how they dealt with the problem?

"Jack admitted that he doesn't know everything but is humble enough to ask for help. Doesn't that send a good message?" Sharon asked.

There were nods in the group acknowledging her point.

"Okay," Sharon shifted to a new topic. "Why do I keep telling you to visit KPI boards no less than weekly?"

"To show support," someone opined.

"Good," Sharon said, "but it's also to keep the pressure on. If you stop coming around, you'll find metrics will start to drift; Action Item deadlines will start being missed; daily huddles will gradually become every other day and then stop altogether.

"And, so far, we haven't talked about the most valuable element of the daily huddle," Sharon continued. "Shouldn't you be talking about the day ahead and what the expectations on this group are? Isn't the morning huddle where you inform your subordinates of changes, new goals, and things to look out for? Isn't this where they bring up problems they're facing and talk through plans?

"If you're not conducting a daily huddle, then people are just showing up to their workstations and doing the same thing they did yesterday, and last week, and last year and … well, you get the point.

"While the overall destination hasn't changed, this is where you make the subtle corrections that keep the ship on course and its sails trimmed. Admittedly, these are small changes, but they gradually build up until, over time, they become a competitive advantage over others in our industry. Then one day you realize your service is better than those offered by your competition.

"Don't get me wrong. There are going to be major breakthroughs planned at the top of the organization as well, but the small improvements coming out of your huddles will complement those changes, making our entire product and delivery system better."

44

Tim and Patty

Patty had insisted that he bring nothing to supper. "Not even flowers or a bottle of wine," she'd stated emphatically.

Tim felt awkward showing up without anything, so he arrived with a small balsawood airplane for Scott. He had hoped the two of them could play either before or after supper. He needn't have bothered, though.

"Scott's at his friends for the evening," Patty told him. She'd spied the small gift in Tim's hand. "I thought it would be better if this evening was just between the two of us. No need to complicate his life. Still, that was very sweet of you," she said.

Tim knew she was right, but he had sort of looked forward to seeing Scott. Seeing Patty, however, more than made up for her son's absence. She'd worn a simple skirt and blouse. There was nothing flashy or "sexy" about the outfit, although her skirt was semi-short and her legs shapely. Her skirt was navy blue cotton and her blouse white linen, but both were fitted well enough for Tim to recall she had a very good figure.

Patty's house was small and in an older suburb of Charleston. Because of its age, the streets were tree-lined, with sidewalks and wide lawns, something Tim hadn't seen since his childhood.

"There are only the two of us," Patty reminded him. "I felt it was far more important that Scott have a safe place to play and ride his bike. The neighborhood is slowly getting younger, but more than half of our neighbors are retired. They are ever so sweet to me and dote on Scott. It's like having a street of grandparents."

Although it was small by present standards, her home was furnished tastefully. Patty had given him a brief tour of the neat house before leading him back to the kitchen, where she had uncorked a bottle of wine and set

DOI: 10.4324/9781003336051-45

out two glasses. "I thought me might want to talk before we grab supper," she informed him. "I hope you like Chinese.

"I know," she admitted, "not much of a first date, but I thought it was far more important that we have time to talk than fussing over preparing a meal. I do work all day," she reminded him with a twinkle in her eye.

They each had a glass of wine before walking to the neighborhood Chinese restaurant. There was no handholding or kissing, but their conversation was one of genuine interest and caring.

Tim admitted that he'd gotten married right out of college. It hadn't taken long to realize that they both intended to have full-time careers. He and his former wife had discussed children while they dated. She'd said she wanted kids but neglected to add that she had seen that occurring later, after she'd established her career.

There were other issues, Tim said. "I was young and had a temper. She did, too. What could have been hammered out in conversation by cooler heads would soon escalate into a major problem for us. Plus, she wanted to keep the lifestyle of a college student, drinking and clubbing during her free time.

"That hadn't been my idea of married life," he admitted. "When I told her that I no longer wanted to do that anymore, she went out with girl-friends. You can imagine where that ended. Suffice it to say the marriage didn't end well."

"Tim," Patty admitted, "I was never married. I got pregnant with Scott during my junior year of high school. Boy, was that a wake-up call. Scott's dad, a senior, wanted no part of being a dad. He was an athlete with pro aspirations. His parents offered to pay for an abortion. I just couldn't. They didn't need to tell him to stay away from me," she added sadly.

"That spring he graduated, and that was that. He's never shown interest in Scott. Neither have his parents. Not so much as a birthday card. So, moving into a neighborhood of grandparents has been a godsend. Besides," she added with a smile, "finding a babysitter is a cinch.

"Does that bother you?" she asked after an awkward pause.

"What?" Tim asked.

"That I got pregnant out of wedlock."

Tim guffawed. "Are you kidding me? How is that worse than divorce? We're both guilty of youthful indiscretions. I'd be more concerned if you still carried a torch for Scott's dad and secretly hoped to restore that relationship. That's not the case, is it?"

It was Patty's turn to laugh. "I don't mean to be crude," she began, "but Scott's dad was little more than a sperm donor. Don't get me wrong. I loved him passionately at the time, but that was behind me by the time I delivered a child by myself. Although my parents are close by and have helped where they could, I've been on my own since Scott was one."

She continued. "I had a job during high school and continued after I gave birth. My parents watched Scott at night while I went to community college. I got an associate's degree and then my bachelors. I'd love to get my CPA someday," she admitted. "I'm really pretty good at my trade and think I could handle being a controller or even a CFO with the proper coaching."

Patty paused and Tim asked, "There's no right answer to this question, but are you open to having more children?"

The question took Patty from her own train of thought. It took her a second to consider it. "I don't know," she finally admitted. "Scott's a little old to have a sibling and I'm no spring chicken," she said with a smile. "Still, if my husband and I agreed, I could see myself having at least one more.

"How about you?" she asked. Tim thought for a second. "You know, I had a brother and sister. I liked having siblings. We didn't always get along, but we had a wonderful childhood. I've missed having a family. I don't think I was cut out for a solo life."

"Then why aren't you married, for heaven's sake?" Patty asked. "You really were such a natural with Scott at the beach."

"It's not that I haven't dated; it's just that I realize, now more than ever, how important it is for a couple to be on the same footing, to be of common accord." He paused for a second, seeming to make his mind up about something.

"The Bible uses a term I've always thought was a perfect description of marriage: 'equally yoked.' If you think of a team of oxen, that yoke implies work, but it's work done together, always moving in the same direction. You can't stray from each other when you see yourself *yoked* and working in harmony."

Patty laid her hand on his wrist as he spoke. She was looking up into his face and her eyes said he'd connected with her somehow.

"So," she asked. "Does that mean you believe in God?"

When he acknowledged he did, she asked, "Do you go to church?"

"I do," he admitted.

"Where?" she asked, then said, "Sorry, I'm getting very intrusive. Forgive me." She withdrew her hand from his arm, looking away.

"It's okay," Tim replied, reaching for her hand. "I go to a non-denominational church on the outskirts of town.

"How about you?" he asked, turning the tables. Mentally, he acknowledged how good her hand felt in his.

"Scott and I attend a small church not far from here. I'm not crazy about it, but it's close. They have a Sunday school where Scott can get instruction. We've met some nice people there, but because it draws from our neighborhood, the other congregants don't always share a lot in common with us. Few have young kids, for instance, and their spiritual needs are different at their age than ours. We don't get invited to small community events, for instance," she said dolefully.

"Sorry, don't know where that line of questioning came from," Patty confessed. Switching the subject, she asked, "Did you save room for dessert? This I *did* make."

Dessert turned out to be peach pie and vanilla ice cream. "Want me to heat your pie?" Patty asked.

"No way!" Tim responded. "I know I'm crazy, but I prefer cold pie."

"Suit yourself," Patty said, slipping her piece into the microwave.

Sitting down, she began a new line of discussion. "Look," she said, "as long as we're getting the tough stuff out of the way, I need to make a confession. As a matter of fact, what I want to talk about is the primary reason I'm still single."

"After becoming pregnant with Scott and then having my partner abandon me, I've made the decision that if I dated again, I wouldn't engage in intercourse until after I was married." Her eyes had been focused on her plate, her spoon absentmindedly moving the now-melting ice cream around in circles. She didn't look up when finished.

Then, just as Tim was about to speak, she continued. "I don't need you to make any commitments. I just felt you should know that at the outset. I know sex often ranks high on a man's list of 'must haves' in a wife.

"Don't get me wrong," she pressed on. "As I recall, I enjoy intercourse ... a great deal." She looked up momentarily, blushing. "I'm not frigid or anything," she assured him, again flashing a lovely smile. This time she met his eyes.

Tim remained silent, eating his pie. Finally, he said, "Not only is that not a turn-off; I actually respect you more for it. You may have set out to give me an *out*, a reason not to develop a relationship, but instead, you have revealed a more compelling reason to get to know you." He paused for a second before adding, "And I'm not frigid, either. More importantly—as I hope this conversation implies—I am not afraid of intimacy. You know what I mean," he said, squeezing her hand. "Revealing who I am and learning who you really are.

"So," he concluded, "if you're trying to get rid of me, you'll have to try harder." They both laughed easily. Patty rested her hand on his wrist, the earlier awkwardness gone completely.

They talked until midnight. They had relocated to the family room, where the furniture was more comfortable. Before leaving, Tim said, "Let me help you with the dishes."

"Maybe I want to wake up to them," Patty replied. "Maybe I want a reminder that tonight happened."

"Hey, I offered," Tim said with a good-natured laugh. Turning serious, he said, "Patty, I've really enjoyed myself. Thank you for the supper and the conversation. I feel like I got to know the real you. I'm grateful for that."

There was a momentary pause before he added, "I'd like to keep seeing you."

"Me, too," Patty admitted.

As they'd moved to the door, Patty had looped her arm through his. "Thank you," she said, looking up. "This has been the best date I think I've ever had."

At the door Patty gave him a tight hug, then, as if making a last-minute decision, kissed his lips. Tim would remember that hug and kiss for years. Even after their marriage.

45

That's a Wrap!

For the full six months, the morale numbers continued to climb. KPI boards were being used as a tool to communicate in both directions, and with the diligent use of the Action Item lists, business performance got better and better.

Sharon's team began holding monthly potlucks with the Accounting organization. As the two groups got to know each other on a personal level, they developed a better working relationship. Even Jerry, a self-described curmudgeon, began to relax the reins of control. He agreed to establish joint Accounting-Operations teams that worked in harmony on the same client accounts.

Something new happened that had never occurred before: Customers began sending thank-you notes to Copper-Bottom corporate (as that was the address on the letterhead and website). In their notes, customers named individual members of the Charleston staff who had gone above and beyond to help them. They acknowledged how seamlessly the Charleston team worked together and how quickly their problems were resolved. Those cards and letters were ultimately forwarded to Jack and his team. Nadine faithfully posted them to the HR corkboard. They became the source of great pride within the Charleston team.

Jack began dialoging with his fellow Branch Managers. Together, they brought pressure to bear on the corporate IT group. Within weeks, the first beta test modules were rolling out to key users. The VPs kept the pressure on until beta tests were completed and the finalized modules were being rolled out to every facility. As new modules rolled out, screens started updating in real time, and CSRs used less paper. Finally, the need to the desktop printers was gone.

DOI: 10.4324/9781003336051-46

With Jack's approval, Skip gathered up the printers and, working with corporate IT, began transferring them to other facilities needing printers. They transferred them with unused ink cartridges, too.

With the improvement of morale, employee resignations slowed to a trickle. Normally, that would have been cause for concern, but because of their service excellence, sales at Copper-Bottom's Charleston branch started to increase. Sales increased the demand for personnel.

When word of their transformation started to spread throughout the Copper-Bottom network, several other branch offices sent delegations to Charleston to see what they'd done.

Then, one day, out of the blue, Jack received an envelope addressed to him by name. It bore the corporate letterhead and handwritten instructions:

Personal and Confidential.
To be opened by addressee only.

Jack's first instinct was to think: "This can't be good." He slid his letter opener under the flap and found a single page inside. On it was a yellow Post-it note with a handwritten message.

180 days ago today, I was making plans to replace you. Without a doubt, I counted you my worst branch manager and was eager to find someone new. Now I'd count you my most valuable VP.

Here's the letter of termination I wrote back then, in anticipation of letting you go. I thought you might want to hold onto it as a memento of all you've achieved.

With great appreciation,

~ George

Index

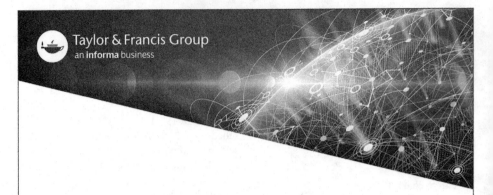

Printed in the United States
by Baker & Taylor Publisher Services